Beginner's Guide to SolidWorks 2012 – Level II

Alejandro Reyes, MSME
Certified SolidWorks Professional

ISBN: 978-1-58503-701-8

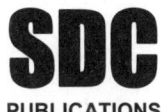

PUBLICATIONS

Schroff Development Corporation

www.SDCpublications.com

Schroff Development Corporation
P.O. Box 1334
Mission KS 66222
(913) 262-2664
www.SDCpublications.com

Publisher: Stephen Schroff

Trademarks and Disclaimer

SolidWorks and its family of products are registered trademarks of Dassault Systemes. Microsoft Windows and its family products are registered trademarks of the Microsoft Corporation.

Every effort has been made to provide an accurate text. The author and the manufacturers shall not be held liable for any parts developed with this book or held responsible for any inaccuracies or errors that appear in the book.

Copyright © 2012 by Alejandro Reyes

All rights reserved. This document may not be copied, photocopied, reproduced, transmitted, or translated in any form or for any purpose without the express written consent of the publisher, Schroff Development Corporation.

IT IS A VIOLATION OF UNITED STATES COPYRIGHT LAWS TO MAKE COPIES IN ANY FORM OR MEDIA OF THE CONTENTS OF THIS BOOK FOR EITHER COMMERCIAL OR EDUCATIONAL PURPOSES WITHOUT EXPRESS WRITTEN PERMISSION.

Examination Copies:

Books received as examination copies are for review purposes only and may not be made available for student use. Resale of examination copies is prohibited.

Electronic Files:

Any electronic files associated with this book are licensed to the original user only. These files may not be transferred to any other party.

Acknowledgements

Beginner's Guide to SolidWorks 2012 – Level II is dedicated to the love of my life, my wife Patricia and my kids Liz, Ale and Hector, who have given me the time, support and patience to write this book. To you, all my love.

Also, I wish to thank the hundreds of students, users, professors and engineers whose great ideas and words of encouragement helped me to make this second SolidWorks training book.

Special thanks to Larry Dixon who sparked the idea to start writing the second volume of Beginner's Guide to SolidWorks.

About the Author

Alejandro Reyes holds a BSME from the Instituto Tecnológico de Ciudad Juárez, Mexico in electro-mechanical engineering and a Masters Degree from the University of Texas at El Paso in mechanical design, with strong focus in Materials Science and Finite Element Analysis.

Alejandro spent more than 8 years as a SolidWorks Value Added Reseller. During this time he was a Certified SolidWorks Instructor and Support Technician, CosmosWorks Support Technician, and a Certified SolidWorks Professional, credentials that he still maintains. Alejandro has over 18 years of experience using CAD/CAM/FEA software and is currently the President of MechaniCAD Inc.

His professional interests include finding alternatives and improvements to existing products, FEA analyses and new technologies. On a personal level, he enjoys spending time with his family and friends.

Notes:

Table of Contents

Introduction .... *vii*

Multi Body Parts, Sketch Editing and Other Tools *1*
- Multi Body Parts 3
- Contour Selection 33
- Part Editing 39
- Equations 63

Sheet Metal and Top Down Design *75*
- Understanding Top Down Design 78
- Sheet Metal and Top Down Design 94
- Sheet Metal Drawings 158
- Sheet Metal Locker Top Down Design 164

3D Sketch and Weldments *231*
- 3D Sketch 233
- Weldments 255
- Structural Member Libraries 297

Surfacing and Mold Tools *301*
- Surface Modeling 303
- Master Model 323
- More About Surfaces 339
- Mold Tools 349

Final Comments *407*

Index *409*

List of commands introduced in each chapter. Note that many commands are used extensively in following chapters after they have been learned.

Multi Body Parts	**Top Down Design**	Convert to Sheet Metal
Multi Body	New Part	Closed Corners
Local Operations	Edit In Context	Selection Filters
Hide/Show Body	Assembly Transparency	Sketch Pattern
Merge	Internal Part	Feature Driven Pattern
Feature Scope	Externalize Part	Hem Feature
Delete Body	Edit Assembly	Creating Forming Tools
Body Pattern	External References	Component Pattern
Combine Bodies	In Context	Collision Detection
Add	Out of Context	Flexible Sub Assemblies
Subtract	Locked	Assembly Features
Common	Broken	
Bodies to keep	List External References	**3D Sketch**
		3D Sketch
Contour Selection	**Sheet Metal and**	3D Sketch Relations
Regions available	**Top Down Design**	Derived Sketch
Contour Selection	Base Flange	Projected Curve
Shared Sketch	Sheet Metal Thickness	
Start From: Condition	Bend Radius	**Weldments**
	Bend Allowance	3D Sketch review
Part Editing	Bend Deduction	Cut list
What's Wrong	K-Factor	Weldment feature
Parent/Child relations	Auto-Relief	Structural Member
Sketch Editing	Rectangular	Corner Treatment
Dangling Relations	Obround	End Miter
Delete Absorbed	Tear	End Butt
Features	Flat Pattern	Locate Profile
Sketch Relations	Forming Tools	Rotate Profile
Over Defined Sketch	Modify Sketch	Trim/Extend
Not Solved Sketch	Link to Thickness	Gusset
SketchXpert	Normal Cut	End Cap
View Sketch Relations	3D Content Central	Weld Beads
	Vent feature	Weldment Cut List
Equations	Miter Flange	Weldment Drawings
Rename Dimensions	Unfold/Fold Bend	Cut List Table
Pattern Seed Only	Edge Flange	Weld Table
Add Equations	Build Library Features	Weld Symbols
Edit Equations	Library Parts	Save Bodies to
Delete Equations	Mate Reference	Assembly
Link Values	Break Corners	Structural Member
	Jog bend	Libraries
	Flat Pattern Drawing	
	Bend Notes	

Surfacing
Revolved Surface
Lofted Surface
Extruded Surface
Direction of Extrusion
Extrude with Draft
Trim Surface
Mutual Trim
Planar Surface
Filled Surface
Knit Surface
Constant Width Fillet
Thicken
Body Split

Face Fillet
Extend Surface
Extrude From
Mirror Bodies
Swept Surface
Twist Along Path
Sweep Cut

Mold Tools
Draft Analysis
Direction of Pull
Positive Draft
Negative Draft
Draft

Neutral Plane
Rollback/Roll Forward
Scale
Parting Line
Parting Surface
Tooling Split
Shut Off Surfaces
Move/Copy body
Delete Face
Face Classification
Manual Parting Line
   Selection
Select Open Loop
Side Core

Notes:

Introduction

Beginner's Guide to SolidWorks 2012 – Level II starts where *Beginner's Guide – Level I* ends, following the same easy to read style, but this time covering advanced topics and techniques.

The purpose of this book is to teach advanced SolidWorks functionality including sheet metal, surfacing, how to create components in the context of an assembly referencing other components (Top-down design), propagate design changes with SolidWorks' parametric capabilities, mold design, weldments, and more while explaining the basic concepts of each trade to allow the reader to understand the how and why of each operation.

We'll use simple examples to allow the reader to better understand commands and environments, as well as to make it easier to explain the purpose of each step, maximizing the learning time by focusing on one task at a time. Keep in mind that this is a SolidWorks learning book, and the specific details of some of the topics that will be covered go far beyond the scope of this book; entire books have been written about sheet metal processes, mold design, welded structures, and such. With that in mind, please remember that this book will teach you how to use SolidWorks' tools for those trades, and at no time will attempt to teach the trade itself, and will only explain the general details in order to understand the processes.

At the end of this book, the reader will have acquired enough skills to be competitive when it comes to designing with SolidWorks, and while there are many less frequently used commands and options available that will not be covered in this book, rest assured that those commands that are covered are most of the commands used every day by SolidWorks designers.

Files required to complete some of the exercises will be available for download on our website (***http://www.mechanicad.com/download.html***) as well as the completed files made throughout the book to help you practice and enhance your skills. We hope you learn many new things and enjoy reading this book as much as we enjoyed making it. We love to hear ideas and comments from our readers. If you have any, please share them with us and our readers; we'll try our best to accommodate any suggestions to improve and expand the content of this book, and while we cannot guarantee that any will make it to the next edition, we can assure you that we reply to all email messages.
alejandro@mechanicad.com

Prerequisites

This book has been written assuming the reader has knowledge of the following topics:
- Familiarity with the Windows operating system;
- General knowledge of mechanical design and drafting;
- Previous experience with SolidWorks.
- A general understanding of sheet metal, structural and molding processes will help to better understand these topics.

Notes:

Multi Body Parts, Sketch Editing and Other Tools

SolidWorks offers a number of tools to help us model components easier and faster with powerful options like multi body parts and contour selection. Multi body parts means that we can have more than one "solid" in a part. Up until now we have been modeling parts as single body parts, meaning that each feature either added or removed material to the part, but always resulted in a single solid body. Designing with multi body parts allows us to do things that sometimes are very difficult or even impossible using a single body component like, among other things, combine bodies, remove one body from another or calculate their common volume. Multi body operations are particularly useful when working with mold design and is the essence of the weldments environment (both are covered in this book).

So far we have worked with single and multiple contour open or closed sketches. In this section we'll cover how to use Contour selection to work with sketches with multiple entities sharing an endpoint and/or having self-intersecting lines. We'll learn how to take advantage of these situations and make the best of them.

Another topic that is very important to modeling in SolidWorks is editing parts to fix errors or change components. After all, when we are designing, most likely we'll have to make changes along the way, and sometimes those changes can cause trouble down the road. In the Editing section we'll cover different options available when editing parts, as well as fixing and recovering from errors.

One last topic we'll cover in this section deals with maintaining design intent; we'll learn how to add, edit and delete equations in a part, giving us powerful tools to make our designs more flexible, robust and predictable when making design changes.

Notes:

Multi Body Parts

As we stated earlier, multi body parts allow us to do certain operations that would be difficult to accomplish with a single body part. First, we'll talk about how to make multi body parts, and after that how to use them.

1. – Multi body parts are made by adding material that is not connected to the current solid body, in other words, that is purposely <u>not</u> merged to it, or by splitting an existing body. To show how it works, make a new part, and add a sketch to the Front plane as shown. Do not worry about dimensions here as we are just illustrating the concept of how multi bodies work.

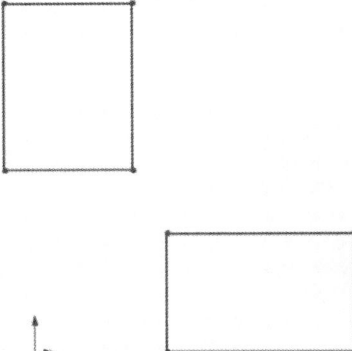

2. – Select the "Boss Extrude" command. Notice that we are not given a warning about having two separate bodies; it just works. Extrude any size that looks similar to the following image (dimensions are not important at this time) and click **OK** to finish. (Making two or more extruded/revolved/swept/lofted features would work just the same.)

3

The first thing we notice is a new folder in the FeatureManager called "**Solid Bodies(2)**." This folder is automatically added when SolidWorks detects multiple disjointed bodies in a part and lists the number of bodies found in the part (in this case, 2). If we expand the folder, we can see the two bodies in our part listed under it. The important thing to know and remember is that **multi body parts are not to be confused or used in place of an assembly**; parts and assemblies have significant differences and each serves a different purpose. A multi body part is used mostly as a means to an end.

3. – The next step is to add a new feature. When working in a multi body part we can make 'local' operations, for example, a shell feature affecting only one body. Applied features like fillets, shells, chamfers, etc. can only be applied to a single body at a time. Select the "Shell" command from the Features toolbar, and shell the bottom body as indicated.

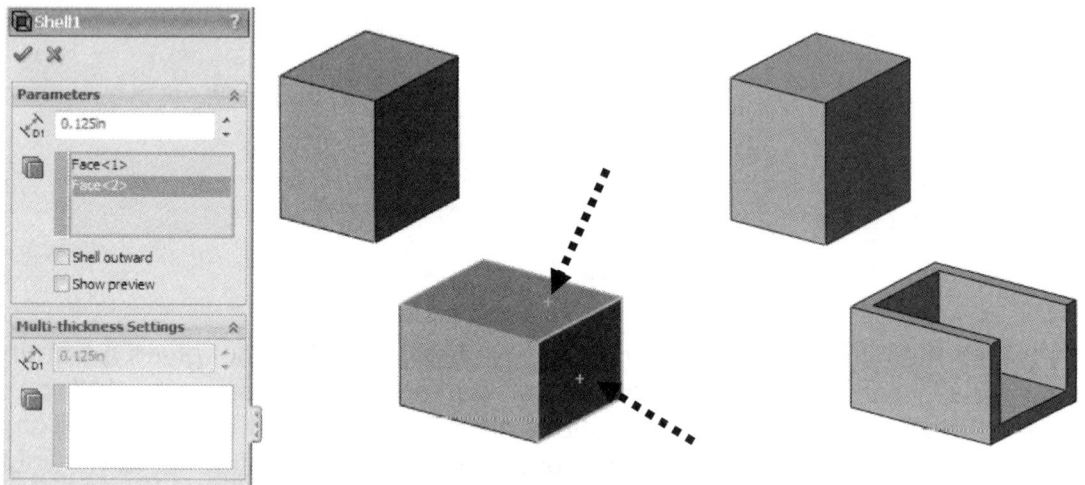

4. – Select the **Fillet** command and round two corners of the top body as shown.

To help the reader understand the concept of local operations better, "local" means that we can add applied features (features that don't require a sketch like Shell, Fillet, Chamfer, Draft, etc.) to one body at a time. Notice the name of a body changes to the last feature applied to it.

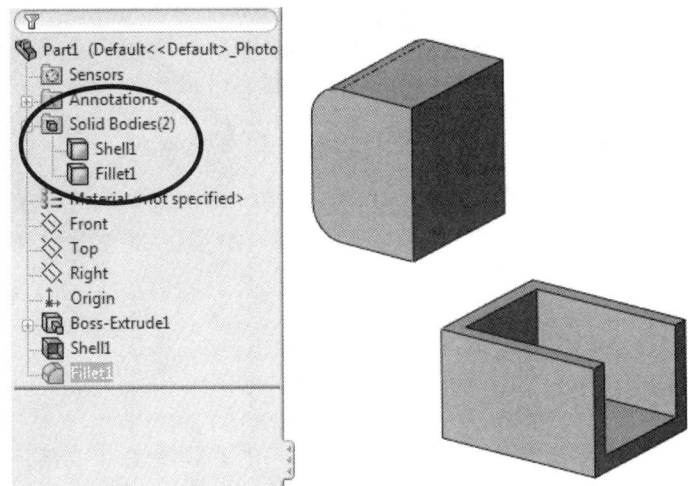

5. – When working with multi bodies, adding more features like a Boss-Extrude automatically selects existing bodies to modify; this is the default behavior. Optionally, we can select which bodies to "merge" (or fuse with) to make a single body, or selectively pick which bodies to merge with. We'll make a new Boss-Extrude and explore the option to merge with existing bodies. Select the front face of a body and make the following sketch in it.

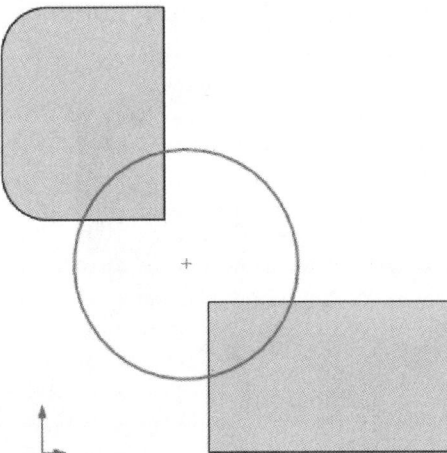

6. – Extrude the sketch *into* the existing bodies. Notice the "**Merge result**" option in the Extrude command. It's always been there (except when there are no solid bodies), and by default is always checked. A new option at the bottom of the Extrude command when we have multiple bodies is "**Feature Scope**." This is where we can select which bodies to affect. We can choose to affect "All bodies" *or* "Selected bodies" either automatically or manually selected. By default the Feature Scope option is set to "**Selected bodies**" and "**Auto-select**." These two options mean that by default the new feature will merge with any body it intersects with. When the "**Merge result**" option is unchecked, *"Feature Scope"* is automatically removed and the new Boss-Extrude will not merge with the existing bodies. Uncheck "Merge Result" and click **OK** to finish.

7. – The result of this operation is three bodies in our part. See how the different bodies' edges intersect each other. If we had left the "**Merge result**" option checked, we would not see these edges overlapping as they would have merged into a single body. Edit the definition of the last extrusion to explore the effect of different "**Merge Result**" and "**Feature Scope**" combinations.

Combination:	Result:
Merge Result: Checked **Feature Scope**: Auto-Select 	Single body. By touching both existing bodies "Auto-select" merges with them, fusing them into a single solid body. The "Solid Bodies" folder is no longer visible. 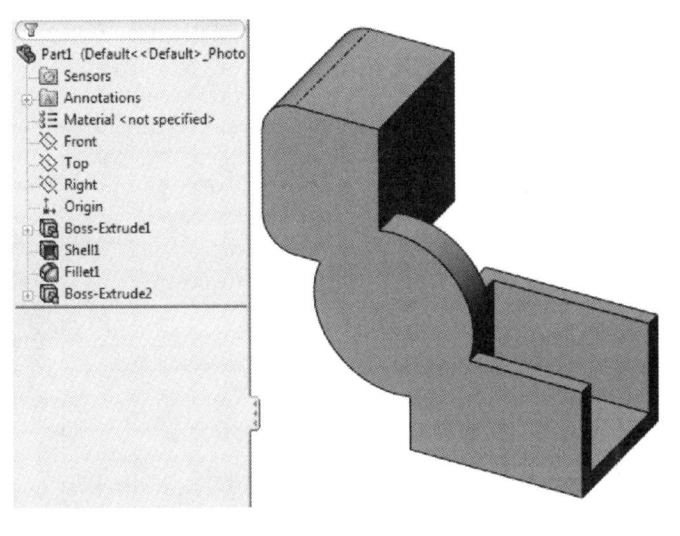
Merge result: Checked **Auto-select**: Unchecked Add shell body to selection box 	Two bodies. We are telling the Boss-Extrude to merge only to the Shell body (or whichever we pick). Notice the edges of the upper body and the Boss-Extrude overlap, as they are different bodies.

8. –The "**Merge result**" option works the same way with any feature that adds material to the part, including revolved boss, sweep, loft, etc. Now we'll see how it works when we remove material. Delete the Boss-Extrude feature and keep the sketch. Select the sketch in the FeatureManager and make a Cut-Extrude "Through All." In this case the "Merge Result" is gone and we only have the "**Feature Scope**" option at the bottom with the same selection options: "All bodies" or "Selected Bodies" with/without "Auto-select." Leave the "Auto-select" option on and click **OK** to finish.

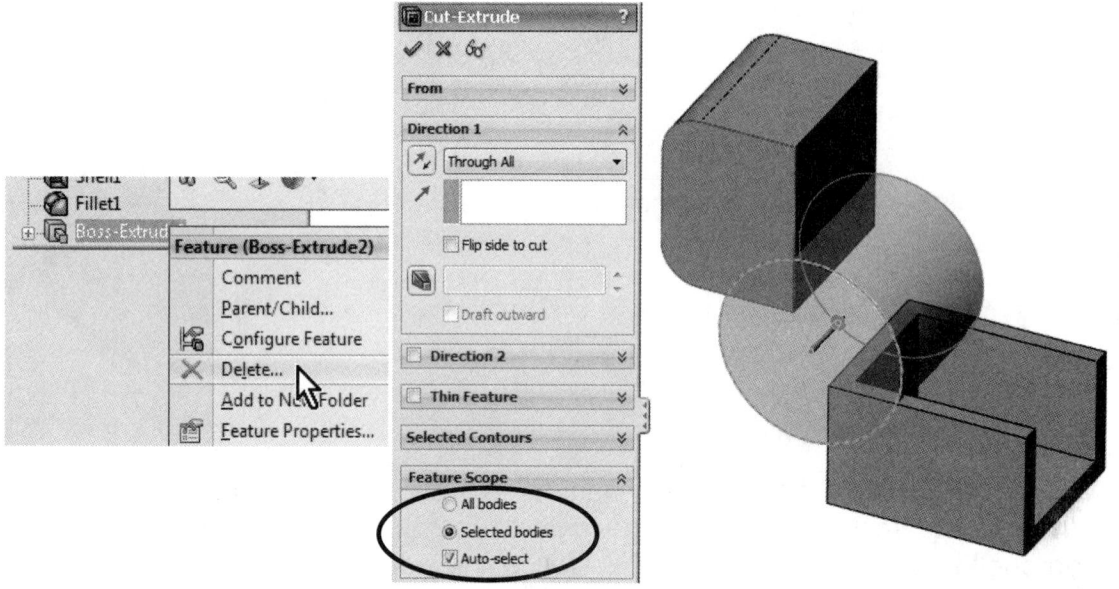

9. – What we end up with is the same two bodies we had before, but now they have a cut through them.

10. – Edit the Cut-Extrude definition, turn off the "Auto-select" option in the "**Feature Scope**," and select only the top body. Click **OK** to finish. Now we are only modifying the top solid, even if the Cut-Extrude overlaps the lower body.

And just as with the features that add material, this technique works the same way with all the features that remove material including revolved cut, sweep cut, loft cut, etc.

11. – Modeling with multi bodies is a powerful technique to model parts that would otherwise be difficult to complete. One frequently used technique is called "bridging"; this means to connect two or more bodies by adding material between them to merge them into a single solid body. Reasons to use this technique may include a model where we know what opposite sides/ends of a part look like, but we may not know what the middle (the "bridge") should be like. For our example we'll assume that we need to design a car's wheel. We know what the actual tire and hub dimensions should be, but we don't know yet what the spokes will look like; we just know it has to look great ☺.

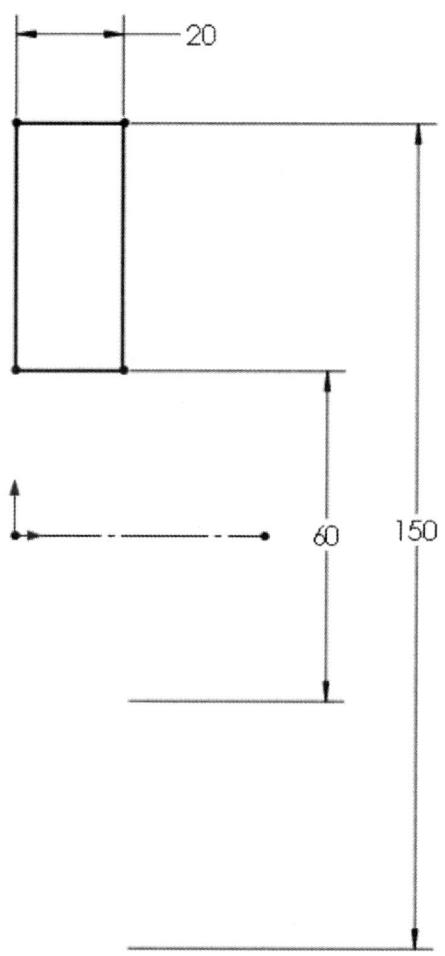

We'll assume the dimensions for the wheel are as shown in the following sketches. The first part of the wheel to design will be the hub or mounting pad. Draw the following sketch in the Right plane and make a 360° Boss-Revolve. Our wheel's dimensions will be in millimeters, so be sure to change your model's dimensions accordingly (**Tools, Options, Document Options, Units,** or in the status bar's **Unit System**). Pay attention to the diameter dimensions (doubled about the horizontal centerline).

12. – Make a pattern of 5 holes to mount the wheel to the car.

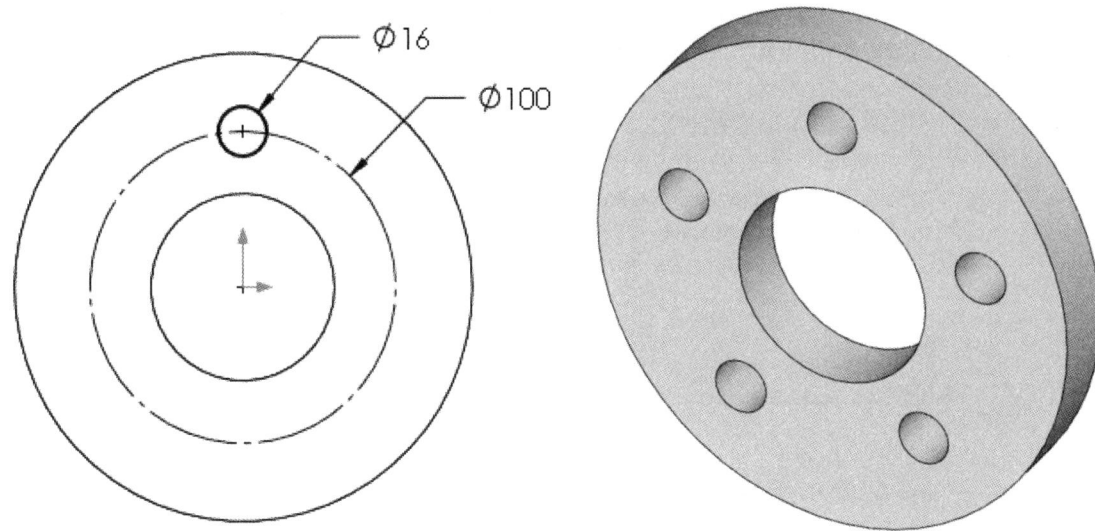

13. – Now we'll make the wheel's rim that matches the tire. Draw the following sketch also in the Right plane. (The 330 mm diameter dimension is doubled about the horizontal centerline as diameter.)

TIP: Make the two short lines on the sides equal, and the two lines connected to the 12mm horizontal line also equal.

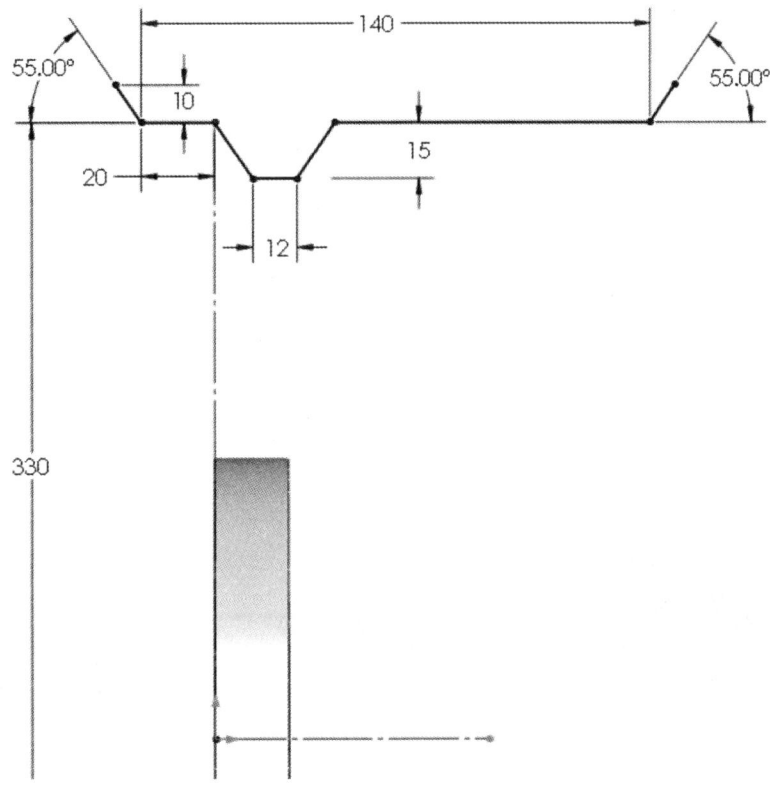

Beginner's Guide to SolidWorks 2012 – Level II

14. – After finishing the sketch, make a Revolved-Boss. Since this is an open sketch we will be warned about closing it if we don't want a thin feature. Select NO when asked. Make a thin revolved feature using the horizontal centerline for axis or revolution, and 5mm thick going inside.

 If we answer YES to close the sketch, a new line will be added going from the first line's open endpoint, to the last line's open endpoint making a closed profile.

12

After finishing the revolved feature, we can see that now we have two bodies.

15. – Now we need to make the spoke in the wheel; this is the part where we can get creative. For this exercise we'll assume our limitations are defined by the hub and the rim where the tire mounts. We'll design the first spoke and will not merge it to any other body; we'll have to make a couple of local operations on the spoke and after it's done, make a body pattern with it. Switch to a Right view and add a sketch in the Right plane. Change to "Hidden Lines Visible" mode for visibility. A shaded model is shown for sketch clarity. Make both arcs tangent to the vertical lines, tangent to each other, and with equal radii. The vertical lines are coincident to the first hole in the hub and the rim's outside edge. This will be the path for a sweep. Exit the sketch and rename it "Spoke path."

16. – Make a new plane parallel to the Top plane and coincident to the top endpoint of the previous sketch. This plane will be used to draw a new sketch that will be the sweep's profile.

17. – Switch to a Top view, add a new sketch to the new plane and draw the following sketch. This sketch will be the Profile for the sweep. The arc is tangent to the edge where the path starts. Exit the sketch when done and rename it "Spoke Profile."

Multi Body Parts, Sketch Editing and Other Tools

18. – Select the **Sweep** command. Select the "Spoke Profile" sketch and "Spoke Path" to make the sweep. In the Options, uncheck "**Merge Result**" as we still need to make a couple more operations before merging all bodies. Click **OK** to finish.

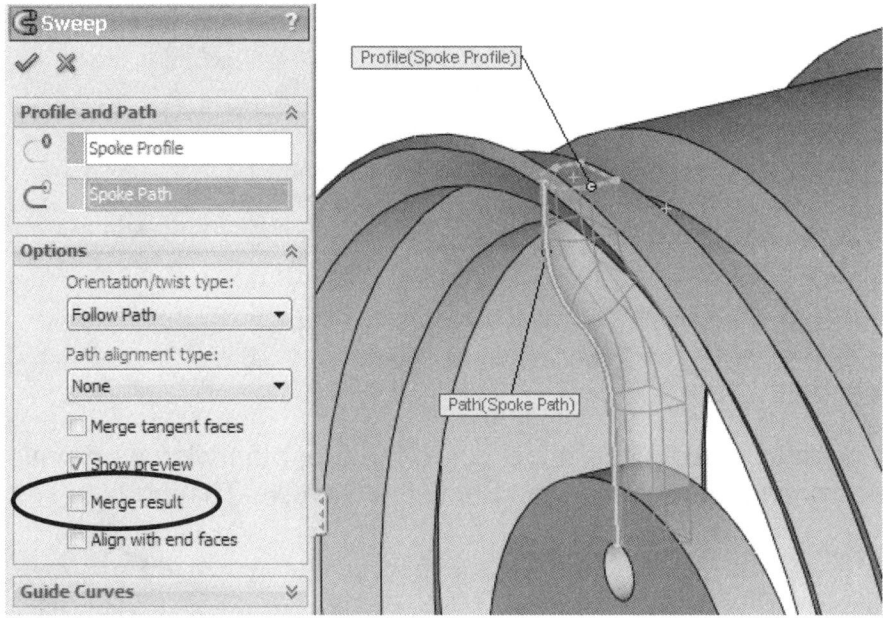

19. – Now we have three bodies. To continue, we'll hide the first two and only leave the Sweep body visible. Select each of the other two bodies and hide them.

15

20. – After we are left with only the Sweep body, select the **Shell** command and remove the ends and back of the body. Make the shell 3mm thick.

21. – We need to make a cylindrical cut to the top; otherwise we'll have a part of the Sweep coming through the top. Show the Revolve-Thin body to see it.

22. – Hide the Revolve-Thin feature again and switch to a Right view. Add a new sketch in the Right plane as shown. We are making the cut just under the top to make sure the Sweep body (now named Shell1) will not go through the top. Add a horizontal centerline at the origin to make a Revolved Cut about it.

23. – Select the **Revolved Cut** command. What we want to do is to cut only the spoke body, and nothing else. Under "**Feature Scope**" uncheck "Auto-select" and select the spoke body only.

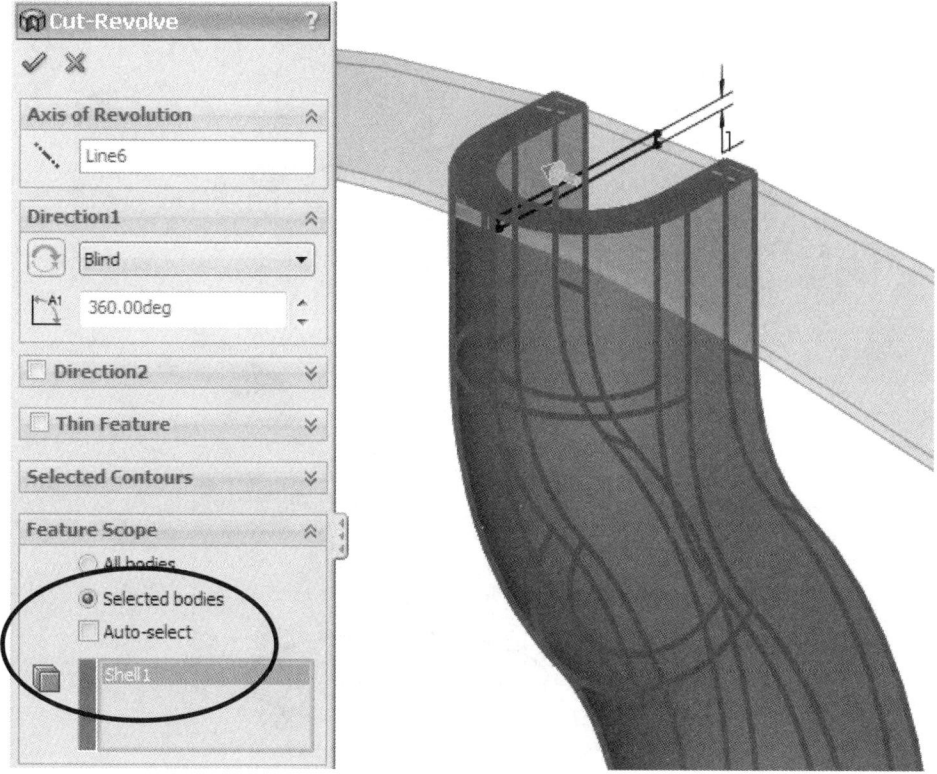

17

24. – After clicking **OK** we get a new dialog box asking us which bodies we want to keep, since the cut we are making divides the spoke in three pieces. Use the "**Selected bodies**" option, and select the spoke's largest body which is the one we want to keep. Click **OK** to finish. In this case we still have our three original bodies and have discarded the two smaller ones.

25. – A different approach, assuming had we opted to keep all three bodies after the Revolved Cut, would be that we have five bodies in our part, and to eliminate the extra bodies we don't need we would have to delete them. To do this, select the two bodies, right mouse click and select "**Delete Bodies**." Make sure the correct bodies are selected and click **OK** to finish.

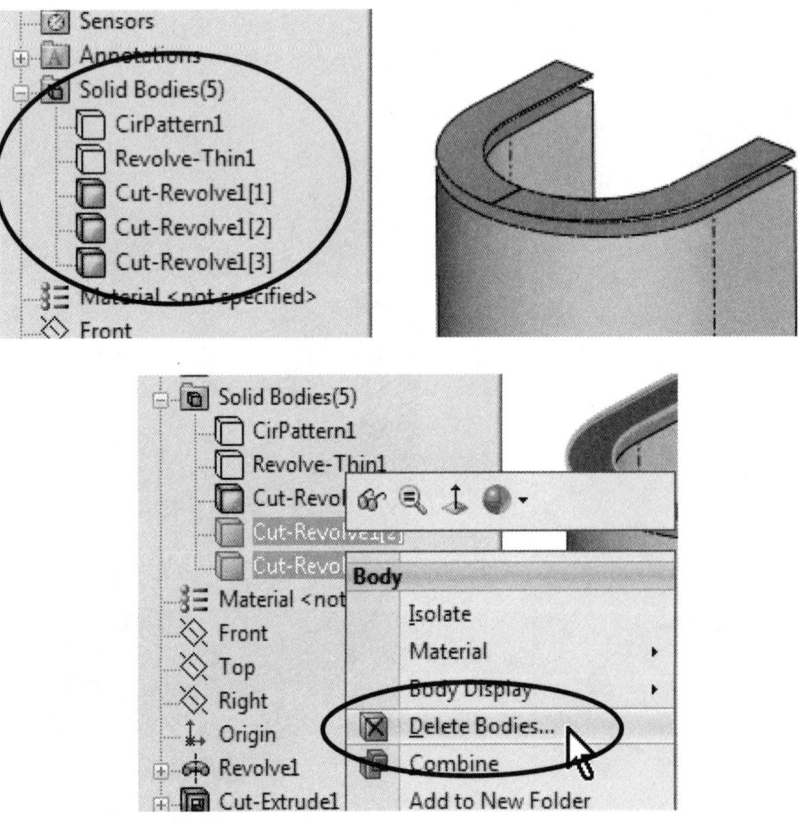

Multi Body Parts, Sketch Editing and Other Tools

A new feature "**Body-Delete**" would be added to the FeatureManager.

 For our example we'll use the approach to select the bodies to keep at the time of making the Cut-Revolve instead of deleting the remaining bodies with an additional operation.

26. – Now add a Full Round Fillet to each side of the Spoke. Select the **Fillet** command with the **Full Round** option. Select both side and center faces to round both sides of the spoke. Two fillets will be added.

19

27. – We are now ready to pattern the spoke body. To show the hidden bodies, select them in the "**Solid Bodies**" folder and click in the **Show** command.

28. – Select the **Circular Pattern** command, but instead of making a pattern of features, we'll make a pattern of bodies. Select a circular edge to define the pattern's axis and expand the "**Bodies to Pattern**" selection box. In the graphics area, select the Spoke and make 7 copies equally spaced in 360 degrees. Click **OK** to finish.

Multi Body Parts, Sketch Editing and Other Tools

29. – Now we have nine solid bodies in our part.

30. – At this time we are ready to combine all solids into a single body. Select all bodies in the FeatureManager, right mouse click on them, and select "**Combine Bodies**" from the pop-up menu, or from the menu "**Insert, Features, Combine**," and select all the bodies in the graphics area.

21

31. – Select the "**Add**" option and click **OK** to finish. All bodies are now combined into a single solid.

32. – Add a 5mm fillet to the faces indicated at the center and each spoke.

33. – To add a similar fillet to the other side of the Spokes, first we need to add a fillet to the Rim's body. If we try to add the fillet after the bodies are combined, the fillet will fail. Move the Rollback bar from the bottom of the FeatureManager before the "Combine1" feature. What we need to do is to add a 20mm fillet to the indicated edge of the rim's body *before* the solid bodies are combined.

34. – Drag the Rollback bar down to the bottom when finished to have the "Combine1" and "Fillet3" features resolved, and have a single body again.

35. – Add a 4 mm fillet to the face of the previous fillet to propagate it to all Spokes at the same time.

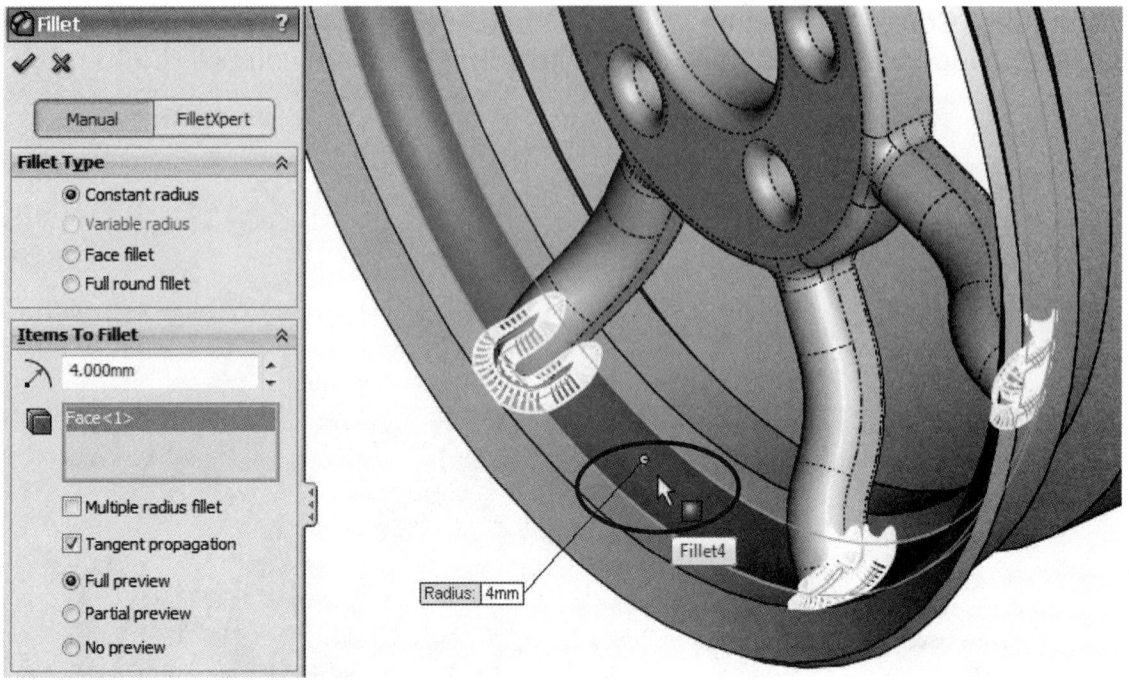

36. – Your finished wheel should now look like this:

I know this may not be the best looking wheel, but it's a good example to show how to work with multi body parts and perform local operations. We'd love to see your designs; please email us a picture to alejandro@mechanicad.com

37. – The next area to cover in the multi bodies topic will be to learn more about combining bodies. What we did in the wheel exercise was to add bodies, in essence merging or fusing them. The other two operations we can do when combining bodies is to subtract one or more bodies from another, or get the common volume between them. To obtain the common volume between bodies, first we need two bodies that intersect. Open a new part and draw the following sketch in the Right plane.

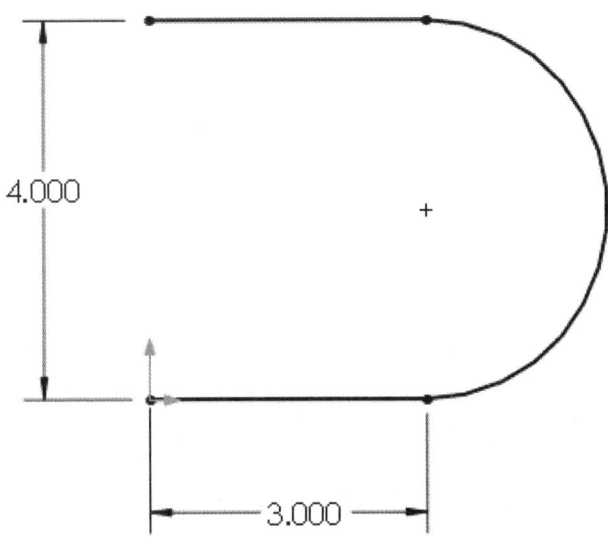

38. – Make a Boss-Extrude as a Thin Feature. The extrusion's depth will be 3" and the thickness of the part 0.5" inside.

39. – For the next feature, add a sketch in the Top face of the first feature. Looking at it from a Top view should look like this:

 Notice the only dimension we need to add is the hole's diameter; everything else is defined with geometric relations.

40. – Extrude the second sketch downwards with the "**Through All**" end condition, and uncheck the "**Merge result**" checkbox. We want to have two overlapping bodies.

41. – Now that we have two separate bodies, we can combine them to get the common volume. Select the menu "**Insert, Features, Combine**" and select both bodies, or from the "**Solid Bodies**" folder in the FeatureManager pre-select BOTH bodies; right mouse click and select "**Combine**" from the pop-up menu.

42. – In the Combine operation select the "**Common**" option under "**Operation Type**." Click on the "**Preview**" button to see what the resulting body will look like and click **OK** to finish.

The finished part will look like this.

43. – The next multi body operation we'll cover is the difference between bodies. One common use for a body difference is to obtain a mold's core and/or cavity, but here we'll show how to obtain the volume capacity of an irregularly shaped bottle. Download the part *Bottle.sldprt* from our website and open it (www.mechanicad.com/download.html). In order to obtain a volume with the inside capacity of the bottle, we need to make a new solid body that will enclose the bottle up to the fill level. Make a new sketch in the Front plane and draw a rectangle as shown. Make the extrusion big enough to cover the entire bottle and uncheck the "**Merge result**" option.

44. – Now that we have the two solid bodies, select the menu "**Insert, Features, Combine**." Select the "**Subtract**" option under "**Operation Type**." In order to get a difference, we need to select the body that we want to remove material from (Main Body) and the body(ies) that we want to remove from it. In the "**Main Body**" selection box, select the body just created, and under "**Bodies to Subtract**" select the Bottle. Click **OK** when done selecting.

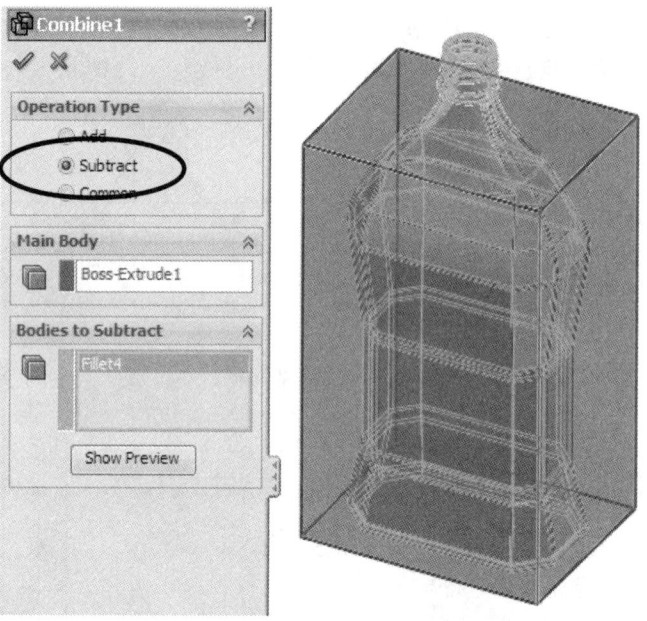

45. – We are immediately presented with the "**Bodies to Keep**" dialog. There are two bodies resulting from the operation, but we are interested only in the inside body. Select the inside body and click **OK** to finish.

46. – Now we have the actual volume of the bottle up to the fill line. Notice that when we subtract one body from another, the original bodies are consumed and we are left only with the difference. After running a "**Mass Properties**" analysis, we can see that the volume of liquid inside the bottle up to the fill line is 25.1 cubic inches. Save and close the part.

Notes:

Contour Selection

Contour Selection is a way to work with a sketch that has intersecting entities, endpoints shared by multiple entities and many of the common problems that prevent us from using a sketch for a feature. We'll also learn how to reuse a sketch for multiple features and a previously unused Extrude/Cut option.

47. – Make a new part and add a sketch to the Front plane as shown. In this example we will not worry about dimensions to simplify the explanation and concentrate on how contour selection works.

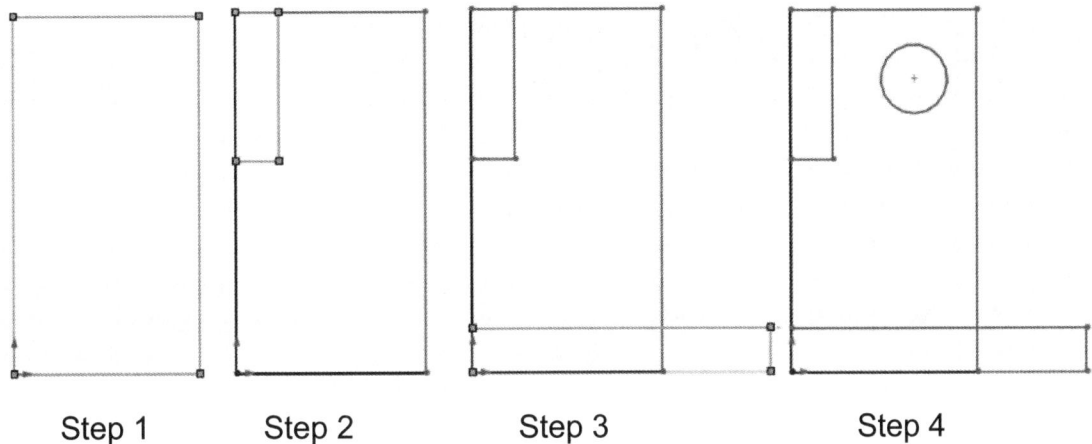

Step 1   Step 2   Step 3   Step 4

 In this sketch we are drawing three rectangles and one circle. Note that the rectangles are overlapping and sharing endpoints.

48. – When we try to create a feature using a sketch with overlapping and/or shared endpoints, the Contour Selection tool is automatically activated and the "**Selected Contours**" selection box is open. Also notice we don't get an Extrusion/Cut preview until we select the region(s) or contour(s) that we want to use in the feature. Select the Boss-Extrude icon. In the graphics area move the mouse pointer around and see the different regions available for selection. We can select single or multiple regions *and/or* complete closed contours.

33

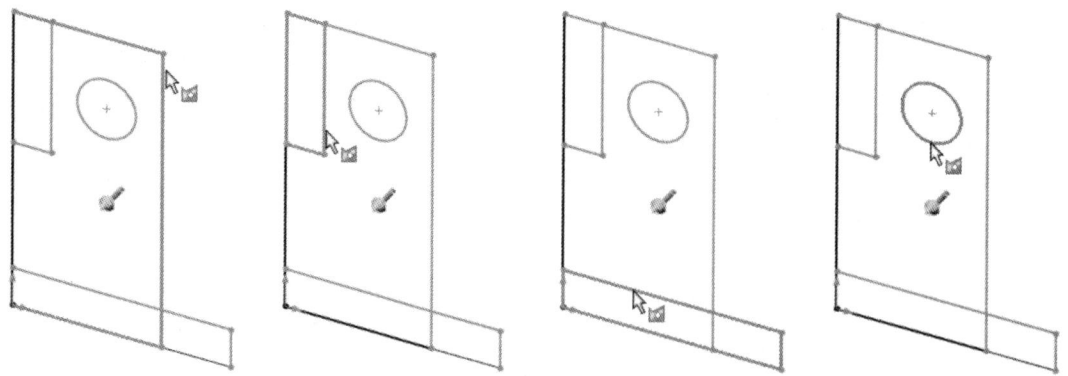

49. – Select the bottom square profile (or both bottom regions) and extrude *approximately* as shown. Just like with any other feature the sketch is automatically hidden after we finish.

50. – To re-use the sketch for more features, select the sketch in the Feature-Manager and click "**Show**" in the pop-up menu. Note the "**Contours**" icon next to the sketch's name.

51. – We will now use the same sketch again for a new feature. To activate the Contour Selection tool we have to make a right mouse click in the graphics area (or the sketch itself). Be aware that by default the "**Contour Select Tool**" option is not available in the pop-up menu; you have to expand the menu at the bottom to make it visible.

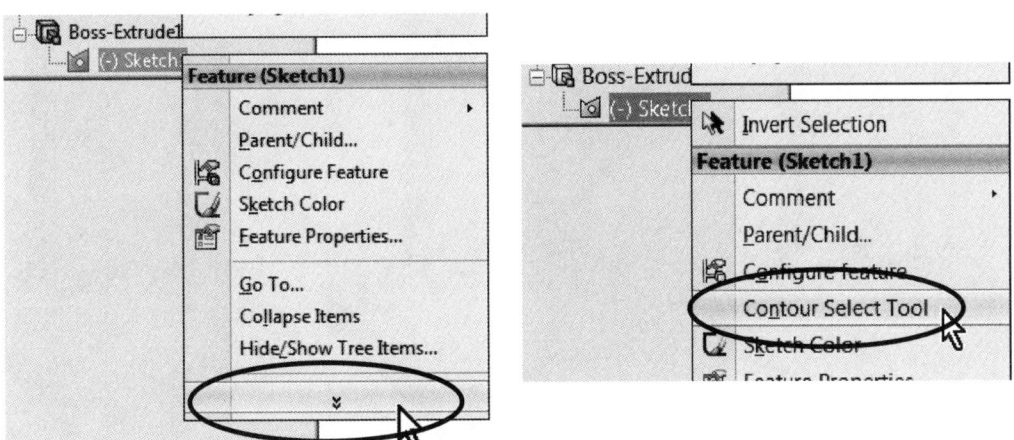

52. – After selecting the "**Contour Select Tool**" option select the regions indicated and extrude *approximately* as shown. You may have to click in the sketch to enable (activate) selection of regions, and either: hold down the Ctrl key to pre-select all three regions and then extrude, OR select the Extruded Base command *and then* select the regions. Either way works the same.

After using the same sketch for two or more features we can see a slightly different icon next to the sketch name with a little hand under it. This means the sketch is "shared" by more than one feature, and the sketch name is the same. Also note that the sketch remains visible after we use the "Show" command.

53. – Repeat the previous process to select the next contour and extrude as shown. Remember at this time we are only showing how it works and are not concerned about the dimensions.

54. – For the final feature select the "**Contour Select Tool**" and select the circle. What we have done up until now is to make features starting in the sketch plane. SolidWorks has a powerful (yet sometimes under used feature) that allows us to start the feature somewhere *other* than the sketch plane. After selecting the circle using "Contour Select," click in the **Extruded Cut** command; in the "**From**" start condition's drop-down menu select "**Surface/Face/Plane**" (we can also use a vertex or distance offset).

Multi Body Parts, Sketch Editing and Other Tools

55. – Now select the front face of the second boss as indicated. Our Cut feature will start here. Make the feature's depth *about* half way deep, and click **OK** to finish. By using the "**Start Condition**" option for feature creation we can easily save time by not having to create auxiliary planes or geometry.

56. – Now that we have made four features from the same multiple contour and self-intersecting sketch, we can hide it.

37

Contour Selection Review

Make the following sketch and make all four features off of it using contour selection.

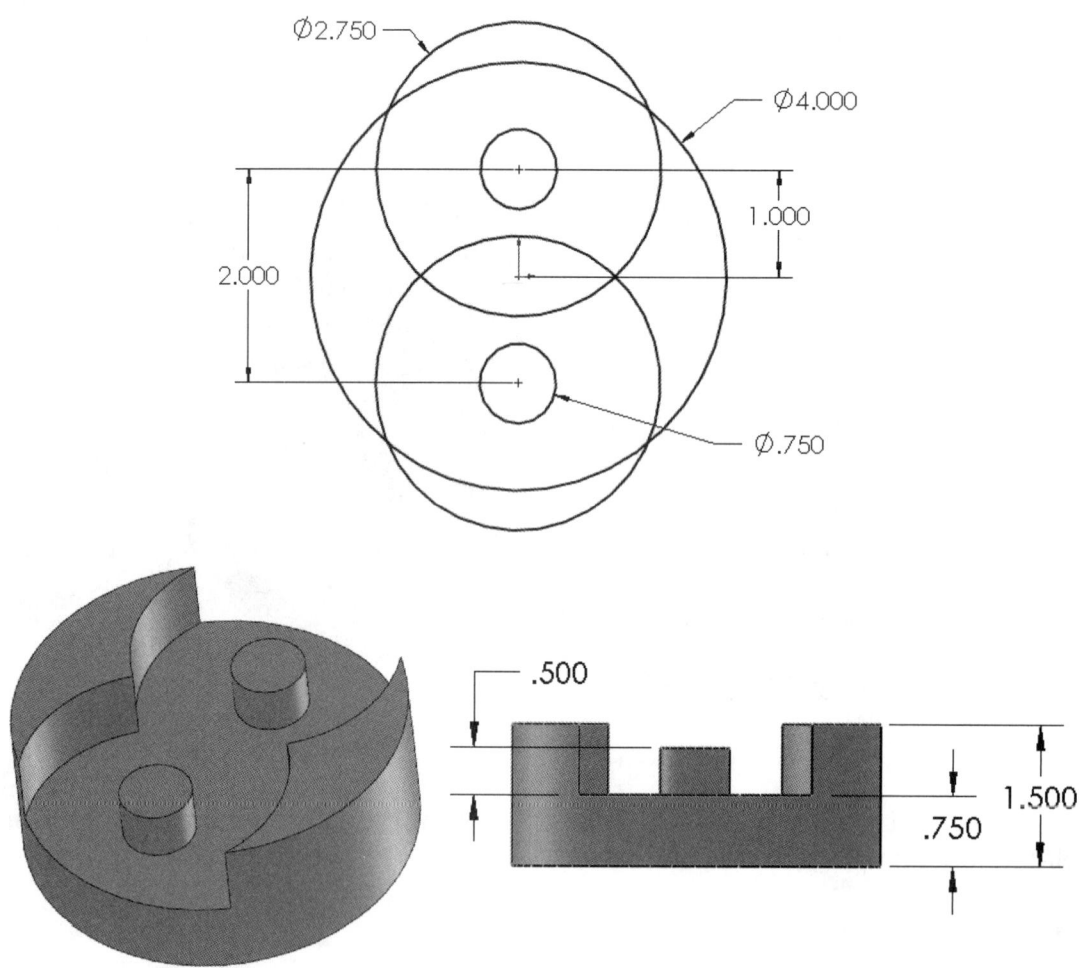

Part Editing

A very important skill to have when modeling in SolidWorks (or any CAD package for that matter) is to be able to change a model and fix errors. Let's face it: the only constant in design is change, and when we make changes to our model, chances are we may cause errors down the road, that is, the Feature-Manager. For example, if we have a part with round edges (fillets) and we change a previous feature and eliminate an edge, the fillet will give us an error because it cannot find it. That's the type of error we are talking about.

57. – To practice editing and fixing errors, download the part *Repair.sldprt* from www.mechanicad.com/download.html and open it. After we are done modifying and fixing the part, it should look like this:

58. – When we open the file we are asked if we want to rebuild it. Select "**Rebuild**" from the dialog to continue.

59. – When rebuilt, we get a list of error messages and no geometry at all.

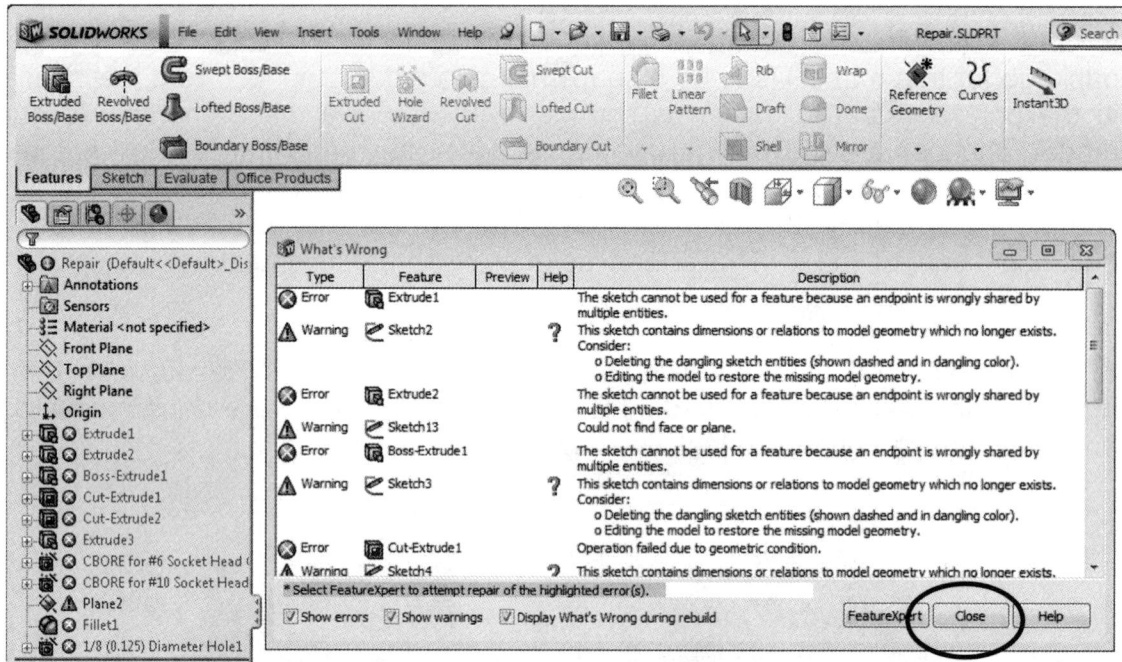

60. – This part has so many errors that no geometry can be generated, and the "**What's Wrong**" dialog contains the full list of things that need to be fixed. Click the "Close" button for now. Since features are added chronologically starting at the top in the FeatureManager, the logical order to start fixing errors is from the top and work your way down. The reason is if a 'parent' feature has an error, it may cause problems in a 'child' feature, therefore the dependency between features is referred to as "**Parent/Child**" relations. For example, if a sketch is added to a face of another feature, or a dimension references another feature's geometry, a Parent/Child relation is generated. To identify these relations, click in the "**Boss-Extrude1**" feature with the right mouse button and select "**Parent/Child**."

 There are two types or errors: a red X means the feature failed to build; the yellow warning triangle means the feature has an error, but SolidWorks was able to build it.

61. – Here we can see the features that "Boss-Extrude1" depends on (Parents), and which features depend on it (Children). The higher we go in the FeatureManager, the more Children a feature may have. Click "Close" to continue.

62. – To start fixing errors, we'll check what the error at the "Extrude1" feature is. Right mouse click on it and select "**What's Wrong?**"

This error means that the sketch has intersecting lines or more than 2 lines connected to the same endpoint. One common cause of this problem is when sketching we accidentally add overlapping lines. Close the "**What's Wrong**" dialog, expand the "Extrude1" feature and edit the sketch.

63. – Sometimes it's easy to see the geometric elements causing the problem in a sketch and we can correct it, but sometimes it's not that obvious. To help us identify the problem, select the menu "**Tools, Sketch Tools, Check Sketch for Feature**."

 Setting the option to show sketch endpoints is usually a good option. Go to the menu "**Tools, Options, System Options, Sketch, Display entity points in part/assembly sketches**."

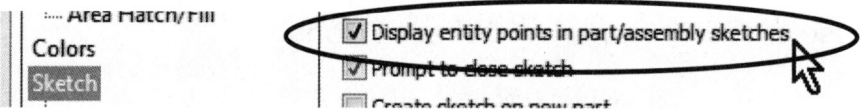

If this sketch has already been used for a feature, that feature type will be pre-selected in the drop-down menu. If the sketch has not been used, we have to select the type of feature that we intend to use it for. In our case "Base Extrude" is pre-selected. Click on "**Check**" to analyze the sketch. Immediately we see the same error message that we got using "**What's Wrong**." Click **OK** to dismiss it and continue.

Multi Body Parts, Sketch Editing and Other Tools

64. – SolidWorks immediately reorients the sketch and places the magnifying glass on top of the geometric element suspected of causing the problem. We are given two areas of concern: the first one is that we have overlapping entities, and the second one multiple (more than 2) elements sharing the same endpoint.

The advantage of using this tool is that we can quickly identify where the problem is and correct it, instead of hunting down small line segments in a sketch. Now that we know where the problem is, window-select the overlapping line and delete it. Click "**Refresh**" to confirm that we don't have any more problems and close the "Repair Sketch" window.

65. – Exit the sketch (or rebuild the model) to continue. We are notified that a subsequent feature has an error and we are asked if we wish to repair it now or continue with the error. Click on "**Continue (Ignore Error)**" and also close the "**What's Wrong?**" message.

43

Now we can see some features and (more importantly) the error from the first feature is gone.

66. – Select the "Extrude2" feature, right mouse click and select "**What's Wrong?**" to view the error. Essentially we have the same problem as the first feature. Edit the "Extrude2" sketch to fix it.

67. – Once we are editing the sketch, select the menu "**Tools, Sketch Tools, Check Sketch for Feature**" to find out what the problem is. Close the error message when it comes up.

In this case, looking at all three problems listed in the "Repair Sketch" dialog (one overlapping entity and two with more than two entities at an endpoint), we can tell that we have two identical lines overlapping. Close the dialog and delete one.

If we use window-selection we'll delete both lines; if we click to select one, only one is selected.

68. – After selecting one of the overlapping lines and deleting it, we may be warned that other entities will also be deleted, most likely dimensions attached to the line selected.

69. – If this is the case click "Yes" to continue. Notice the top horizontal line's dimension is also deleted. This is because that dimension was referencing the line we deleted. Add the missing dimension and exit the sketch. Select "Continue (Ignore Error)" and close the "What's Wrong?" message.

70. – Now our model is starting to look better. Notice that we have fixed only two features and we have cleared many errors, better illustrating the importance of understanding parent/child relations.

71. – After reviewing the next error with "**What's Wrong?**" we see that it's the same error as the two previous features. Editing the sketch we can see an extra diagonal line. We can either delete it, or convert it to **Construction Geometry**. The second option is usually safer, as we could lose dimensions and/or relations if we delete it, and we can always revert it if needed. Select the diagonal line and convert it to construction geometry from the pop-up toolbar.

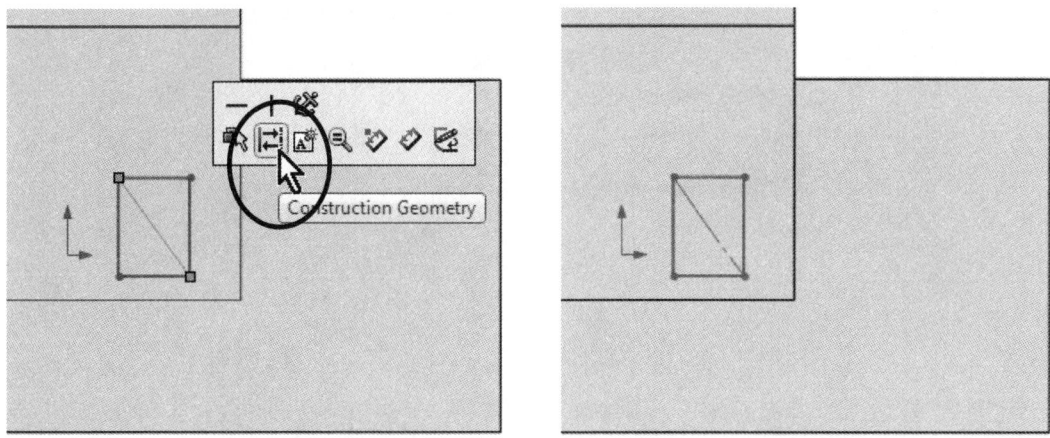

72. – Exit the sketch to rebuild the part. Since the newly created feature does not seem to be part of the original design, the logical step would be to delete it. Select the feature with the right mouse button and after selecting "**Delete**" we get the confirmation dialog:

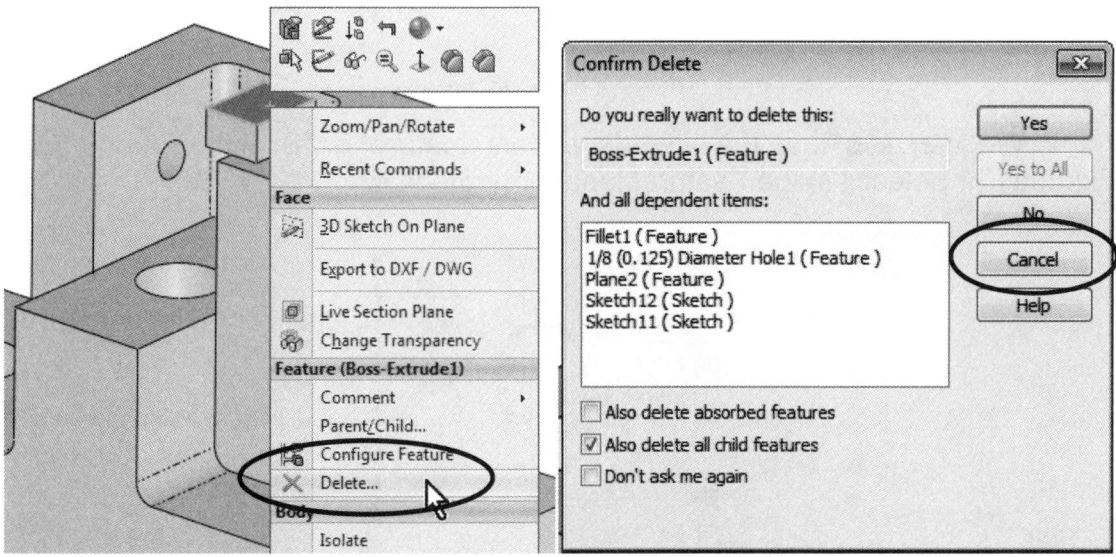

73. – In the confirmation we can see that if we delete this feature we'll also delete its dependent features, but we need to have them in our part. The reason those features would also be deleted is because they are "children" features of "Boss-Extrude1." Select "**Cancel**." We don't want to delete anything at this time; we'll edit those features to remove the dependencies *and then* delete this feature. Select the extrusion's "**Parent/Child**" relationships.

74. – We can see that the first dependant feature is "Sketch3" (from "Cut-Extrude1"). Select it in the FeatureManager and edit it.

75. – Change to a Top view for clarity. We can see a dimension colored in brown (0.603). The brown colored dimension (or geometric relation) tells us it is '***dangling***,' which means that it is referencing something that no longer exists. What we need to do is to is to fix the dimension's reference.

Here we can do one of two things:

a) Delete the dimension and add it again to a valid reference, or
b) Re-attach the dimension to a valid reference.

Deleting the dimension is straightforward and often a good solution, so we'll talk about the second option. After selecting the dimension, we see a witness line ending with a red dot; this is the witness line missing the reference. It may look as if it was referencing the existing edge, but in fact it lost the edge it was attached to, even if it was rebuilt. To re-attach it, <u>drag the red dot</u> onto a valid reference. Here we'll use the right side edge. After re-attaching, note that the geometry does not change; the value of the dimension is what updates.

76. – Exit the sketch and review the "**Parent/Child**" relationships again (dismiss the "**What's Wrong**" dialog). As we can see, Sketch3 and Cut-Extrude1 are no longer listed as children features of Boss-Extrude1, since we changed the dimension to reference a different edge, in essence, breaking the relation.

77. – From the relationships dialog we can see that the only children left are Plane2 and Fillet1. Reviewing the Parent/Child relations for Plane2, we see that the only child feature is the "1/8 (0.125) Diameter Hole1." A Hole Wizard feature has two automatically made sketches; the first sketch locates the hole's position, and is created in the plane/face where the hole is made, the second sketch is the hole's profile.

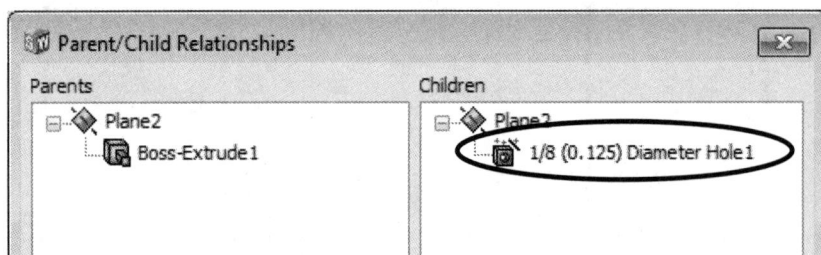

The most likely reason why the "1/8 (0.125) Diameter Hole1" feature is a child to Plane2 is that it was probably made in Plane2. We can find out in which plane or face a sketch is made by editing the sketch plane; to do this expand the Hole Wizard feature, select the first sketch (Sketch12) which is the hole's location sketch, and from the pop-up menu select "**Edit Sketch Plane**." Since Plane2 is listed it confirms it as the current sketch plane.

Multi Body Parts, Sketch Editing and Other Tools

78. – To change the sketch to a different plane (or face) and delete the relationship to Boss-Extrude1, select a new face for the sketch. Select the face indicated and click **OK** to finish. Close the "**What's Wrong?**" dialog to continue.

79. – Review the Parent/Child relationships again for Boss-Extrude1 and Plane2. Now the only children of Boss-Extrude1 are Plane2 and Fillet1, and Plane2 has no children. Close the dialog to continue.

80. – Select Fillet1 and check "**What's Wrong**?" Note that the icon is different; in this case the error is a warning. The Fillet was built but it's missing one or more edges. Close the dialog and edit the Fillet feature.

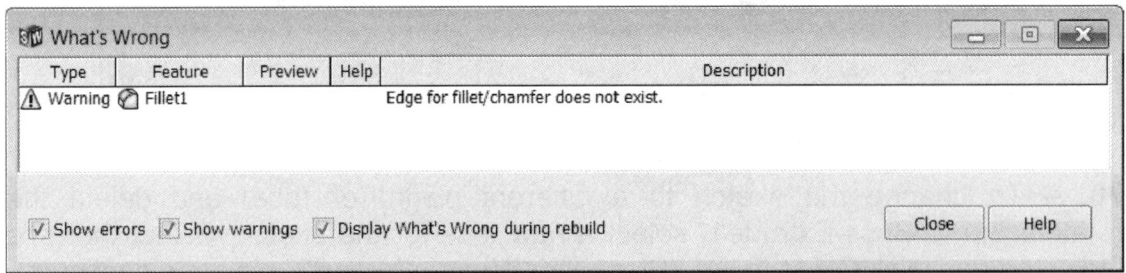

81. – The selection box is listing a missing edge in the same 'dangling' brown color, and the missing edge is shown with a faint red phantom line. Since we no longer need the fillet in that missing edge, delete it from the selection list and click **OK** to finish; the error will be cleared.

82. – After fixing Fillet1 we can delete the Boss-Extrude1 feature. Select it in the FeatureManager and delete it. This time the confirmation dialog only lists Plane2, which we don't want (or need) and it's OK to delete. Be sure to click on the option "**Also delete absorbed features**" to delete its sketch, too.

83. – Now we have one error left to fix. This error means that the cut is not cutting through the model.

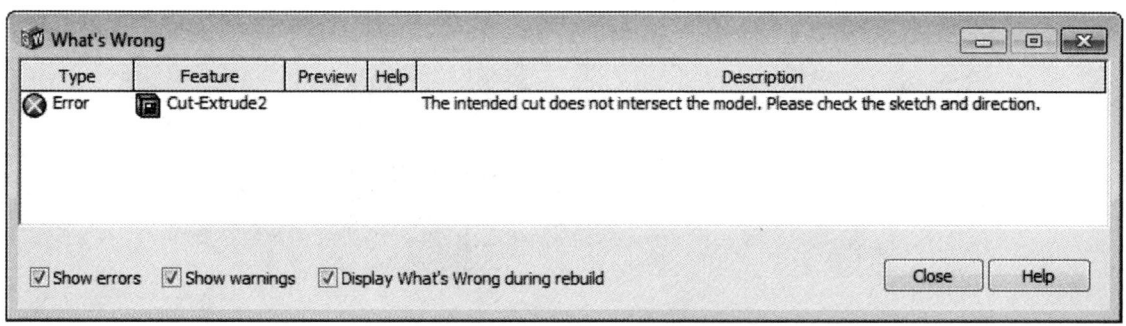

84. – Close the "**What's Wrong**" dialog and edit the Cut-Extrude2 feature. We can see the preview is not going deep enough and we want it to be 0.375" deep into the lower step.

85. – Change the cut's end condition to "**Offset from Surface**" and select the lower step's face as indicated. This end condition will make the cut the offset distance going to either side of the selected face; if needed, turn on the "**Reverse offset**" checkbox to cut into the part as shown. Click **OK** to finish.

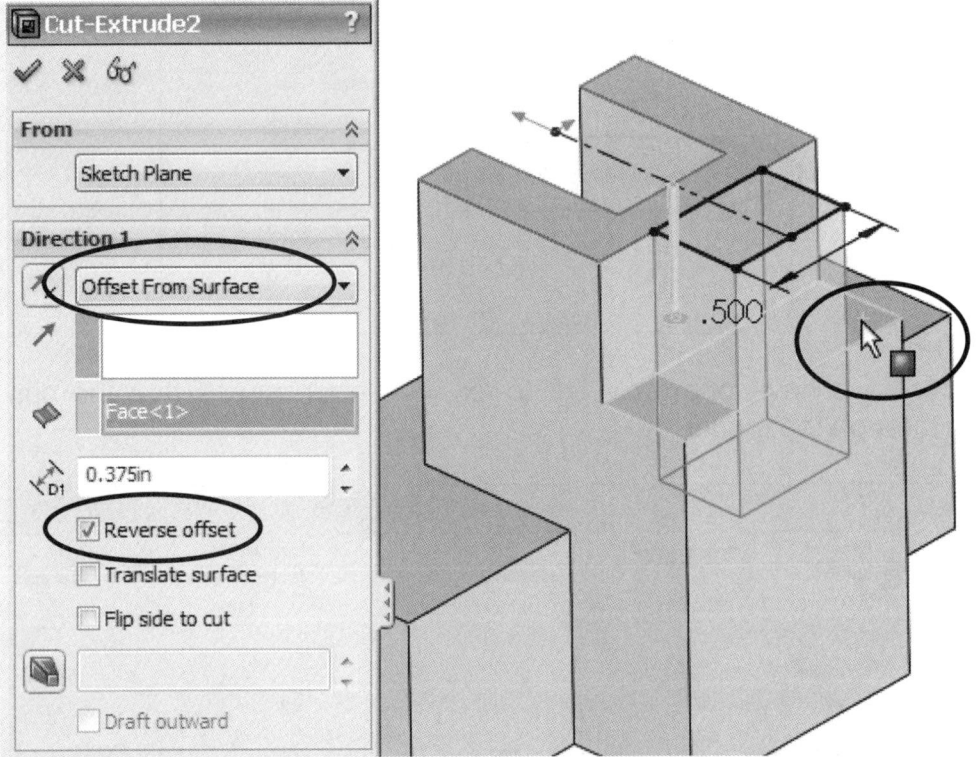

The finished part fully repaired looks like this:

86. – When working in a sketch we can have different errors, so we decided to show them with a different part. Download the part *Sketch Relations.sldprt* from www.mechanicad.com/download.html. Just like the part before, we have a number of errors in this part's sketch. Close the "**What's Wrong**" dialog after opening the part and edit the sketch. We'll show the use of diagnostic tools to help us correct the errors.

In a sketch we can have many types of geometric relations. What we are going to focus on is when relations are not solved correctly and generate warnings or errors.

An Under Defined or Fully Defined sketch can be used in a feature without a problem, the latter being the desired state. When we add conflicting relations that cannot be solved, a sketch's geometry can be in one of the following states:

State	Color	Description
Over defined	Red	Conflicting relations cannot be satisfied.
Not Solved	Yellow	Relations cannot be solved; geometry cannot meet the required relations.
Dangling	Brown/Gold	Relations to geometry that no longer exists.
External	Can be under, fully or over defined, not solved or dangling.	Relations to geometry outside the sketch;
In Context *		Relations referencing other part's geometry added in an assembly.
Locked *	Can be any color	'Frozen' *In context* relations.
Broken *		*In context* relations that have been broken.

* Will be covered more in depth in the **Top Down Design** section later.

A sketch can become Over Defined, Not Solved or Dangling when geometry is deleted, modified, or when the user adds conflicting relations and/or dimensions.

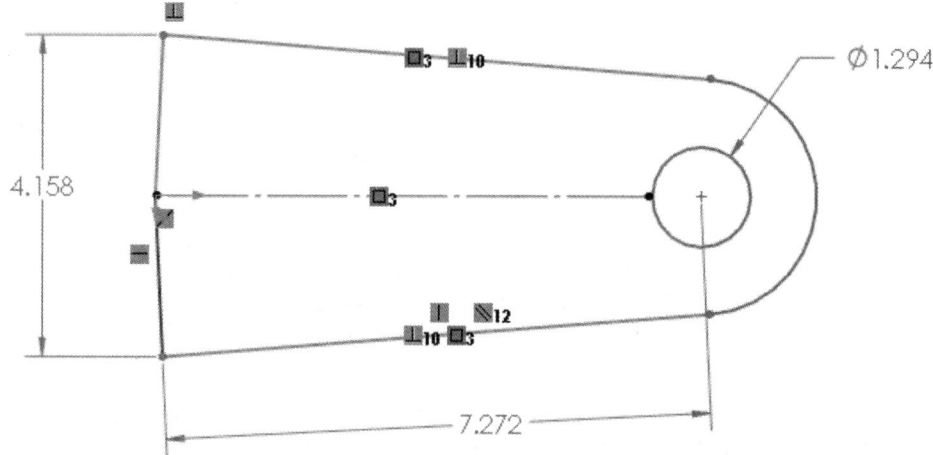

87. – After editing the sketch we see red and yellow entities. There are two ways we can approach this: we can manually sort through the geometric relations and delete the conflicting ones, or we can use the **SketchXpert** tool to fix them. We'll show the manual mode first. Select the "**Display/Delete Relations**" icon from the Sketch toolbar, or the menu "**Tools, Relations, Display/Delete**."

88. – In the PropertyManager we can see the list of existing relations in the sketch. We can see the relations highlighted with different colors, and their state listed under the list. At the top of the list we can filter the relations displayed by state, or if we select an entity, its relations will be listed.

Multi Body Parts, Sketch Editing and Other Tools

As the user can see, having a large number of conflicting relations can be difficult to sort manually. This is a good diagnostic option when we have problems with a few relations. On the other hand, this is a good tool to identify and/or delete relations, especially External, In context, Locked or Broken, if needed.

89. – Using this tool we'll remove the "**In Context**" relations. By deleting this relation, our part will no longer be referencing geometry outside the part (more on this in the Top Down Design section). Select the drop down filter menu and select "**Defined In Context**." In our sketch we only have a Parallel relation and its status is "Out of Context." Click the "Delete" button at the bottom or select the relation and press "Delete" on the keyboard. Click **OK** to close the "**Display/Delete Relations**" dialog.

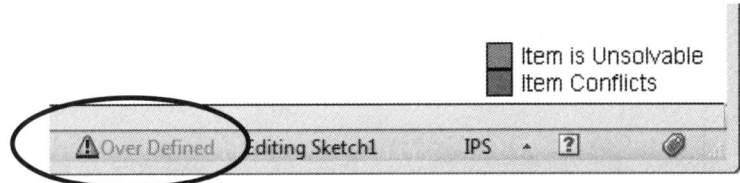

Our sketch still has errors, but we'll fix them using **SketchXpert**, which is a great tool to quickly review multiple possible solutions. We can load it by clicking in the "**Over Defined**" message in the status bar or the menu "**Tools, Sketch Tools, SketchXpert**."

57

90. – In the **SketchXpert** dialog select "**Diagnose**" to automatically analyze the sketch and evaluate possible solutions.

91. – **SketchXpert** quickly diagnoses the sketch and offers possible solutions. We can view each option by advancing in the "Results" box. In the "More Information/Options" box we are shown the relations and/or dimensions that would be deleted if we accept the solution displayed. Scroll until you see the following solution and click "**Accept**" when done.

We see the message "The sketch can now find a valid solution" with a green background. Click **OK** to finish.

92. – We want to make the lines on the left to be collinear and horizontal (along the short origin arrow; the sketch is shown sideways to save space). What we need to do is to find what relations are keeping the lines fully defined, delete/edit them, and then make the lines horizontal. Turn on the display of sketch relations using the menu "**View, Sketch Relations**" if not already activated; this way we can see all the relations in every geometric element.

93. – We can see that there are only three relations in the two lines that we are interested in: a perpendicular, a coincident and a "**Fix**" relation. The Fix relation is the equivalent of artificially and arbitrarily constraining an element in space. Think of it as putting a nail in a geometric element and hammering it in. Read: brute force. Select this Fix relation and delete it.

94. – If we pay attention, we'll see that we have a relation colored brown/gold in the centerline. This relation is "**On Edge**," and is the type of relation created when we use the "**Convert Entities**" command in a sketch. The brown/gold color means that it is "dangling;" in other words, it lost the reference from where it was converted from, and we have to delete it. Delete this relation and make both lines on the left "**Horizontal**."

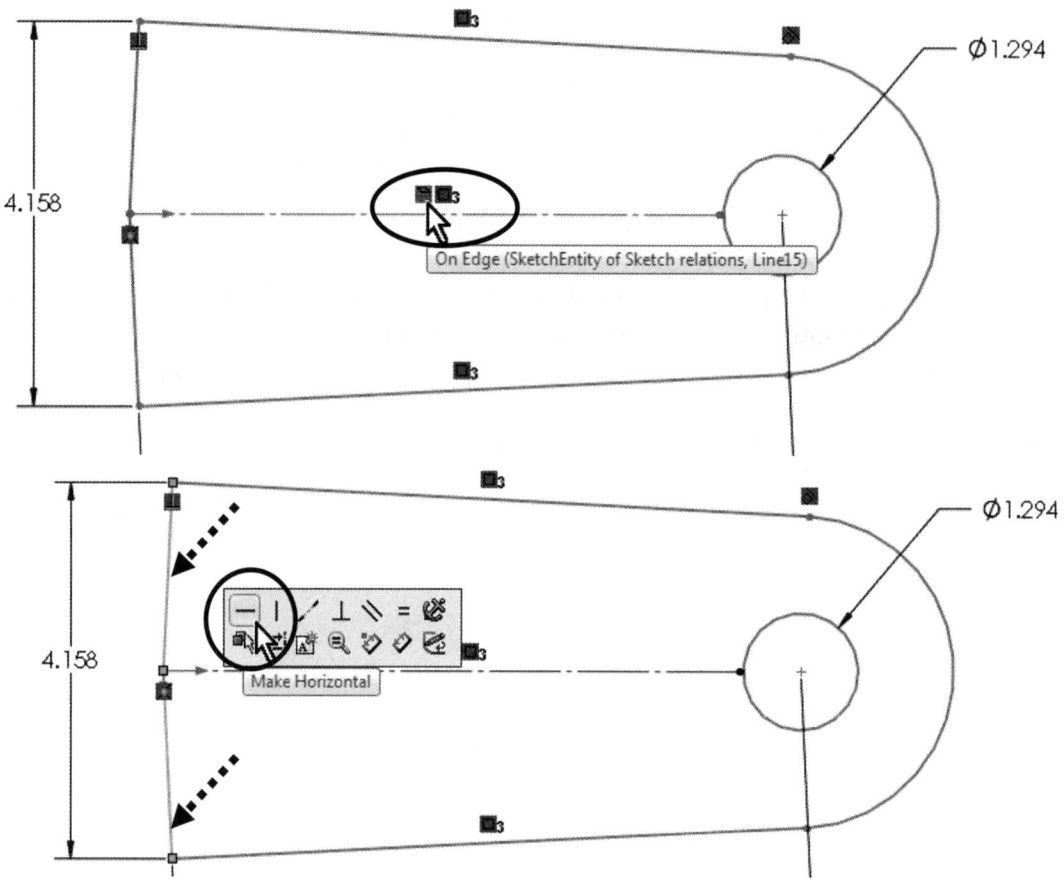

95. – Make one of the long lines "**Vertical**;" the other two lines will also become vertical as they have a "**Symmetric**" relation between them about the centerline.

96. – To complete the changes and fully define the sketch we need to add a "**Tangent**" relation between the lower long line and the arc. Note that the other side of the arc is already tangent to the top long line. If desired, click and drag the endpoint (blue) to see the effect of not having the tangent relation.

We can read in the status bar that our sketch is now "Fully Defined."

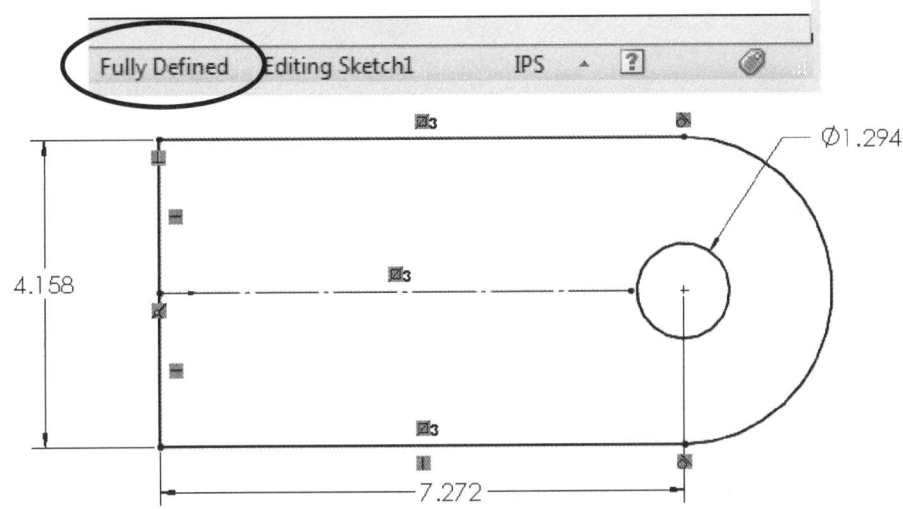

97. – Now the part is complete. Exit the sketch to finish, save and close the file.

Notes:

Equations

One way to help us maintain design intent in our models is by using equations. Equations are commonly used to evenly space features, add or remove instances to a pattern, change a feature's dimensions when other features are modified, etc. All equations in SolidWorks have the following format:

variable=expression
where:

variable is the dimension/value to change (dependant value).
expression is the algebraic combination of other dimensions and values that will define the value of **variable**.

For example, if we have a part of length "L" where we want to evenly space a pattern of "N" number of holes spaced a dimension "S," the **variable** dimension will be "S," because that's the value we want to change when the number "N" and length "L" values change. Our equation would look like:

S = L / N

A good practice when working with equations in SolidWorks is to rename dimensions and features, so instead of an equation looking like this:

"D1@LinearPattern1" = "D3@Sketch1" / "D2@LinearPattern1"

it would look like this:

"Spacing@Holes" = "Length@Base" / "Number@Holes"

which is more descriptive and easier to understand. If we have one, maybe two, equations in our part it may not be a problem, but with more it becomes difficult to manage and modify them if needed; besides, it's easier to edit if necessary.

98. – To show how equations work, we'll make a simple part, rename features and dimensions and add an equation to it. Draw the following sketch (any plane will do) and extrude it 0.5".

63

99. – Add a through hole in the corner...

100. – Add a linear pattern. In this case the pattern will be made in two directions. Select a diagonal edge for Direction 1, three copies spaced 0.5", and a horizontal edge for Direction 2, seven copies spaced 0.5" (don't finish it yet).

101. – Since we need a single row of copies in each direction, check the option **"Pattern seed only"** under the "Direction 2" options box. Using this option allows us to only copy the original hole, not the copies of the copy. Click **OK** to finish.

102. – We'll now rename the dimensions. To show feature dimensions, right mouse click in the "**Annotations**" folder and select "**Show feature dimensions**;" to view dimension names, activate the menu "**View, Dimension Names**."

103. – Rename the dimensions for the side's length and linear pattern as shown; this way when we add the equations, it will be easier to identify them. Select each dimension and type the name in its PropertyManager.

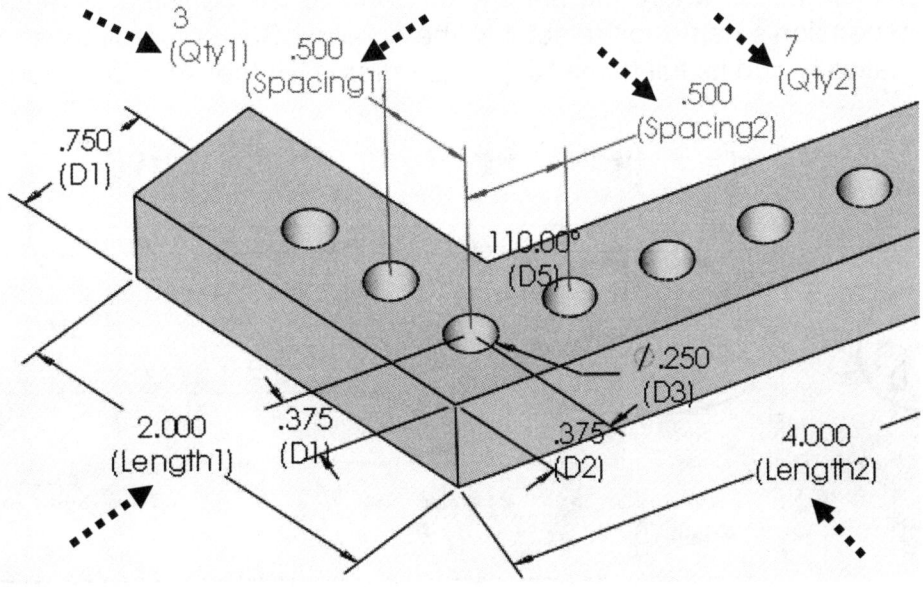

65

104. – Our design intent is to have a pattern of holes equally spaced to fill each side and update accordingly if the length or spacing change. To accomplish this, we'll need two equations to calculate the quantity of holes (one for each direction). Our "dependant" dimensions will be "*Qty1*" and "*Qty2*," and the driving dimensions will be "*Length1*," "*Length2*," "*Spacing1*" and "*Spacing2*." Based on this, our equation's general format has to be:

$$Qty1 = Lenght1 / Spacing1 \qquad Qty2 = Length2 / Spacing2$$

105. – There are two ways to add equations; we'll learn both, one with each equation. For the first one, select the menu "**Tools, Equations**." We are immediately presented with the Equations dialog box. Here we can define Global Variables to use in our equations as constants, set feature's suppression states and of course, add equations.

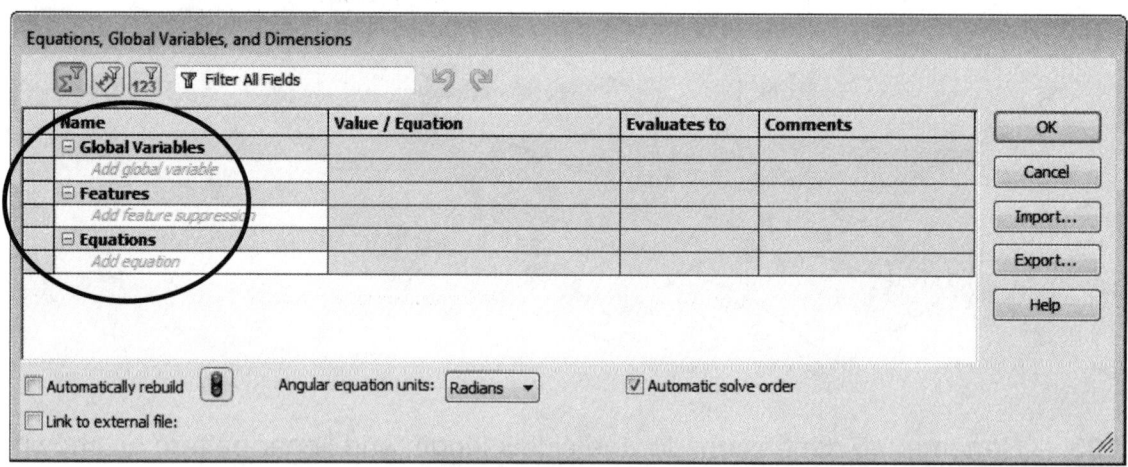

106. – To create the first equation click in the "Add equation" field in the Equations list; this is where the dependant variable will be listed. We can either type a dimension's name, or select it in the screen. Select the dimension "*Qty1*" to automatically add its full name "*Qty1@LPattern1*" in the "Add Equation" field.

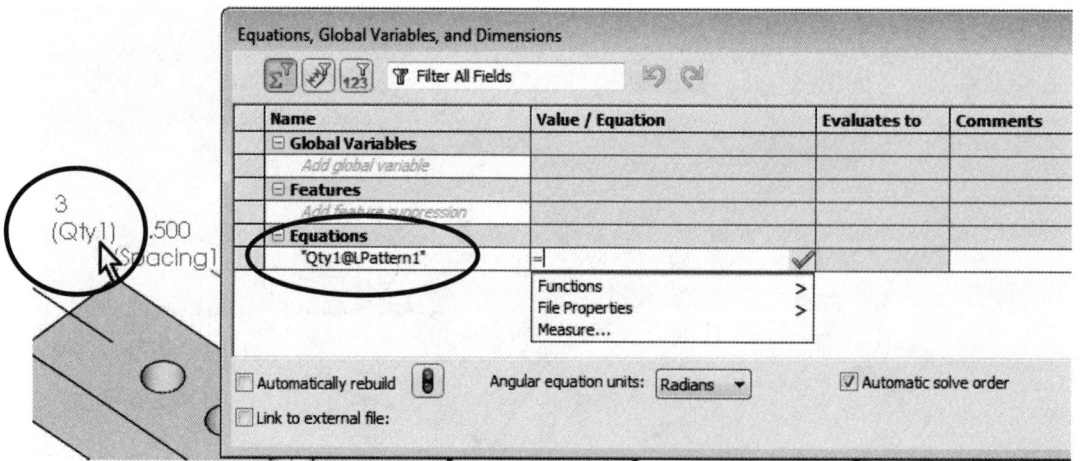

107. – After selecting the *Qty1* dimension, the equal sign is automatically shown in the Value/Equation field, waiting for us to type the rest of the equation to evaluate *Qty1*. In order for our equation to calculate the correct number or holes, we have to subtract a small distance from the length in order to have a minimum space at the end. Otherwise we may get an extra hole at the end. After the equal sign, open a parenthesis, select the *"Length1"* dimension (its full name will be copied), type '**- 0.375**', close the parenthesis, type '**/**' to divide and finally select the *Spacing1* dimension. The green checkmark next to the equation indicates that the expression is valid. Our first completed equation looks like:

"Qty1@LPattern1" = ("Length1@Sketch1" - 0.375) / "Spacing1@LPattern1"

108. – In the "**Equations**" dialog we see the first equation is added, and the value for the *Qty1"* dimension evaluates to 3. Click OK to finish.

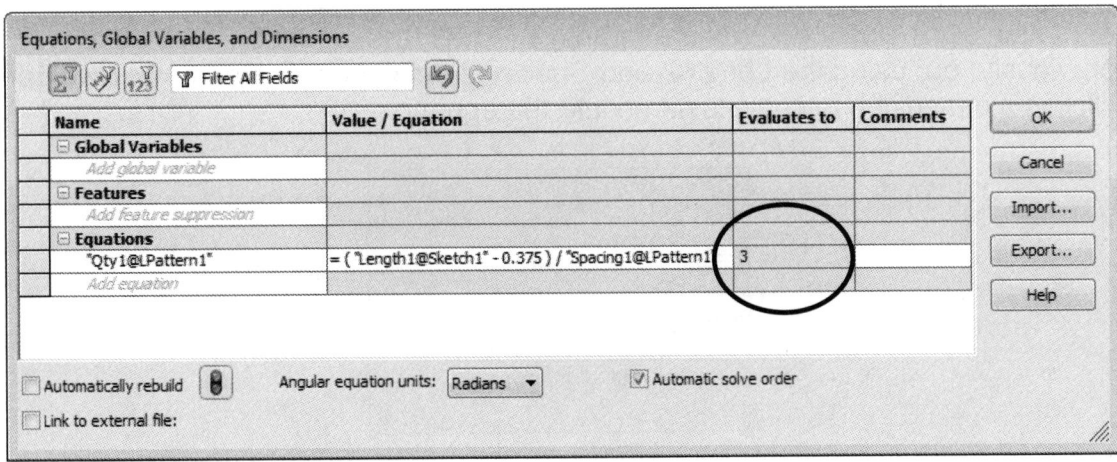

109. – After adding the equation, we see a red ∑ symbol next to the dimension indicating that it is driven by an equation and therefore its value cannot be changed directly. It can only change when the dimensions driving it change.

 A folder named "Equations" is automatically added to the FeatureManager after we add equations to our model.

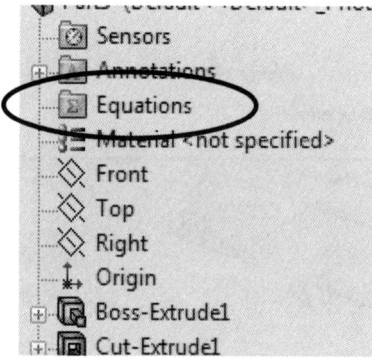

110. – To add the second equation, double click in the "*Qty2*" dimension as if to change its value. In the second line, where we enter the dimension's value, enter = (equal sign) and now we are ready to enter the equation just as we did previously, but using the Length2 and Spacing2 dimensions. Remember we can click in a dimension to copy its name into the equation.

111. – Just as we did with the first equation, we'll open a parenthesis immediately after the equal sign, click in the "*Length2*" dimension, enter '**- 0.375**', close the parenthesis, add ' **/** ' and click in the "*Spacing2*" dimension. The completed second equation entered in the Modify dialog box looks like:

=("Length2@Sketch1" - 0.375) / "Spacing2@LPattern1"

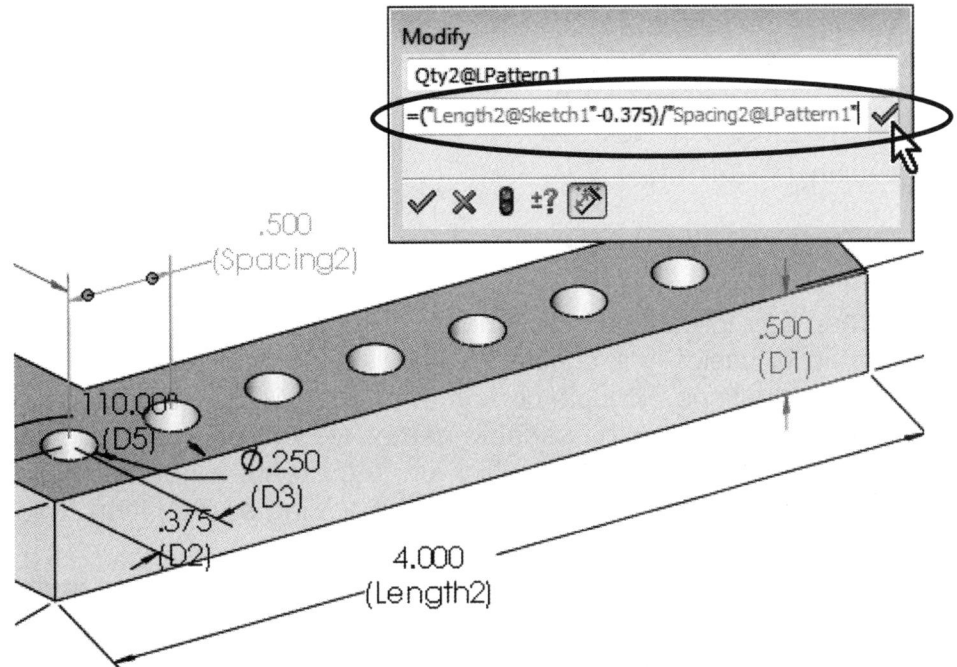

After clicking the green checkmark at the right side, the equation is created and the ∑ symbol is added. Click OK to finish adding the equation.

Click **OK** to finish. Now "*Qty2*" evaluates to 7. Click **OK** to close the "Equations" dialog. Both "*Qty1*" and "*Qty2*" have the red ∑ symbol added to alert us that these dimensions are equation driven.

69

112. – To test the equations, change "*Length1*" to 2.75" and "*Length2*" to 4.5". Rebuild the model. Now we have 5 holes in the left side and 8 holes in the right side.

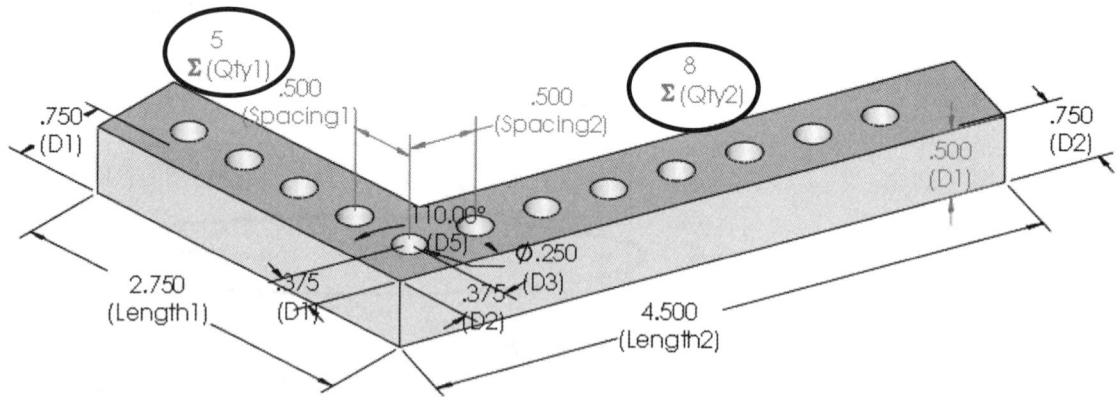

113. – Another way to maintain design intent is by using "**Global Variables**." A Global Variable is basically a constant with a name; after creating a variable it can be used in equations. Double click in one of the 0.75" dimensions and enter a "=" equal sign followed by the variable name "*Width*." After entering the name, a Global Variable icon is displayed. Click on it to create a new Global Variable, and make the dimension's value equal to it by adding an equation. Click **OK** to link this dimension.

 We can switch from viewing the value or the Global Variable using the toggle button on the left side of the Modify dialog box.

114. – After creating the Global Variable, the value is displayed with the red ∑ symbol letting us know that the value is now driven by an equation. What happened was that the Global Variable was created, and at the same time an equation was added making the dimension equal to the variable "*width*."

115. – To show how to make a dimension equal to a Global Variable, double click in the other 0.75" dimension, enter an "=" equal sign, and from the drop down menu select *Global Variables, width*. Click **OK** to finish.

By doing this we are creating a new equation and this dimension is also equal to the Global Variable "w*idth.*" Global Variables are automatically listed under the "**Equations**" folder in the FeatureManager and in the "**Equations**" dialog box. To change a Global Variable or equation, right mouse click in the Equations folder and select "Manage Equations."

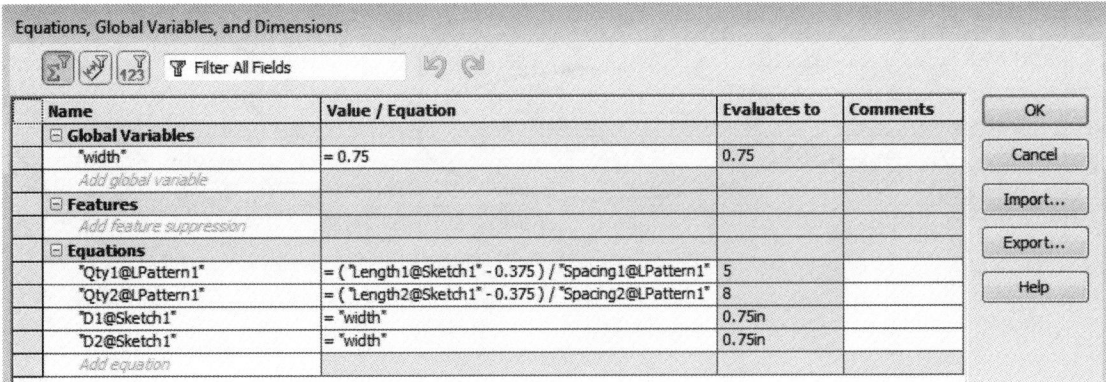

71

In equations we can't change the dependent dimensions directly ("*Qty1*" and "*Qty2*"), only the referenced dimensions ("*Length1*," "*Length2*," "*Spacing1*" and "*Spacing2*"). Using Global Variables allows flexibility when using values that are referenced by equations, and variables are updated anywhere they are used when their values are changed.

116. – In the "**Equations**" dialog we can Add, Edit, Delete or configure equations. To Suppress, Unsuppress or delete an equation, right mouse click in each equation and select the desired option from the pop-up menu. Do not delete or suppress equations; this step is only to show how to do it if needed.

Name	Value / Equation	Evaluates to	Comments
⊟ **Global Variables**			
"width"	= 0.75	0.75	
Add global variable			
⊟ **Features**			
Add feature suppression			
⊟ **Equations**			
"Qty1@LPattern1"	= ("Length1@Sketch1" - 0.375) / "Spacing1@LPattern1"	5	
"Qty2@LPattern1"	= ("Length2@Sketch1" - 0.375) / "Spacing2@LPattern1"	8	
"D1@Sketch1"	Suppress	0.75in	
"D2@Sketch1"	Unsuppress	0.75in	
Add equation	Delete Equation		

117. – To illustrate the effect of not subtracting 0.375" from the length and show how to edit equations, remove the '**– 0.375**' portion from the two equations (it doesn't matter if we leave the parenthesis or not). Our equations should now be:

"*Qty1@LPattern1*" = ("*Length1@Sketch1*") / "*Spacing1@LPattern1*"

"*Qty2@LPattern1*" = ("*Length2@Sketch1*") / "*Spacing2@LPattern1*"

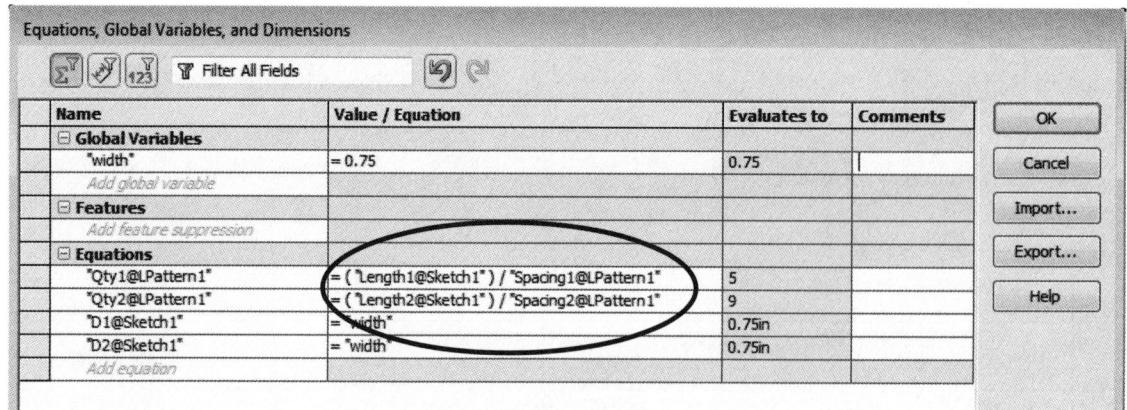

Multi Body Parts, Sketch Editing and Other Tools

118. – Now the equations evaluate to 5 and 9 respectively. We can see the effects of the changes by rebuilding the model at the bottom of the dialog, or have them automatically rebuild as we make changes to them. Click **OK** to finish and rebuild the
model to see the changes. What just happened with this change is that a sixth instance is added that breaks the edge of the part; the equation resolves to 5.5, and is rounded up to 6. That is the reason why we subtract 0.375" from the length in the equations. Edit the equations again to subtract the 0.375" again as originally done.

119. – Add two new equations to center the holes about the "*width*" dimension.

120. –Change the "*width*" variable to 0.875". The holes should remain centered about the width of the part. Save and close the part to finish.

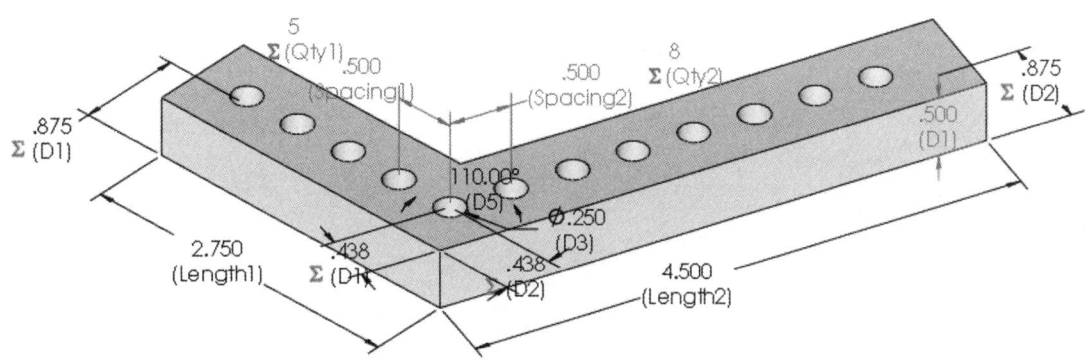

73

Equations Review

121. – Download the part *Equations-Review.sldprt* and give all dimensions used in an equation a meaningful name. Add equations and Global Variables to:

a) Make the bottom thickness equal to the wall thickness (10mm dimension).
b) Make the number of "Copies" equal to the outside diameter divided by 8.
c) Make the "ShaftCut" diameter ¼ of the "Body" inside diameter.

 When making equations we can use almost any algebraic expression to evaluate values. As a general guide, you can write equations with the same algebraic format as you would in Excel formulas.

Sheet Metal and Top Down Design

When we talk about a sheet metal process, we are talking about trimming and bending sheets of metal beyond their yield strength causing a permanent deformation. Sheet metal components are made from steel, aluminum, bronze or pretty much any malleable metal and, while the sheet metal process can produce components with tight tolerances, this process is more frequently used when high precision is not required and the components manufactured need to have flexibility in an assembly process, like the power supply we'll be making in this lesson or a school's locker.

Due to the inherent nature of the process of cutting and bending metal, this manufacturing technique is used mostly for internal components that are "out of sight" or don't have a high aesthetical requirement, since the resulting components are not always as pretty or good-looking as a plastic injection molded part and have a more "industrial" look. A very good example is a computer's case. If you look at the back of a your PC's case, you'll see that most likely it is made from sheet metal, and the front (more visible parts) are likely made of plastic to give it a more attractive look as a consumer product.

Sheet metal tends to be a relatively cheap manufacturing process, and lends itself very well for mass produced components using multiple stations or progressive dies, where a long sheet metal strip is fed in one end, and is progressively trimmed, cut, punched and bent until a finished part is completed at the other end. Other manufacturing techniques include cutting the metal with computer controlled torch, plasma, laser or water jet machines and bending the part afterwards using presses and bending tools.

Example of a progressive die sheet metal part

Understanding Top Down Design

In designing the power supply, we'll use different sheet metal and advanced assembly techniques including Top Down Design.

Top Down Design is generally referred to as the process where we create and/or add features referencing other components in the assembly; in our example, we'll design a sheet metal enclosure for the power supply *around* the actual electronics of the power supply. In other words, we'll make an enclosure where the internal components fit, instead of building an enclosure and *then* trying to fit the components inside. That's the main difference.

One of the biggest advantages of Top Down Design is that when the component referenced is modified, the components designed around it (driven), also change. Looking at this example, the base component is the DRIVING component, the circular hole's edge is the driving feature, and the DRIVEN part will update when the BASE part updates. Here the hole's diameter is changed from 1" diameter to 1.625" and the pin's size changes accordingly.

Sheet Metal and Top Down Design

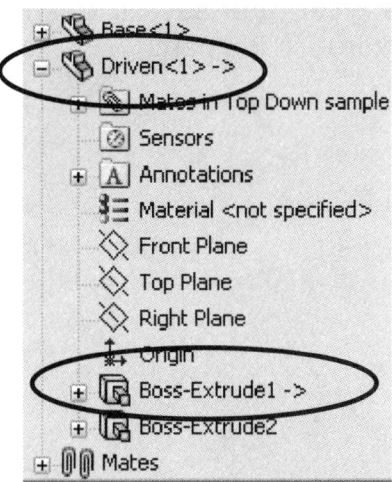

When designing components in the context of an assembly (**Top Down Design**), you can reference other parts or assemblies, including geometry, sketches, planes, axes, etc.

The relations created this way are called **External Relations** and are indicated in the Feature Manager with "**->**" both in the part's name and each feature that references external geometry. External relations are created every time dimensions, geometric relations or feature end conditions reference other components (parts or assemblies) while editing them in an assembly.

As a primer to **Top Down Design** before we jump into **sheet metal**, we'll make the components illustrated on the previous page as a simple example of working in the context of an assembly, or Top Down Design.

In a **Bottom Up Design** approach (as we've done until now), we would make both parts and then assemble them together; the problem is that if a part is changed, the other has to be manually changed. In a **Top Down Design** approach, only one change is needed. For our simple Top Down example we'll make the "Base" part, add it to a new assembly, create the "Driven" part while in the assembly and finally modify the hole's dimension to propagate the changes.

The steps we'll follow for the Top Down Design example are the following:

79

122. – Make the following part using the dimensions given and save it when done. Name this part *Top Down Base*. The hole is centered in the part.

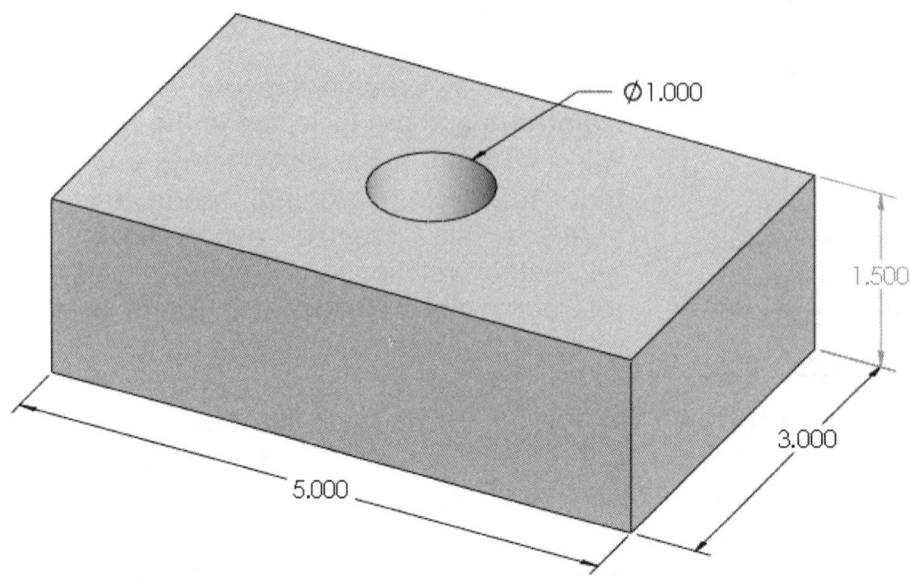

123. – Add the *Top Down Base* part to a new assembly. The location of this part in the assembly is not important for this example. Save the assembly with the name *Top Down Assembly*; saving the assembly is a requirement to working in the context of the assembly.

 It is important to save the assembly before external references can be added. The reason for this is because SolidWorks needs to know in which assembly the external reference was created.

Sheet Metal and Top Down Design

124. – The next step is to add a new component. The new component will be created *inside the assembly* or *in context*. Click on the drop-down arrow from the "**Insert Components**" icon in the Assembly toolbar, and select "**New Part**" or from the menu "**Insert, Component, New Part**."

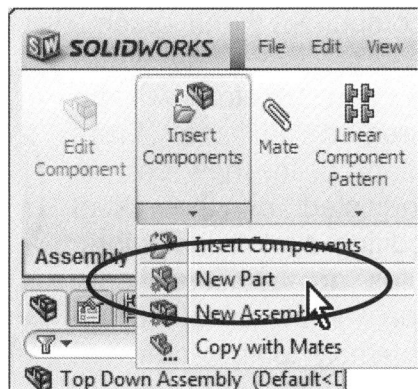

125. – Immediately after selecting the "**New Part**" icon, SolidWorks will ask us for a plane to locate the new part. Select the Top face of the "Base" part in the assembly. By selecting the Top face, we are creating the first external reference in the new part; the Front plane of this new part will be coincident with the face selected. This is an "**InPlace**" relation and will fix the new part to the selected face. In other words, the new part is immovable; all six degrees of freedom fixed.

126. – After selecting the Top face several things will happen:

A new part will be added to the FeatureManager tree and its name will be shown (by default) in blue. The name in blue indicates that we are *editing* this component in the assembly.

A new Sketch will be created in the Front plane of the new part as indicated by the usual editing sketch indicators, plus an additional one: an "**Edit Component**" icon will be added to the CommandManager (or assembly toolbar) and will be activated. This indicates a component (part or subassembly) is being edited *in* the assembly. This icon will be visible in every CommandManager toolbar.

The most obvious indicator to know that we are editing a new part in the assembly is that the existing component(s) will become (by default) transparent. This is a System option in the "**Display/Selection**" section, and it has three options:

Opaque Assembly will force every component in the assembly to be opaque regardless of the component's transparency setting in the assembly.

Maintain Assembly Transparency will leave components as they were; no changes to transparency will be made. Using this setting it will be less obvious that we are editing components in the assembly.

Force Assembly Transparency (default setting) will make every component transparent except the one being edited. The level of transparency can be set with the slider.

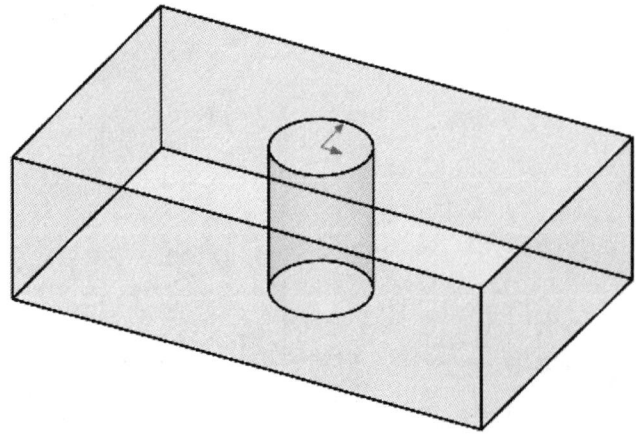

Sheet Metal and Top Down Design

 If, after selecting the face to insert a new part, you are asked to name the new part, the System Option "**Assemblies, Save new components to external files**" is set. The default setting is *off*.

127. – The next step is to design the Driven part. What we want to do is to make the pin 0.025" smaller than the hole. Since we are editing the first sketch in the new part, we'll use the **Offset Entities** command to offset the hole. The only new thing here is that when we make the offset we are selecting the edge of a *different* component. Select "Reverse" if needed to offset the edge to the inside of the hole; click **OK** to finish.

83

Your sketch will now look like this:

128. – Extrude the sketch to the bottom of the *Top Down Base* part using the end condition "Up to Surface" and select the bottom face of the *Top Down Base* part.

Our assembly should now look like this:

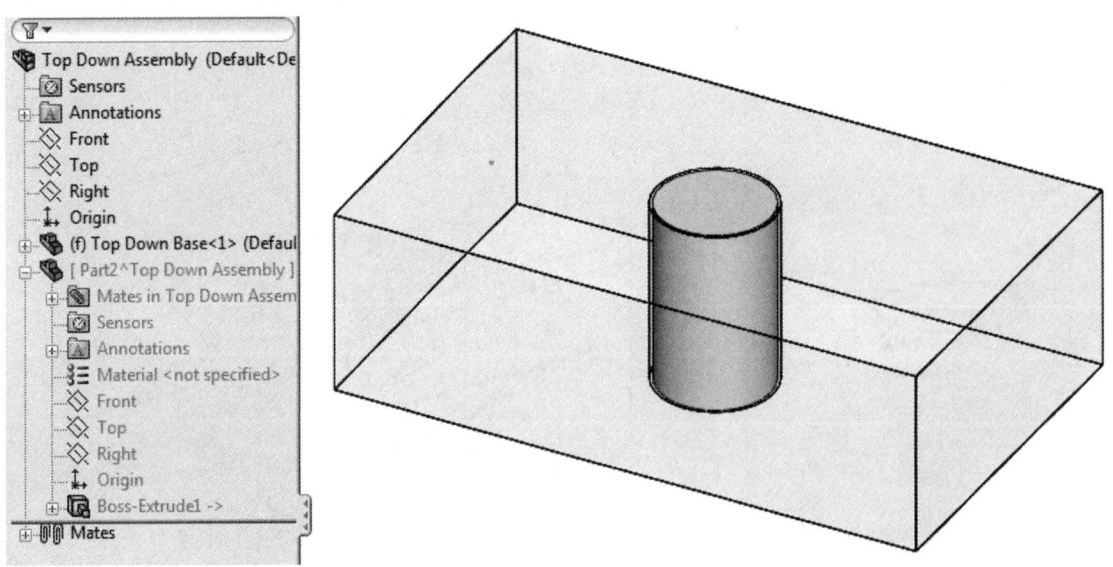

Sheet Metal and Top Down Design

Take a look at the FeatureManager for a second; there are a few things we have to pay attention to:

The part we added was automatically named, in this case **[Part2^Top Down Assembly]**. Notice the name is in rectangular brackets [ ]; this means that the part is *internal* to the assembly, meaning that while the part is a separate component, there is no external file for it (yet). In this case we only have 2 actual files on the hard drive: the assembly (*Top Down Assembly.sldasm*) and the Base part (*Top Down Base.sldprt*).

The name of the new part and all of its features are shown in blue; this means that the part (or subassembly if that was the case) is being edited.

At the end of a part's name, the Boss-Extrude1 and Sketch1 names, we can see

->; this means that the feature has *at least* one external reference. If you remember, Sketch1 was made by making an offset from the hole's edge and Boss-Extrude1 was extruded up to the bottom of the *Top Down Base* part.

We'll talk more about external references and internal/external components later in the lesson.

129. – The second feature for the new part will be the top of the pin. Remember that we are editing the new part in the context of the assembly, and EVERY part modeling command is available here as well. Add a new sketch on top of the part we just made. Using the **Offset** command, make a sketch 0.5" bigger than the hole in the Base part, just as we did for the first sketch.

85

Extrude the sketch 0.5" up to finish the part.

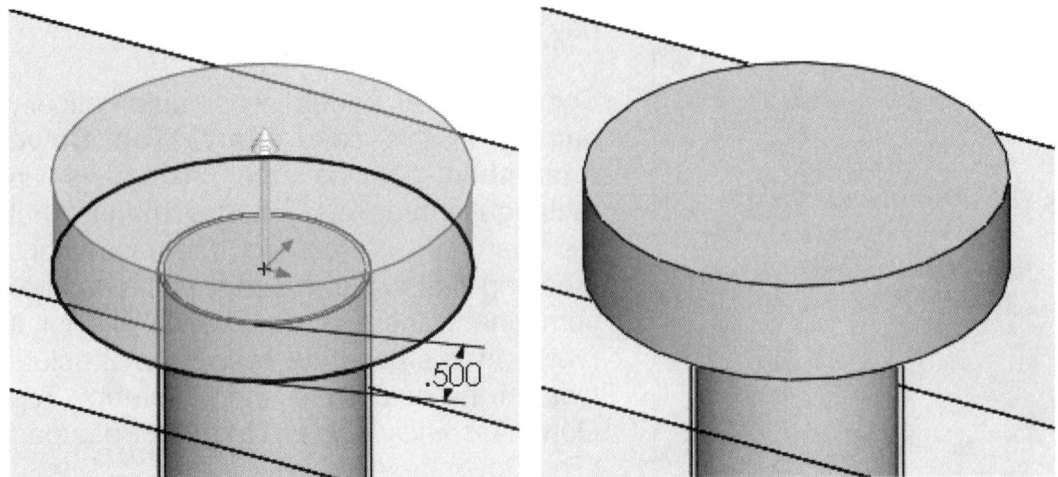

130. – We have finished the new part in the context of the assembly. What we need to do now is return to editing the assembly. As a reference, the different editing levels within SolidWorks are:

Icon	Editing Level
	Part Sketch
	Part Feature
	Part
(Yellow & Blue)	Part in Assembly
(Yellow & Blue)	Subassembly
* As many Subassembly levels as needed.	
(Yellow & Blue)	Subassembly
(Yellow & Green)	Main Assembly

 Additionally, SolidWorks has assembly sketch and assembly features in assemblies and subassemblies which will be covered later.

 When we are at the part (or subassembly) editing level inside an assembly, we can right mouse click in the graphics area, and change the assembly transparency from the pop-up menu "**Assembly Transparency**" or select the "**Assembly Transparency**" icon in the CommandManager.

Sheet Metal and Top Down Design

Currently we are editing the part *inside* the assembly. To return to editing the main assembly, select the "**Edit Component**" icon in the CommandManager (or Assembly toolbar if visible) or,

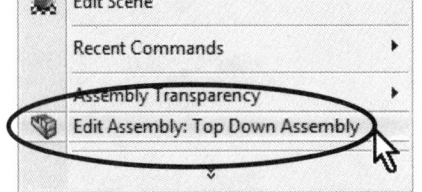

...right mouse click in the graphics area and select "**Edit Assembly: xxxx**" or,

...select the **Edit Assembly** confirmation corner (just like when we close a Sketch).

Now that we are editing the assembly, everything should look as we are used to, and the status bar at the bottom will read "**Editing Assembly**." Notice that when editing a part in the assembly, the assembly tools are disabled.

131. – At the assembly editing level, add an exploded view and pull the Driven part out for visibility.

87

132. – Double click in the hole to display its diameter dimension and change it from 1″ to 1.625″. Rebuild the assembly to see the changes propagate to the driven component.

133. – Save the assembly and when asked, select "**Save All**," and "**Save internally**" for now.

 It may seem a little confusing at first, but it's very simple. Edit assembly or Edit part. Just like that. The rest is what you do while you are editing the part or the assembly. The important thing is to *be aware* if we are editing an assembly or a part.

Sheet Metal and Top Down Design

134. – Saving the part "internally" means that there is no file that we can reference, and therefore we cannot make a drawing of it while it remains an internal part. To *externalize* the part and make a file for it, we have to rename it like a regular feature (with a slow double click or in its properties) and then save it. Rename the internal part as *Driven Part*. Right mouse click on it and select "**Save Part (in External File)**." Select the path to save the file and click **OK**. Now that the part has been *"externalized,"* we have a file for this part and the FeatureManager shows the part's name as any other component, except that it shows that it also has external references (**->**).

More about external references

 External references can have four different states: In Context, Out of Context, Locked and Broken. Here is a description and example of each.

In Context:
When a part with external references and the assembly where those references were created <u>are open in SolidWorks</u> (loaded in memory), if a referenced part (driving) is modified, the driven part updates automatically, as in the previous example. **In context** external references show "**->**" in the FeatureManager.

Assembly view   Part view

Out of Context:
Out of Context is when a part with external references is open, but the assembly in which those references were created is not (not loaded in memory). If a part referenced (driving) is modified, the driven part **WILL NOT** update until the assembly where the external references were made is opened.

Open the *Driven Part* and *Top Down Base* parts but **not** the assembly. Change the *Top Down Base* part's hole size and then go back to the *Driven Part*; notice the changes do not propagate to the driven part. Finally, open the assembly to see the changes propagate. **Out of Context** references show "**- >?**" in the FeatureManager.

Sheet Metal and Top Down Design

Locked:
When external references are locked changes will not propagate, even if the assembly is open (loaded in memory or In context). To lock a part's external references right mouse click at the top of the part's FeatureManager and select "**List External Refs...**"

In the "**External References**" list we can see the features with external references, status (In context, Out of context, Locked or Broken) and which part and entity is being referenced. To lock references means that we can temporarily *freeze* them. This is useful when we are working in an assembly and we don't want to propagate changes immediately. Open the *Driven Part* file, list the external references and select "**Lock All**." When locking external references, ALL references are locked. There is no way to lock individual references selectively; it's an "all or nothing" thing. When locking references, we'll see the following message; click **OK** to continue.

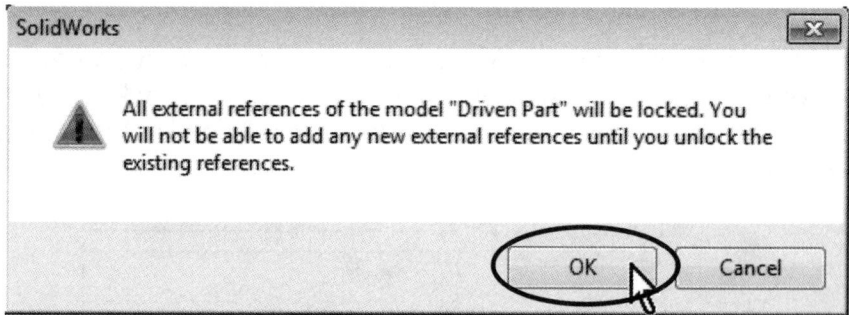

When the external references are locked, we cannot add more external references until they are unlocked. Open both parts and the assembly, with the *Driven Part* external references locked. Make a change to the hole's diameter in the *Top Down Base* part. Return to the *Driven Part* and confirm that changes have not propagated, even when the assembly is open. Locked external references are listed in the Feature Manager with "**->*.**"

To unlock external references, repeat to show the part's external references and select "**Unlock All**." After unlocking, changes will propagate following the rules when parts are "**In Context**" or "**Out of Context**."

Broken:

Broken external references work exactly the same way as "**Locked**;" the difference is that Broken references **CANNOT** be re-established. Once a part's external references have been Broken, there is no way to recover them. To break external references list the part's references as before, but select the "Break All" option. Broken external references are listed with "**-> x**" in the Feature Manager.

 When listing External References for a part with Broken references, the list will be empty unless we use the "**List Broken References**" checkbox.

Sheet Metal and Top Down Design

135. – Now that we have a basic understanding of what **Top Down Design** is and how it works, let's design a computer's power supply enclosure. For our example we'll start with the assumption that the electronic components are already designed and they will drive the size of the enclosure. Download the *Power Supply.sldprt* part file from www.mechanicad.com/download.html.
Our electronics board looks like this:

136. – The first thing we need to do is to make a new assembly, locate the electronics board at the assembly's origin and save the assembly as "**Power Supply Assy**." Remember that the assembly must be saved to edit parts in the context of the assembly.

Sheet Metal and Top Down Design

137. – The first component we are going to design in the context of the assembly is the bottom half of the enclosure. Select "**New Part**" from the drop down list in the "**Insert Components**" icon in the Assembly toolbar, or from the menu "**Insert, Component, New Part**."

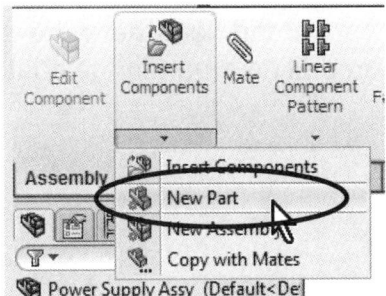

138. – Select the assembly's Right plane in the FeatureManager to locate the new part's Front plane, adding the "InPlace" mate.

Immediately after selecting the assembly's Right plane in the FeatureManager, this is what will happen:

- The electronics board will become transparent (if the option is set in "**Tools, Options, Display/Selection, Force assembly Transparency**").
- The "**Edit Component**" icon in the CommandManager will be enabled.
- A name will be assigned to the new part in the FeatureManager tree if the option "**Tools, System Options: Assemblies, Save New Components to external files**" is NOT checked; if set, you will be asked for a new part name.
- The new part's FeatureManager will be blue (default setting).
- A new sketch will be created in the new part's Front plane.
- The status bar will read "Editing Sketch."
- The title bar will read:
  Sketch1 of Part#^Power Supply Assy -in- Power Supply Assy.SLDASM
  Which means:
  Sketch1: We are editing the new part's first sketch (Sketch1)/
  of Part#^Power Supply Assy: of **internal** Part# in the Power Supply Assy.
  -in- Power Supply Assy.SLDASM: in the "Power Supply Assy.sldasm" file.
- An "**InPlace**" mate will be added automatically fixing the Front plane of the new part to the selected plane or face, in our case, the assembly's Right plane.

As we can see, there are plenty of visual clues to alert us when we are working on editing a part in the context of an assembly.

139. – If not already visible, activate and select the Sheet Metal toolbar in the CommandManager and/or individual toolbar by either a right mouse click in the CommandManager's tabs and selecting "**Sheet Metal**" from the pop-up menu, or in the menu "**View, Toolbars, Sheet Metal**."

The Sheet Metal toolbar has most of the commands needed, and looks like this:

140. – When designing sheet metal components with SolidWorks there are different techniques available:

　　Make a bent part (Base Flange) and add more sheet metal features.

　　Start with a flat pattern (unbent sheet metal) and add features and bends.

　　Convert a solid model to sheet metal by adding bends and rips.

In this example we'll start with a **Base Flange**, and add many features available in the Sheet Metal environment as we move forward. But before we start our part, let's take a look at the most common sheet metal features and terminology.

Icon	Description	Example
Sheet-Metal	Definitions of default bend parameters including sheet metal thickness, bend radius, relief type and related options.	N/A
Base Flange/Tab	Base Flange/Tab will be the first sheet metal feature (or additional tabs) in the part. If it's the first feature, it will create the required Sheet Metal features automatically (Sheet-Metal, Base-Flange and Flat-Pattern).	
Base Flange/Tab	Tab: Tabs are used to add more material to an existing sheet metal part using a sketch. Tabs can be bent later.	
Flat-Pattern	Represents the sheet metal part in its unbent state. If this feature is suppressed, the part is bent; if it's unsuppressed, the part is unbent (flat).	
Convert to Sheet Metal	Used to convert a solid, surface or imported model to Sheet Metal by adding rips and bends to allow the part to be flattened.	

Edge Flange	Used to add flanges to model edges. Flange shapes can be modified and do not need to be the full length of the edge. Circular edge flanges are allowed.	
Miter Flange	Used to automatically add flanges to a series of adjacent edges, including non-planar flanges.	
Hem	Used to add a hem to a linear edge. Mostly used to remove sharp edges.	
Jog	A jog will add two bends on a model using a single sketch line.	
Sketched Bend	A sketched bend will add a bend to a flat area defined using a single sketch line.	

Sheet Metal and Top Down Design

Corners	Used to close corners after relief cuts are made.	
Forming Tool	Used to create indentation forms using forming tools like louvers, lances, flanges, etc.	
Unfold / **Fold**	Used to selectively unfold and re-fold bends to make additional operations that can only be done while in the flat state.	

| | Used to rip corners in a solid, surface or imported model to convert it to Sheet Metal. Rip is included in the "Convert to Sheet Metal" command. | |

141. – Now let's design the lower part of the sheet metal enclosure. Select a Left view orientation (Assembly view orientation), and draw the following sketch. Remember, we are already working in a new sketch in the new part in the assembly. Note that this is an open sketch and is dimensioned referencing the lower and outer edges of the electronic board and both vertical lines are Equal.

A sheet metal component is essentially a thin extrusion with a few more parameters that we'll explain in the next step. With our sketch complete, create the Base Flange feature selecting the "**Base-Flange/Tab**" icon from the CommandManager's Sheet Metal toolbar. Remember, we are designing the enclosure in the context of the assembly using a Top Down design approach.

142. – Extrude the Base Flange 7" using the "**Mid plane**" end condition. In addition to the end condition for the extrusion we see more options to control the sheet metal's thickness, bend radius, bend allowance and auto relief type. For our example, use a thickness of 0.030" with a bend radius of 0.05" and a K-Factor of 0.5. Auto Relief will be set to Tear. Be sure to turn on the "Reverse Direction" checkbox.

What these options mean:
In the "Sheet Metal Parameters" options we'll enter:

Thickness of the material: This is the uniform thickness of the material that will be used to make the part.

"Reverse direction" checkbox: Since a sheet metal part is a Thin Feature (with constant thickness) we need to define on which side of the sketch we want the material to be added; in other words, if the given dimensions are *inside* or *outside* dimensions. In our example we want them to be *inside* dimensions and the material will be added *outside*. It may not seem to be important, but if we don't pay attention to which side we add material to in our designs, the result will be a part that is one material-thickness bigger or smaller, and that will ruin your design. Remember to pay attention to this important detail when designing sheet metal components and not ignore it.

Default bend radius: The radius measured on the inside of the bend.

The "**Bend Allowance**" section refers to the way SolidWorks calculates how much material will be consumed by a bend. When we bend a sheet metal component, the material on the inside face of the bend is compressed and the material outside is stretched. For example, if we take a 4" long strip of metal, and bend it 90 degrees at the center, the length of the flat portions plus the bent region will not necessarily add to 4". SolidWorks has three methods to calculate the flat pattern length: **Bend Allowance**, **Bend Deduction** and **K-Factor**.

Bend Allowance: When we use the Bend Allowance method we specify a length of metal that will become the bent region and is calculated by adding a specified length to the flat regions.

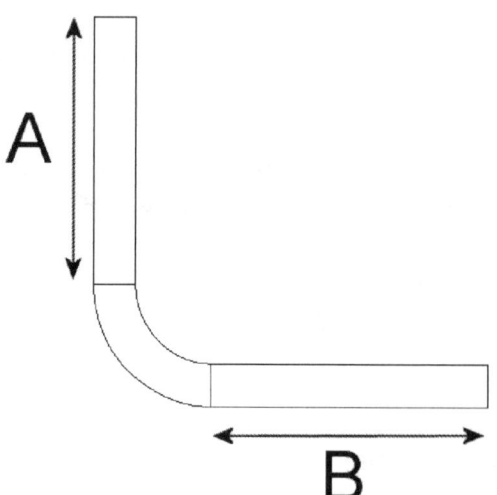

Flat Pattern Length = A + B + Bend Allowance (BA)

Bend Deduction: If we use a Bend Deduction we <u>subtract</u> a specified length to obtain the flat pattern length.

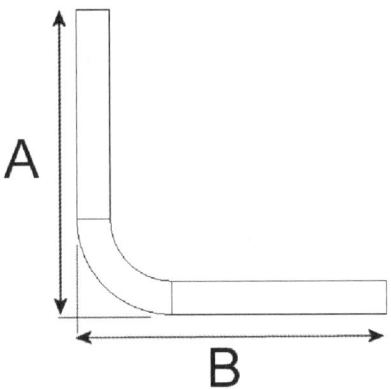

Flat Pattern Length = A + B − Bend Deduction (BD)

K-Factor: As we explained before, the material inside the bend is compressed and the material outside is stretched. The line between them is known as the neutral axis, which in essence does not change length. The relation between the distance of the neutral axis to the inside face and the sheet metal's thickness is known as the K-Factor.

K-Factor = t / T

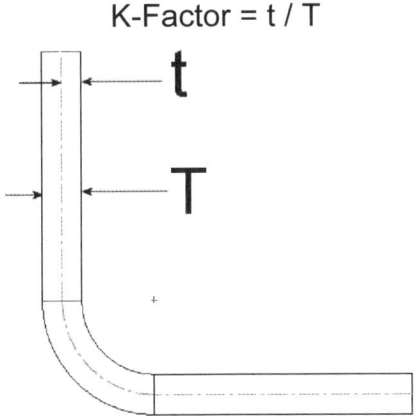

The bend allowance (BA) is then calculated by:

BA= π (R + KT) A/180

Where:

R= inside radius (Bend Radius)
A= Angle in Deg.
T= Thickness
K = K-Factor (t/T)

The method to calculate a sheet metal's bend allowance varies by preference, experience, availability of data, material, etc. There are numerous tables, books, references and guides to calculate it, and since these parameters vary by material, thickness, bend angle, grain direction, process and even temperature, we will not go into those details as it's well beyond the scope of this book and instead we'll use a generic K-Factor value for our examples.

The "**Auto Relief**" section refers to the relief cuts generated by SolidWorks for sheet metal fabrication processes. These cuts are added as needed for bending purposes. During the bending process, it's common to make small cuts (reliefs) at the end of bends to allow the metal to bend properly and not deform the material unexpectedly.

The types of reliefs available are:

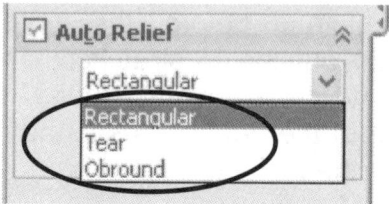

Rectangular: In a rectangular relief, a cut is made using a ratio or by specifying dimensions. The ratio is the cut's size (Dim) calculated based on the sheet metal's thickness as follows:

$$Dim = (Material\ Thickness) \times (Relief\ Ratio)$$

Obround: Is just like the Rectangular relief, but the relief's cut is rounded.

Rectangular Relief   Obround Relief

Tear: In a tear the smallest possible relief cut is made, just enough to allow the metal to bend as intended. This is similar to ripping the material at the time of bending during fabrication.

143. – After extruding the "Base-Flange" with the defined parameters, our part looks like this. Keep in mind that we are still editing it in the context of the assembly, and that's the reason why the electronics board is still transparent.

144. – The FeatureManager now shows the new part and the Sheet Metal features.

In *"Part1^Power Supply Assy"* (in blue because we are editing it in context of the assembly) we see the new sheet metal features added with the Base Flange operation.

"**Cut list**": Shows the number of bodies in the part. If multiple sheet metal bodies are added to a part, they will be listed under this folder.

"**Equations**": Lists the equations and Global Variables in the part. For sheet metal components, a variable is automatically added called "Thickness" which is used to make dimensions equal to the material's thickness.

"**Sheet-Metal1**": The feature that defines the sheet metal parameters of the part including material thickness, default bend radius, bend allowance and relief type.

"**Base-Flange1**": The first feature of the sheet metal part. Just like other sketch-based features, it includes the sketch used to make it and the bends created when the feature was made. Notice the "In Context" icon (->) next to the feature, letting us know that the part has external relations in the context of the assembly.

"**Flat-Pattern1**": This feature is suppressed when the part is bent (default). To show the part's flat pattern (*un-bent part*) we can unsuppress it. It includes a sketch (Bend-Lines1) automatically generated with the part's bend lines and a list of all the bends in the part.

145. – The next step is to add features to screw the board to the enclosure. The way we are going to create these supports is by using a feature called "**Forming Tool**." A Forming Tool works as a die that forms the sheet metal by bending, cutting and stretching as if it was pressed into the part, hence the "*Forming*" part of the name. SolidWorks has a number pre-loaded tools to make flanges, louvers, lances ribs, etc. In this step we'll learn how to use an existing forming tool and in a later step we'll see how to create one.

Sheet Metal and Top Down Design

Expand the Design Library, and from the "**forming tools**" folder select the "lances" subfolder. We'll use the "bridge lance" forming tool. To apply it to our model, drag it onto the bottom part of the model, and before dropping it make sure the tool is going 'into' the part (pressing the metal from the outside in), as in the following image. To reverse the direction of the forming tool press the "Tab" key before 'dropping' the forming tool with the mouse.

If SolidWorks asks "*Are you trying to make a derived part?*" when dropping the forming tool, the "forming tools" folder is not defined as such. To fix it, right mouse click in the "**forming tools**" folder in the Design Library and turn on the "**Forming Tools Folder**" option.

146. – After dropping the forming tool, we see the "**Form Tool Feature**" PropertyManager where we can define the face where we want to locate it, if we want to rotate it, flip the form tool to go in or out, etc.

147. – If needed, we may have to rotate the Form tool. Make sure the "Rotation Angle" box has "90deg" to have the alignment we need.

148. – After making sure the form tool has the correct orientation, we have to locate it accurately. Select the "Position" tab at the top of the properties; change to a bottom view and Hidden Lines Visible mode for easy visualization.

149. – The process to locate the form tool feature is similar to the hole wizard. Notice we have the sketch point tool active, and we can add all four locations needed at the same time. Since we want to locate the form tool features concentric with the mounting holes in the board, touch the edge of each of the other three holes in the electronics board to reveal their centers, and add a point concentric to each one.

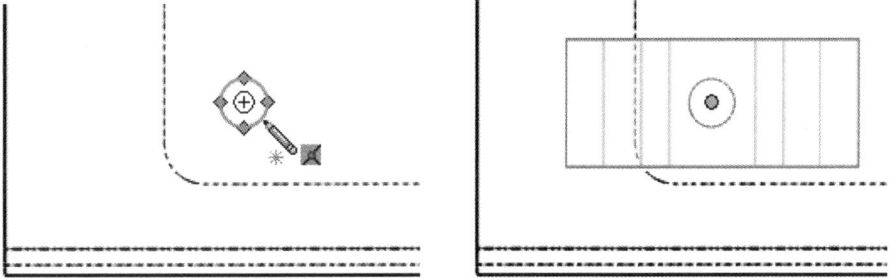

150. – Remember we still have one point close to one corner where we dropped the form tool at the beginning.

To locate the last form tool, turn off the sketch Point tool and add a concentric relation between the point and the edge of the last mounting hole.

151. – After locating the last form tool, click OK to finish The finished part should now look like this.

152. – After adding the lances to the bottom, we need to make holes for the screws. Switch to a Top view, select the top of any of the form features just added and make a new sketch. Add four equal circles concentric to each of the electronics board mounting holes. Dimension them 0.1" in diameter.

153. – After drawing the four equal circles, select the "**Extruded Cut**" icon to make a cut using all circles at the same time. Notice the extra options under "Direction 1." Using the "**Link to Thickness**" option will make the cut exactly as deep as the sheet metal thickness, essentially making the depth equal to the "Thickness" global variable.

The second new option is "**Normal Cut**." A normal cut means the cut will be made perpendicular to the sheet metal, even if the cut is being made at an angle. The reason to do this is because sheet metal manufacturing processes cannot make cuts at an angle in thin metal, it's not practical or easy, and therefore this option is driven by the nature of the manufacturing process itself.

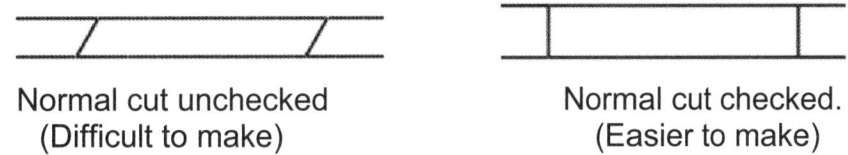

Normal cut unchecked. (Difficult to make)

Normal cut checked. (Easier to make)

154. – After adding the mounting holes we need to add a fan to help us cool the power supply. In many cases we'll need to include purchased components in our designs, like electrical components, hardware, etc. Many suppliers provide 3D models of their products, saving designers the trouble of modeling purchased parts, reducing the risk of design errors and at the same time improving the chances of having their products selected for our designs, making it a win-win situation. There are multiple sources of 3D models, from manufacturer's web sites to portals that consolidate multiple suppliers and user submitted models, like SolidWorks' 3D Content Central. 3D Content Central is a free portal that is also integrated in SolidWorks, and can be accessed directly from within SolidWorks or on the web at www.3dcontentcentral.com.

Remember that at this point we are editing the sheet metal part *in* the assembly, and now we need to add a new component to the assembly. To do this we need to stop editing the part for now, and return to editing the assembly. Select the "**Edit Component**" toggle button in the toolbar or CommandManager, *or* the confirmation corner *or* right mouse click and select "**Edit Assembly: xxxx**" to stop editing the sheet metal part and return to the assembly.

When we stop editing the part and return to editing the assembly,

- The sheet metal part's FeatureManager is no longer blue.
- The Power Supply electronics will become opaque again.
- The status bar will read "Editing Assembly."
- The "Edit Component" button will be disabled (since no component is being edited).
- The confirmation corner will be off.
- The title bar will read "*Power Supply Assy.sldasm*."

Basically, the assembly looks like any other assembly and now we can add more components to it.

155. – In SolidWorks, select the Design Library, go to "**3D ContentCentral**, **User Library, Home Page**" and click on the icon at the bottom to display the **User Library**.

A web browser will be launched where we can search the online catalog for components. As of the writing of this book, you have to register (free) in order to download files. In our example we'll use a user supplied model instead of a supplier certified component for the power supply we need.

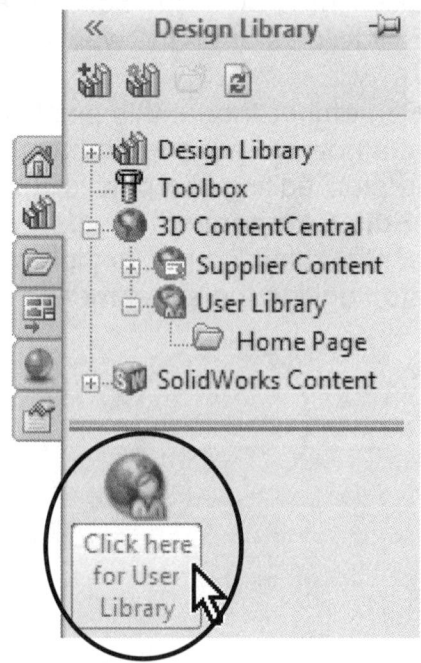

112

Sheet Metal and Top Down Design

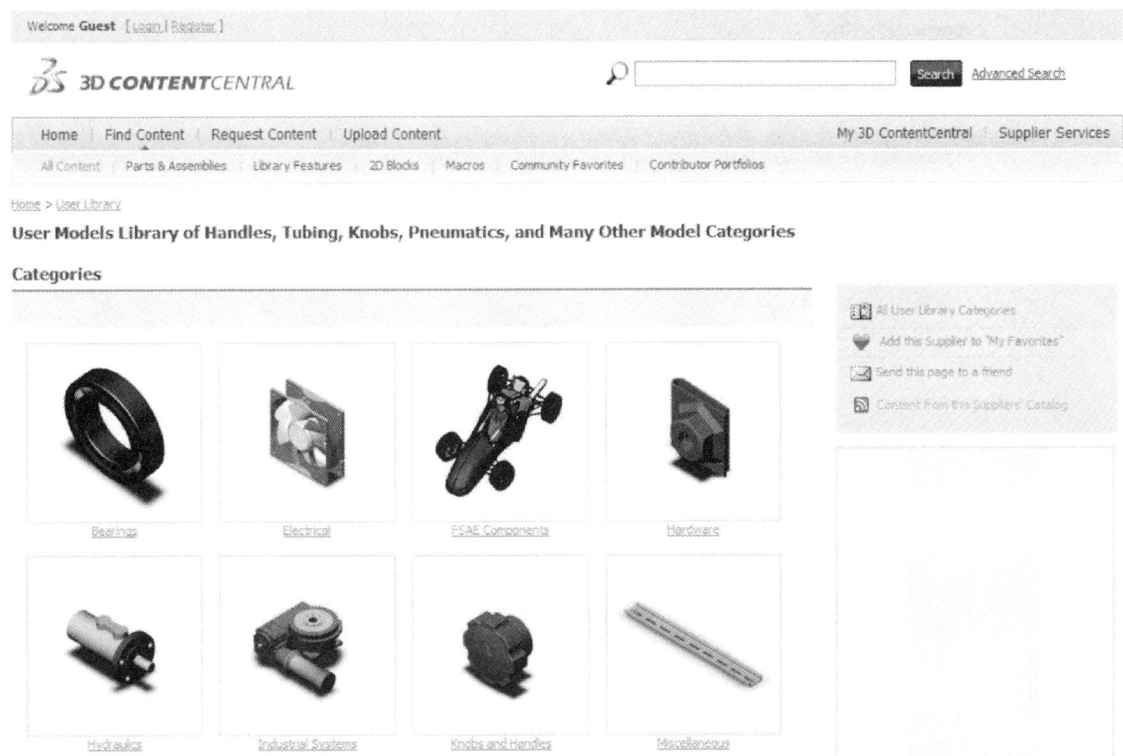

In the search box, type *PABST 512F*. This is the exact model we'll use; however, users would typically search by model or part number, make a general search for "Fan," and select a suitable model from the available options. The search now shows the part we are interested in.

Select the model; in the next screen make sure the format selected is SolidWorks 2012 (or earlier) and download the 3D model. After we are presented with the download window, drag the model's name into the assembly to add it to our Power Supply. When asked for a part name, select the folder to save the downloaded part and save as "**Fan-PABST 512F**." The model will be automatically added to your model. Save it and return to the assembly.

113

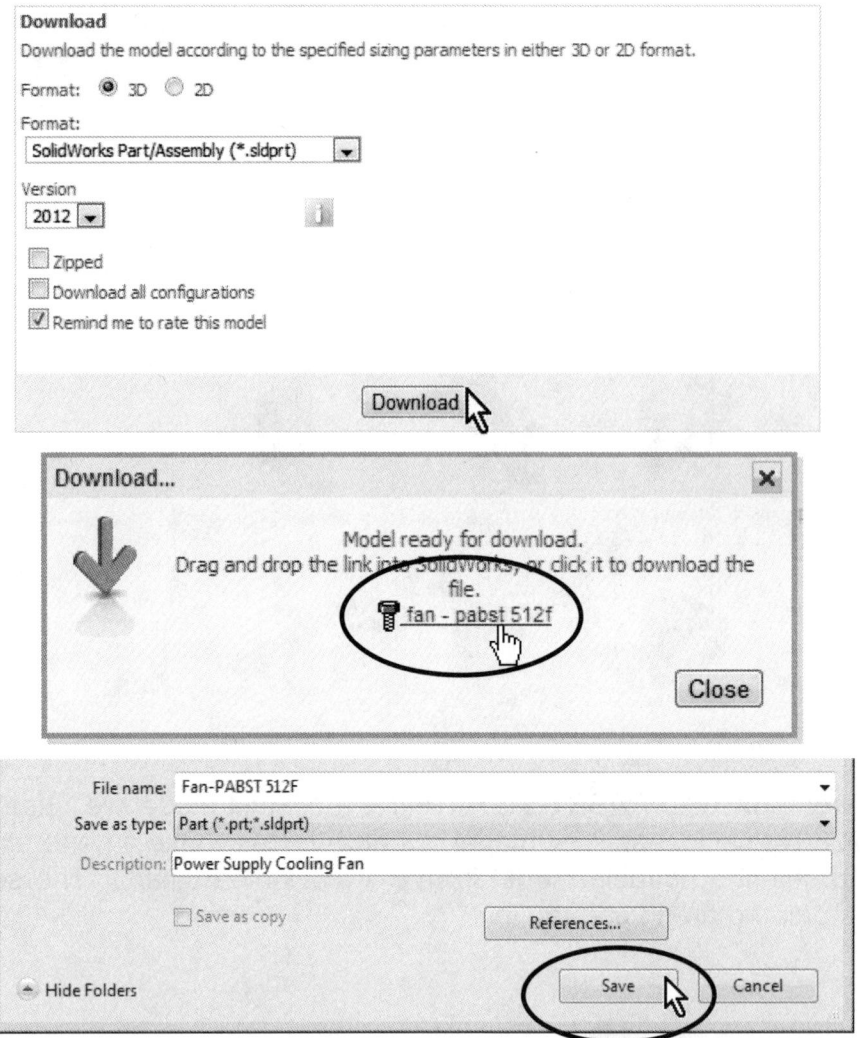

After adding the Fan to our assembly, locate it approximately as indicated.

156. – Add a Coincident mate between the Fan and the inside wall of the enclosure.

...then a second Coincident mate between the Right plane of the Fan and the face indicated in the electronics board.

157. – To finish locating the Fan, add a 0.2″ Distance mate from the Top face of the Fan to the top of the enclosure. Our Fan is now fully defined in the assembly.

158. – Now with the Fan in place, we need to edit the sheet metal part to make a cut for ventilation. Select the sheet metal part in the FeatureManager or in the graphics area and from the pop-up menu select "**Edit Part**."

159. – We are now editing the sheet metal part again; the electronics board and the fan are transparent and the box is opaque. Switch to a Back view and hide the electronics board component for visibility. Change the display mode to "Hidden Lines Visible."

 While editing a component in the assembly, we can hide, show and change the transparency of other components in the assembly.

160. – To add ventilation to our power supply, we need to make a cut using the "**Vent**" feature, and we'll use the fan's location for reference. Select the face in the back of the sheet metal part and make the following sketch. By matching the vent's location to the fan, if the fan's position needs to be changed the vent location will change as well; that is the idea behind designing in the context of an assembly. Notice the sketch used for the vent has intersecting lines, and the only reference to the fan is a Concentric relation to the fan's center.

Hidden lines visible (for relation)   Hidden lines removed (for clarity)

161. – From the Sheet Metal toolbar select the "**Vent**" feature. This icon is also located in the "**Fastening Features**" toolbar, or in the menu "**Insert, Fastening Feature, Vent**."

162. – In this step the fan was hidden for clarity. Select the outer (2") circle as the "**Boundary**" and set the "**Radius for the fillets**" value equal to 0.05" (this will be the fillet radius for all inside edges). In the "**Ribs**" selection box select all straight lines and make their width 0.1". For the "**Spars**" selection box select the 1" and 1.5" diameter circles and make them 0.1" wide. Finally, select the inner circle in the "**Fill-In Boundary**." The Fill-In Boundary is an area that will be covered. Note the "**Flow Area**" section lists the total area and the open area percentage for reference. Click **OK** to complete the Vent feature.

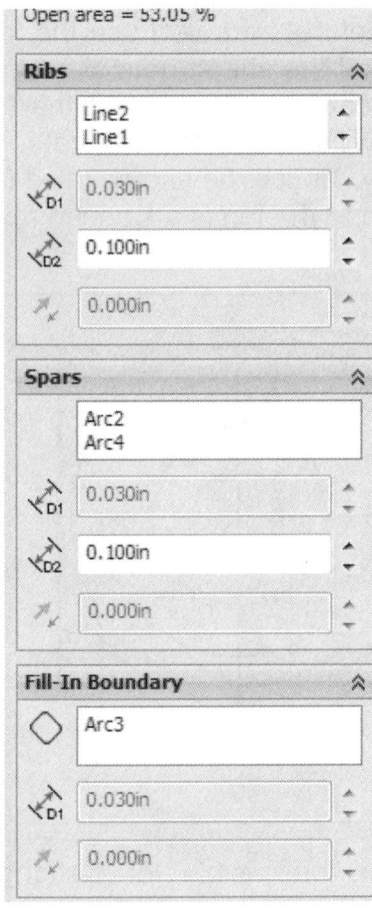

Sheet Metal and Top Down Design

Fan and electronics board hidden for visibility

163. – So far the sheet metal component has been an '*internal*' component in the assembly. If you remember, this means that it only exists inside the assembly; there is no file on the hard disk that we can make a reference to. Since we need to have a *part file* to make a drawing of it, we need to *externalize* the part. (It's not possible to make a drawing of a part internal to an assembly.) If you remember, we never gave the part a (file) name; it was automatically assigned by SolidWorks. In this step we'll make the part external. To externalize the part, select it in the FeatureManager with a right mouse click, then select "**Rename Part**" from the pop-up menu and change the name to "*Box Bottom*."

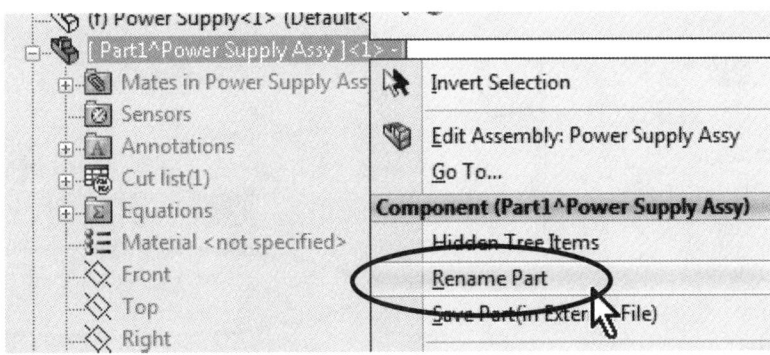

164. – After renaming the part, select it again with a right mouse click and select "**Save Part (in External File)**" from the pop-up menu.

119

Make sure the path is correct and click **OK**. The *Box Bottom* has been saved as a part file and looks the same as any other part in the assembly.

165. – At this point we can stop editing the part in the assembly and open it in its own window, or continue working in the context of the assembly. We'll edit the part in its own window as much as possible to make it easier to visualize the process, and revert to editing in the assembly as needed to take into consideration other components. To stop editing the part in the assembly, turn off the "**Edit Component**" icon and open the *Box Bottom* part in its own window.

or

Sheet Metal and Top Down Design

166. – The next step is to reinforce the sides to make our component stronger. To add a Miter flange, we need to make a sketch perpendicular to the edge. One way to do this is to select the thin face at the end of the part and insert a sketch in it (which is difficult unless we zoom in really close), or select the **Miter Flange** icon and click near the end of the edge where SolidWorks automatically creates a plane perpendicular to the selected edge where we can draw the miter flange sketch profile.

Zoomed in VERY close (harder)   Select the edge (easier option)

167. – Draw a single line perpendicular to the edge and dimension it 0.25" long. This will be the profile of the miter flange. Notice the new plane created at the end of the edge where our sketch is made.

168. – Click on the **Miter Flange** command icon (or Exit Sketch) to continue. Notice the preview in the first edge. To continue the flange along the bottom and other side, either click on the "**Propagate**" icon to automatically select these edges, or manually select them. Leave the "**Use default radius**" checkbox selected to make the flange's bends the default radius as defined when the sheet metal parameters were defined. "**Gap Distance**" is the gap at the corners of the miter. "**Trim side bends**" removes material when a bend of the miter touches an existing bend (no difference in this case). Select the "**Material inside**" flange position for our part. See the differences for flange position below. Click OK to complete the miter

The different "**Flange Position**:" options mean:
Material Inside: The Flange added will not extend beyond the existing edge of the part, maintaining the original part dimensions.

Material Outside: The flange added will be *one material thickness* outside the existing edge.

Bend Outside: The flange will leave the existing edge intact and add all the material and the bends outside. The part will increase in size by one thickness and one bend radius.

169. – Add a second Miter Flange to the other side of the enclosure using the same parameters as the first one.

170. – Now we need to add a cut on one side to allow the power supply wires to exit the enclosure. Go back to the Power Supply assembly and make the electronics board visible and edit the *Box Bottom* part in the assembly to continue.

171. – To make the cut, first we need to unfold the miter edge closer to the wires. We'll use the "**Unfold**" command from the Sheet Metal tab, or from the menu "**Insert, Sheet Metal, Unfold**."

 The cut can be made without unfolding the flange, but we chose to do it this way to show the reader a different approach.

In the "**Fixed face**" selection box select the model's face that will remain fixed; in other words, when we unfold the miter flange, the flange will move out instead of the other way around. In the "**Bends to unfold**" select the bend region of the flange. Click **OK** when done.

The miter flange will unfold.

125

172. – While unfolded we can add the cut for the wires and then re-fold the flange. Switch to a Front view and make the next sketch around the wires. Make a cut using the "**Link to thickness**" option.

173. – To re-fold the flange after making the cut, select the **Fold** icon from the Sheet Metal toolbar or from the menu "**Insert, Sheet Metal, Fold**."

The "**Fixed face**" is automatically selected; all we have to do is select the bend region (SolidWorks will only let us select bends). Clicking in the "**Collect All Bends**" button will add all unfolded bends.

174. – The next step is to add flanges at the top of the box to screw the cover in place. Select the "**Edge Flange**" command from the Sheet Metal toolbar, or the menu "**Insert, Sheet Metal, Edge Flange**."

In the "**Flange Parameters**" selection box, select the top edge of the side with the vent. As soon as the mouse pointer is moved, you can see a preview of the edge flange. Click towards the center of the box to make the flange inside. Then click on the "**Edit Flange Profile**" button to modify the shape of the flange. (If we want the flange to be the full length of the edge, there is no need to edit the profile.)

We can modify the sketch as much as we want, as long as we end with a single closed profile. Drag the lines on the sides towards the inside, delete the short line in front and replace it with a tangent arc. The end lines can be dragged even if they appear fully defined. Add dimensions as needed to complete the sketch.

127

175. – Click the Back button to return to the **Edge Flange** command when the sketch is complete.

 If you click Finish, the flange will be completed with the parameters entered before editing the sketch.

In the "**Flange Parameters**," set the angle to 90 degrees. In the "**Flange Position**" selection box, select the "Material Inside" option, and turn on the "**Custom Relief Type**" checkbox. We'll use an Obround relief for the flange with a 0.5 ratio. Click **OK** to finish.

 For rectangular or obround types we can optionally define the relief by width and depth.

128

Sheet Metal and Top Down Design

176. – Now we need to add a hole for a screw to the tab we just made. In this case we'll use one of the built in Form Tools to do it. Open the "**Design Library**" in the task pane, and scroll down to "**forming tools, embosses**." From the list of tools select "**extruded hole**." Drag-and-drop it in the Top face of the tab just made. Make sure it is going *into* the part, and not out. Remember that we can reverse the direction of the tool by pressing the TAB key before releasing the mouse.

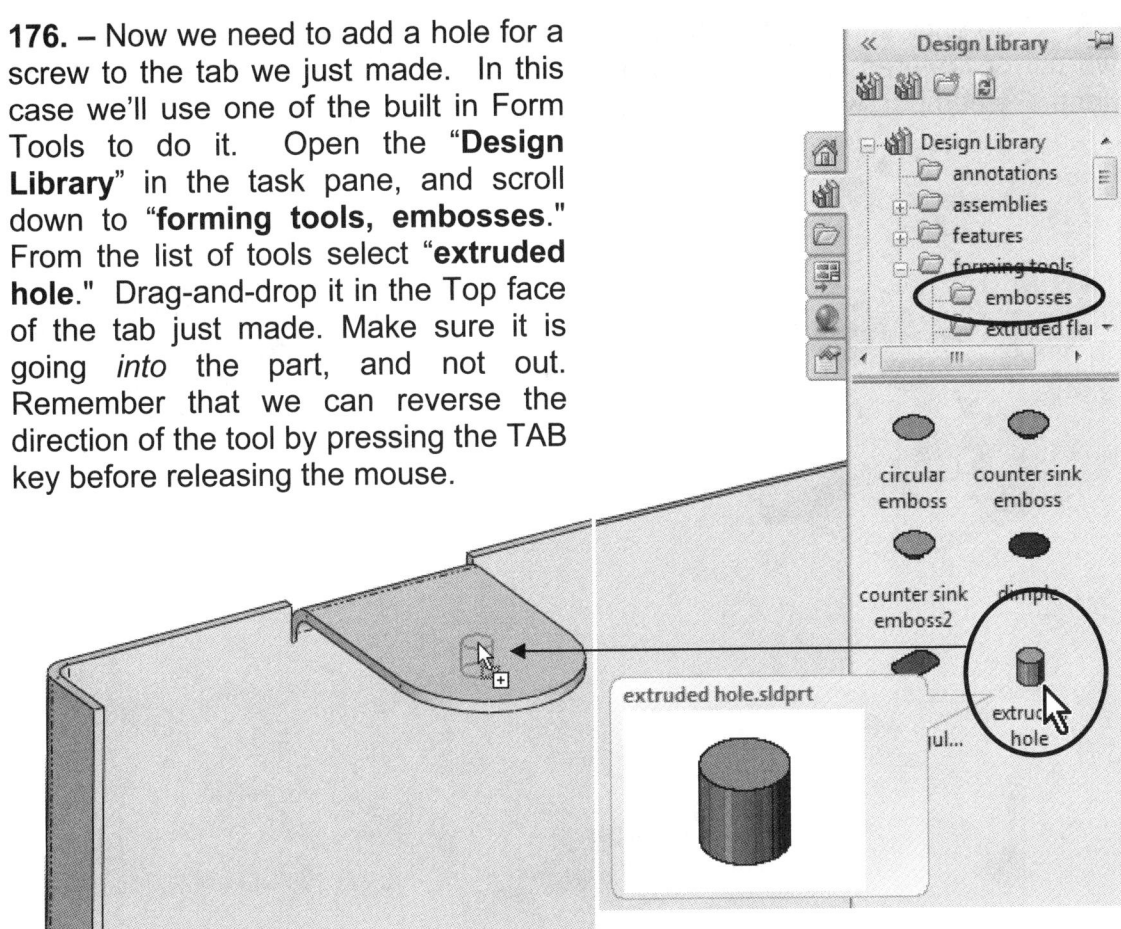

177. – In the "Position" tab of the form tool properties, make the locating point concentric with the edge of the round tab and click OK to finish. Your part should now look like this:

178. – The enclosure requires four flanges (and holes); add the other three using two mirror features first about the part's Front plane, and then about the Right plane. Remember, we are still working in the context of the assembly.

179. – Form tools can be used only in sheet metal parts, but a **library feature** can be used in any part. To make a library feature that we can reuse in our designs, first we need to make a new part (outside the assembly), add the feature(s) we want the library to have and save it as a Library Feature.

For our example we'll make a Library Feature of a cutout for a power supply connector, and add it to our part next to the vent. To build a library feature, make a new part (NOT in the assembly), add a new sketch (any plane) with a 3" x 2" square and extrude it 0.125" thick. After extruding it, make the following sketch and make a cut using the "Up to next" end condition. The size and thickness of the first feature are not really important; it just has to be big enough to hold the feature we want to make a library from.

Sheet Metal and Top Down Design

180. – Once the cut is made, select the Cut-Extrude1 feature in the Feature-Manager, select the menu "**File, Save as...**" and from the "Save as type" drop down selection box select "Lib Feat Part (*.sldlfp)." Name it *Power Connector Cutout*. Notice as soon as the library feature type is selected, we are switched to the "Design Library" folder. Save the library in this folder.

 If the feature(s) to be saved as a library is(are) not pre-selected in the FeatureManager, saving a library feature will not work.

The FeatureManager changes to reflect it is now a library feature. A green letter "L" is superposed in the feature(s) that are the library, and the icon at the top is changed to a library feature.

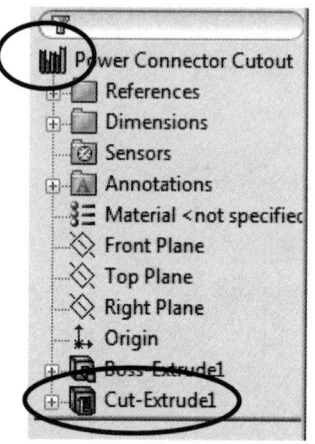

When the library is saved, the folder "**Dimensions**" is added to the Feature-Manager tree. Right mouse click in the "Annotations" folder, turn on "**Show Feature Dimensions**," and display dimension names from the menu "**View, Dimension Names**." Rename the indicated dimensions as shown.

132

181. – The reason for renaming the dimensions is that in the library file we can define which dimensions will be used to locate the feature when inserted into a part, which dimensions are user modifiable, and which are not. Expanding the "**Dimensions**" folder we can see all the dimensions listed. What we need to do is drag-and-drop the "*Locate_Top*" and "*Locate_Side*" dimensions to the "Locating Dimensions" folder, and the rest in the "Internal Dimensions" folder.

Locating Dimensions will be used to position the feature when we add the library to a part. **Internal Dimensions** cannot be changed by the user and the dimensions not added to either folder can be changed when adding the library. After adding the dimensions to the folders, turn off the dimension display, save the changes and close the library file. The library we just made is now listed under the "Design Library" folder in the task pane.

 We can drag the library files to one of the folders in the top to keep libraries organized. More folders can be added as needed.

 Library features can have more than one feature. The best way to make multi feature libraries is to make the second and subsequent features referencing the first feature only (including sketch locations if possible). This way the external references and locating dimensions can be kept to a minimum.

182. – We are now ready to add the "Power Connector Cutout" library to the *Box Bottom* part either in its own window or editing it in the assembly (your choice). Open the task pane, select the "Design Library" folder, and drag-and-drop the library onto the part. Notice we are editing the sheet metal part in the assembly.

After dropping the library, a preview pop-up window will show us the edge that we need to select in the part for each of the locating dimensions. When an edge is selected, the "References" selection box will show a checkmark next to each edge listed. Select the reference asked for, in this case it is "Locate_Top" (yours may be the Side); select the edge at the top.

Immediately after selecting the first reference we are shown in the preview window, select the second reference. Select the indicated reference in the part.

Click inside each dimension in the "Locating Dimensions" box, and change their values. Locate_Side = 1.25"; Locate_Top = 1.5". Click **OK** to finish.

If a dimension is not designated as "*Internal*" or "*Locating*" in the library, its value can be changed in the "*Size Dimensions*" box after selecting the "*Override dimension values*" checkbox. Also, if no locating dimensions are added to the sketch when the library is added, we'll see an "Edit Sketch" button to locate the library.

 A library feature can have configurations, and each time it's used, a different one can be selected.

183. – We can also make libraries of parts and even assemblies, not just features. In the next step we'll create a library part and use it in our assembly. The part we want to make a library of is the Power Connector for which we just made a cut out.

A library part can be any SolidWorks part, and can be used as such by putting it in the "**Parts**" folder of the "Design Library." What makes library parts useful is that we can define mate references so that when we drag it into an assembly, the mate references will attempt to find a matching face or entity. Download and open the part *Power Connector* from our website www.mechanicad.com/download.html. As a challenge, feel free to download the part's drawing and build the part.

Sheet Metal and Top Down Design

184. – Once the connector is open, go to the menu "**Insert, Reference Geometry, Mate Reference**." Mate References will automatically add mates when the library part is inserted into an assembly, and will try to match the references defined.

 Up to three mate references can be defined in a part; for our example we'll only use a Concentric and a Coincident mate.

For the "**Primary Reference Entity**" select the circular edge in the left mounting hole of the connector.

For the "**Secondary Reference Entity**" pick the flat face shown. Select "Coincident" mate and "Anti-Aligned" for the orientation. This is the mate that will be added. Click **OK** to add the Mate References.

137

Mate Alignment refers to how the mated faces will be oriented. For flat faces imagine an arrow (Vector) going out of each face. "**Aligned**" means both arrows are pointing in the same direction; "**Anti-Aligned**" means they are pointing at each other. There is no analogy for cylindrical surfaces; just flip them as necessary. A good practice is to position parts as close to the desired orientation before adding mates; SolidWorks will not rotate a part more than 180 degrees to add a mate.

185. – Save the *Power Connector* part with the Mate References. After adding the Mate References, a new folder is added to the FeatureManager listing the references defined.

Before adding the part to the library, we need to keep the Design Library visible by clicking on the auto-show pin.

Expand the Design Library and drag-and-drop the part from the top of the FeatureManager to the task pane in the desired folder. We'll select the "**parts**" folder for our example.

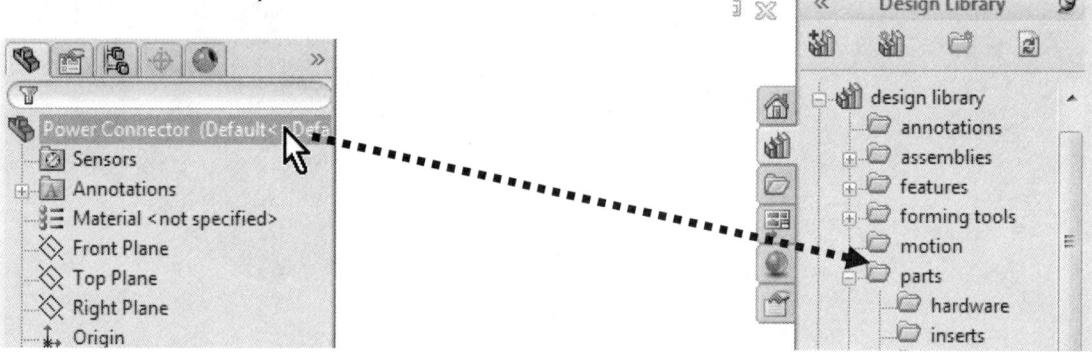

We are asked to select the folder to add the library to, and optionally give it a different name. Click **OK** to continue and close the *Power Connector* part.

138

186. – Now, back to our assembly. After making the library part, it's time to add it to our assembly. Be sure we are editing the assembly before adding the library part. From the "**Design Library**," drag-and-drop the *Power Connector* into the assembly. Notice, as we move it close to a hole or a flat face, the part automatically snaps, trying to find a match using the defined mate references. When we drop the part at the cutout, a concentric and a coincident mate are added. Close the "**Insert Components**" message to continue.

The only thing left for us to do is to add a Parallel mate to align the connector using the faces indicated.

187. – In order for the fan to properly cool the power supply, we'll add a series of slots for air to go into the enclosure and then out through the fan's vent. Open the *Box Bottom* part in its own window, add the following sketch using the "Slot" tool and make a cut with the "Link to thickness" option.

188. – Make an array of 15 copies spaced 0.25".

Sheet Metal and Top Down Design

189. – The last operation to complete our first sheet metal part is to eliminate all the sharp edges. When fabricating sheet metal components, it's common to see sharp edges due to shearing and punching operations and eliminating them will prevent accidents. The "**Break Corners**" command is in the Sheet Metal toolbar, under the drop-down "**Corners**" icon.

190. – There are two options for the "**Break Corners**" command, to add a chamfer or a fillet. For this part of the enclosure, we'll use a 0.050″ chamfer. Select all edges that could potentially have a sharp corner.

 When using the "Break Corner" command. a filter to select small edges is automatically enabled to make selection easier. Small edges can also be window-selected. Selecting a face will add all of its small edges, too.

191. – Save the *Box Bottom* part. Our finished component now looks like this:

192. – Sheet metal components can be flattened at any time. The "**Flat-Pattern**" feature at the end of the FeatureManager is suppressed while the part is in the bent state, and when we select the "**Flatten**" command from the Sheet Metal toolbar, it is unsuppressed and the part unfolds.

A flat pattern is required for manufacturing to know what size the metal needs to be cut and how to bend it. Using the correct bend allowance is extremely important, because otherwise when the calculated flat pattern is bent, the resulting part will not have the expected design dimensions. To see the flat pattern for the *Box Bottom* select the "**Flatten**" command.

The "Flat-Pattern1" feature is now unsuppressed, and we can see the flattened sheet metal part and a sketch that represent the minimum material size needed to make this part.

Sheet Metal and Top Down Design

193. – Editing the "**Flat-Pattern**" feature will show the following options:

 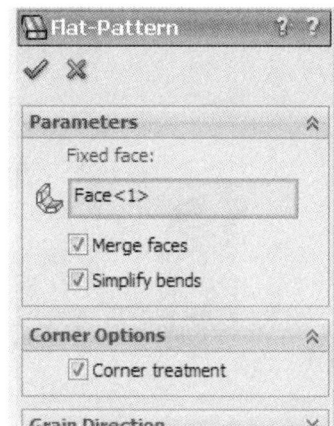

More on Flat Pattern Options

Merge faces: When this option is checked, no bend regions are shown in the flat pattern, merging every flat face together. If left unchecked, all the bend regions will be displayed.

 Merge faces is useful when the flat pattern is exported to a computer numerical control (CNC) software to avoid multiple broken lines and faces.

Merge faces unchecked   Merge faces checked

143

Simplify bends: When flattening complex bends (like bends across a curved area), this option will make a straight edge in the bend region, making the manufacturing process easier.

Simplify bends checked

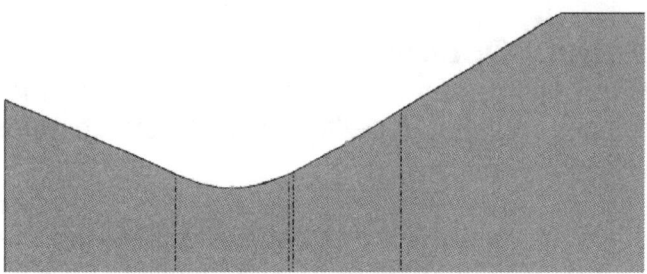

Simplify bends unchecked

Corner Treatment: Will make a flat pattern easier for manufacturing to fabricate by eliminating complex cuts in the corners.

No corner treatment

With corner treatment

Sheet Metal and Top Down Design

194. – The second component to be designed is the power supply's cover. Just like the bottom part, we'll design the cover in the context of the assembly. Change to the assembly window, if not already there, and make sure we are editing the assembly and not a part.

Add a new part to the assembly. Select the "**Insert Components**" drop-down icon and select "**New Part**," or from the menu "**Insert, Component, New Part**."

145

195. – In the FeatureManager, select the Front plane to insert the new part. Remember, the Front plane of the new part will be aligned and constrained to the selected plane with an "**InPlace**" mate.

As soon as we select the assembly's Front plane, a new part is added to the assembly and it's displayed in blue in the FeatureManager. The other assembly components become transparent (if the option is set), and a sketch is ready for us to start working in the new part's Front plane.

Sheet Metal and Top Down Design

196. – Switch to a Front view. Hide the electronics board, the fan and the connector; they will not be needed to design the cover and keeping them visible makes the screen unnecessarily busy. Draw the sketch as three lines; add the necessary Coincident relations to make the lines coincident to the top and side edges.

197. – After completing the sketch, select the "**Base-Flange**" icon from the Sheet Metal toolbar.

198. – This sketch represents the inside dimensions of the sheet metal cover; therefore, we'll change the settings to add material *outside* the sketch. Extrude the base flange in Direction 1 "**Up To Surface**" and select the Front face of the *Box Bottom*; in Direction 2 "**Up To Surface**" and select the Back face. Select the same sheet metal parameters as we did for the bottom part, except make the default Bend Radius 0.015". "K-Factor" is 0.5 and "Rectangular" relief ratio of 0.5.

Sheet Metal and Top Down Design

199. – The next step is to add two jogs, one in each side; these jogs will help us assemble the cover to the bottom. To add a jog we need a sketch with a line, and we can draw the sketch before or after selecting the Jog command.

Before option: Select the side of the cover, and draw a single line sketch. (Remember we are editing the cover in the assembly.)

 The sketch line does not have to go all the way across the face that we intend to bend, but the jog will.

200. – Select the "**Jog**" icon from the Sheet Metal toolbar or the menu "**Insert, Sheet Metal, Jog**."

In the "**Jog**" command, under the "**Fixed Face**" selection box, click anywhere in the sketch face above the line; this is the part of the face that will not move. Leave the option "**Use default radius**" checked. In the "**Jog Offset**" section we'll define the parameters for the jog bends.

We can make the jog a fixed distance, up to a surface, vertex or offset. The purpose of the jog is to bend the cover inside the miter flange of the base part to assemble them together. When using the fixed distance, there are three different ways to define how the Jog distance is measured, and the icons for each one are self explanatory:

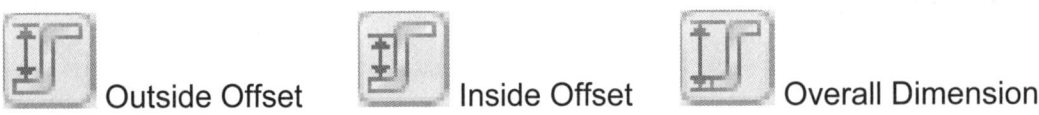
Outside Offset   Inside Offset   Overall Dimension

The "**Fix projected length**" option means that material will be added equaling the jog distance plus the jog bends, making the flat pattern bigger as seen below. If it's un-checked no material will be added.

Fixed projected length option:

Unchecked   **Checked**

Flat pattern:

The "**Jog Position**" is essentially the same definition as when making flanges. Change to a Front view and zoom in the jog area for visibility. Select "Blind," 0.1" going into the enclosure (use reverse direction if needed); use the "**Overall Dimension**" and "**Material Inside**" options, and enter 90 degrees for the "**Jog Angle**."

Notice the option "Fix projected length" is not checked; if it was checked, the jog would be extended and go through the bottom part. Click **OK** to finish.

Sheet Metal and Top Down Design

201. – For the other side, select the "**Jog**" command first. When asked to select a face on which to draw the sketch, select the cover's opposite side face, draw the same sketch and add the second jog with the same settings as the first one, also going inside. The second jog should now look like this:

202. – With the jog we bent the entire length of the cover to fit behind the miter flange of the *Box Bottom* part, but now we have interferences at the corners (Assembly Transparency set to "Opaque" for visibility).

203. – To correct this situation we'll have to make a cut in the corners. Add a sketch on one side of the cover (either side will work). Dimension the inside of the rectangle 0.050″ past the miter flange corner. Make the rectangle coincident relation with the bend and the lower outside corner of the jog to fully define the sketch.

Mirror the sketch about the part's center and make a cut using the **"Through All"** end condition to cut all four corners at the same time.

Sheet Metal and Top Down Design

Cover part opened by itself to show the corner cuts

204. – The next step is to add holes to screw the cover to the *Box Bottom* part. In the assembly, switch to a Top view and add a sketch on the Top face of the cover. Change to "Hidden lines visible" and add four circles concentric to the holes in the tabs. Dimension one circle 0.150" diameter and make all four circles equal. Make a cut using "**Link to thickness**." (The "Shaded" view was added for clarity, as it's difficult to distinguish the sketch with hidden lines visible.)

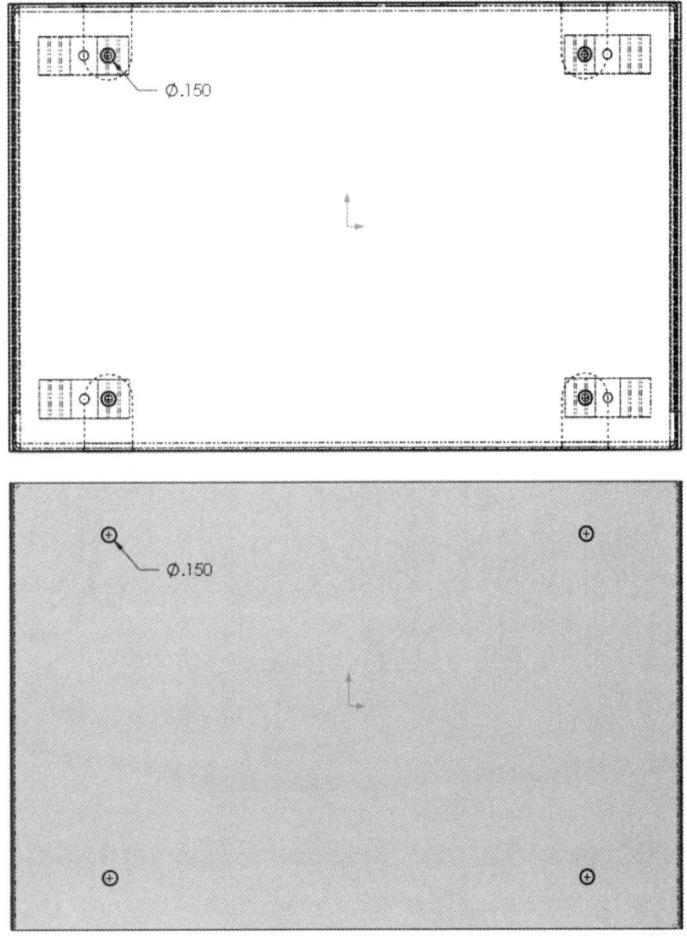

205. – Now add ventilation slots to the cover. Add a new sketch in one side of the cover and dimension it as shown. Just as with the corner cuts, make a Cut Extrude using the "**Through All**" end condition to cut both sides of the cover.

206. – Make a linear slot pattern with 12 instances spaced 0.250".

Sheet Metal and Top Down Design

207. – As a final step, break all sharp corners using the "**Corners, Break-Corners**" command from the Sheet Metal toolbar. Add a 0.1″ chamfer break. Select the side and the jog faces to automatically select all corners.

208. – Now that the part is finished we'll *externalize* it from the assembly. All this time the part has been internal, meaning it only exists in the assembly and there is no "file" we can reference.

Stop editing the cover in context of the assembly and return to editing the assembly. Press the "**Edit Component**" button in the CommandManager *or* right mouse click in the graphics area and select "**Edit assembly: Power Supply Assy**."

209. – Rename the part *Box Cover* with a slow double-click, or from the right mouse click menu select "**Rename Part**." Right mouse click in it again and select "**Save Part (in External File)**" from the pop-up menu. Make sure the path is correct and click **OK** to save the file.

210. – Open the *Box Cover* part in its own window and view the flat pattern by selecting the "**Flatten**" command in the Sheet Metal toolbar. Turn off the "Flatten" command and return to the assembly.

211. – Show the Power Supply, Fan and Power Connector parts in the assembly and if wanted, make an exploded view to finish. We'll work on the sheet metal drawings next.

Sheet Metal Drawings

Sheet Metal and Top Down Design

212. – There are a few differences when we talk about a Sheet metal part's drawing. When we make a new drawing, the first thing to notice is that we have the option to add a "**Flat Pattern**" view besides the standard views we are used to. Open the *Box Bottom* part and make a new drawing. Drag the "**Flat pattern**" from the View Palette into the drawing.

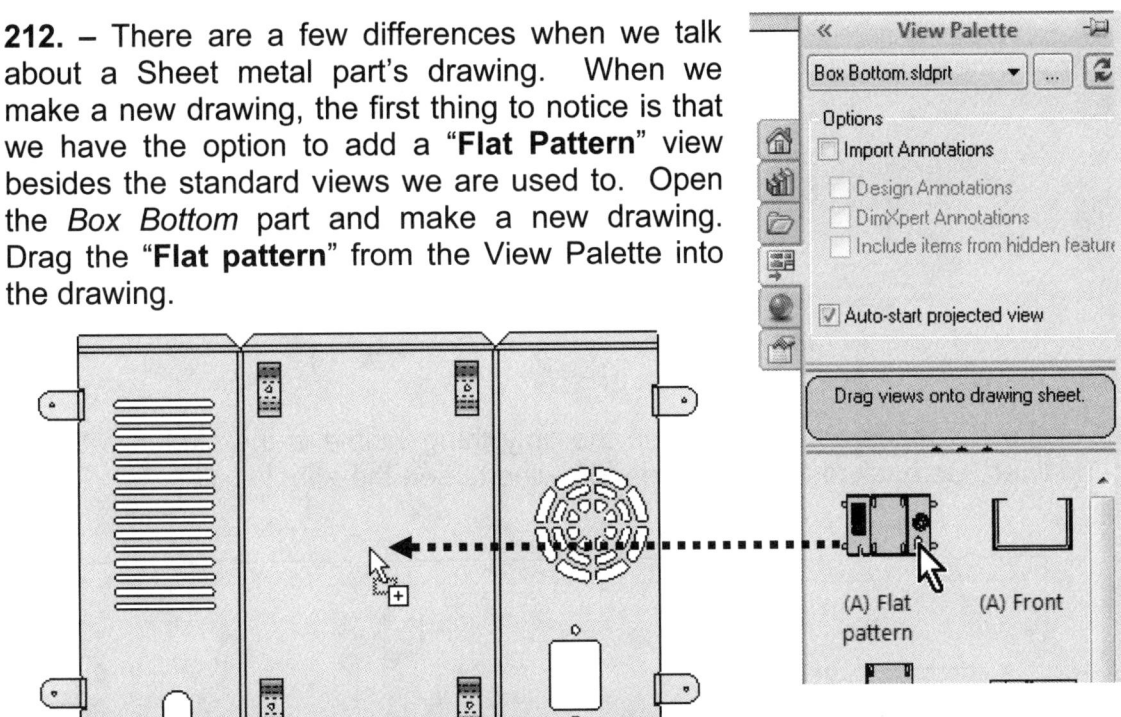

As soon as we drop the flat pattern in the drawing, the sketch with bend lines and bending notes is added automatically. These notes will help you to bend the part correctly. Adjust the drawing view's scale and/or bending note's font as needed.

213. – Open the *Box Bottom* part, edit the "**Flat-Pattern1**" feature and turn on the "**Merge faces**" option.

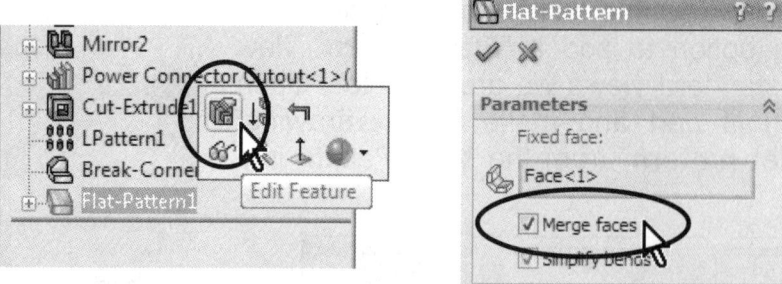

All of the flat faces are merged and the only thing visible is the sketch with the bend lines. Go back to the flat pattern drawing to see the effect.

214. – It is common practice to export a 1:1 scale drawing in DWG or DXF with "Merge faces" on for manufacturing (CNC) purposes, and you may or not want the bend lines and notes in this file, as a CNC program only uses the contours to trace the part. To turn off all notes and bend lines in the drawing, you can right mouse click in the "**Annotations**" folder of the drawing and turn off "**Display Annotations**," or hide the sketch with bend lines in the "**Flat pattern**" feature.

Sheet Metal and Top Down Design

If needed, flat patterns usually have to be manually dimensioned.

 To enable or disable the option to add sheet metal notes in the flat pattern when making a drawing, go to the menu "**Tools, Options, Document Properties, Sheet Metal**" and turn off "**Display sheet metal bend notes**."

215. – One more thing to know: the flat pattern is a part sub-configuration where the "Flat pattern1" feature is unsuppressed, showing the sheet metal part flat.

CHALLENGE:

Make manufacturing drawings from the power supply sheet metal parts including a flat pattern.

Notes:

Sheet Metal Locker Top Down Design

216. – For our next sheet metal project we'll build a metal locker also using a top down design approach. Our locker will have a base to raise it from the floor. In this example, we'll learn how to convert solid parts into sheet metal. A solid or shelled part can be converted directly as shown here:

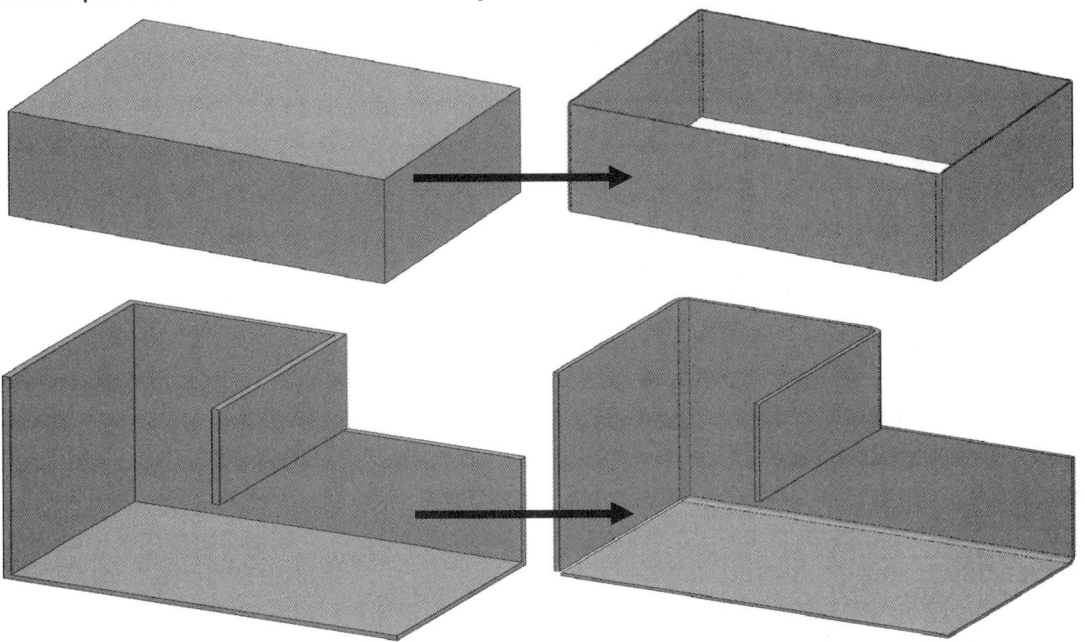

What happens after converting the solid part into sheet metal is that the face selected as "fixed" will remain static, the faces connected to it by edges defined as "Bends" will be part of the sheet metal component and the rest of the faces will be deleted. If the part is made of surfaces or a shelled part before converting it to sheet metal, some of the faces not connected by "Bend" edges will also be removed. Let's make one to practice.

217. – The first part we'll make is the locker's base. Make a new part; draw the following sketch in the Top plane and extrude it 10″ up. Note the square is centered in the origin.

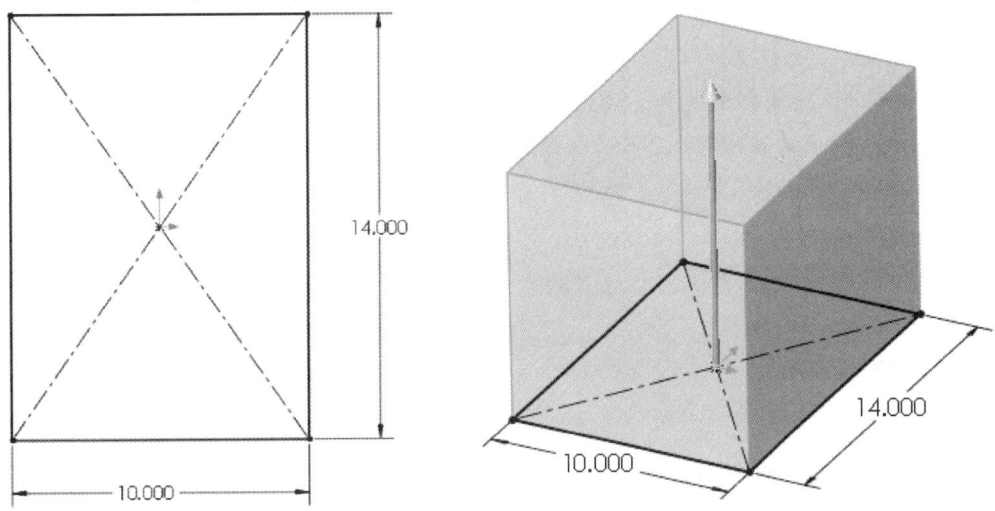

218. – From the Sheet Metal toolbar select "Convert to Sheet Metal."

219. – We have to select a face that will be the fixed face in the sheet metal, the edge(s) of the part that will become bend(s), and the edge(s) that will be ripped (open). Select the left face of the part to be the fixed face (here we used "Select other" to select the face). For our locker's thickness, we'll use a 22 gauge sheet metal. From standard gauge tables for steel* we see that the thickness is 0.03". Enter the thickness and a default bend radius of 0.05". Make sure the thickness of the sheet metal is added *'inside'* as we want to maintain the dimensions given as external dimensions. You can zoom into a corner to see if the material is added inside or out and check (or uncheck) the "Reverse Thickness" option as needed...

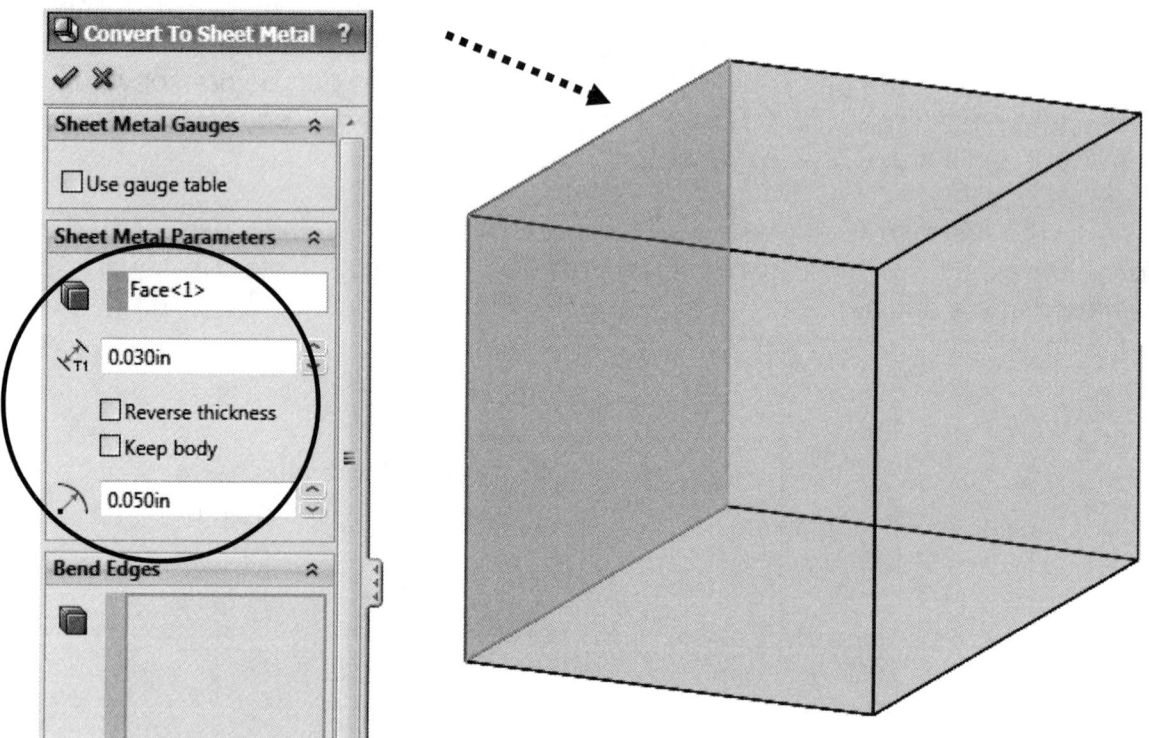

* "Standard" sheet metal gauge tables vary by country, material, etc.

220. – ...select the 3 vertical edges (labeled "Radius") that will become bends. The remaining vertical edge (labeled "Gap") is automatically selected as a "**Rip Edge.**" Set the default gap for rips to 0.01" and "**Auto Relief**" type to Obround with a 0.5 ratio. Click OK to convert the part to sheet metal.

 In the fly-out labels we can override the default settings for bend radius and gap distance if needed.

The part has been converted to sheet metal, the top and bottom faces have been automatically removed and the sheet metal features added to the Feature Manager.

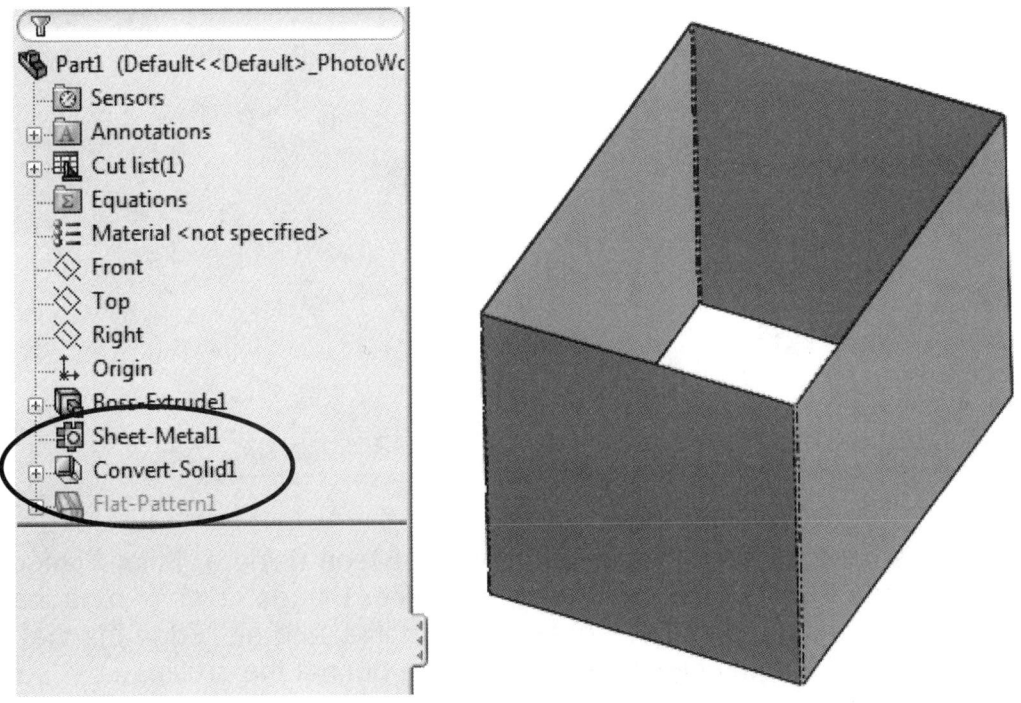

221. – Now we need to add miter flanges in top and bottom, but instead of using the "**Miter Flange**" command, we'll use "**Edge Flange**." Select the Edge Flange command, and click to select all the edges indicated;

the miter cuts will be automatically added to the corners. Make the flange 0.5" long, with the option "Material Inside." The arrows in each flange can be used to reverse the direction individually if needed.

 In this case there is no real difference between using a "Miter Flange" or an "Edge Flange," but remember, the "Miter Flange" always runs the full length of the edge and can change the profile, and an "Edge Flange" can change the length and shape of the flange but not the profile.

Sheet Metal and Top Down Design

Miter Flange
Different profile, full length

Edge Flange
Different shape, not full length

222. – After adding the flanges, we need to close the gap in the corner that was ripped when we converted the solid to sheet metal.

Select the "**Corners, Closed Corner**" drop down icon. This command will extend one sheet metal side to match the other using a butt, overlap or underlap extension. In the "**Faces to Extend**" selection box, select the flat face on one side, and in the "**Faces to Match**" select the other flat face.

 Closing the corner is an option when converting to Sheet Metal, but we chose to show how to use this command instead.

169

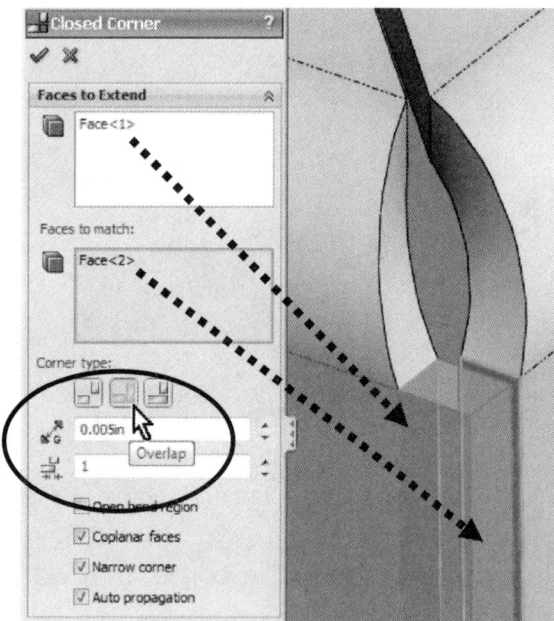

Select "Overlap" to make the first face extend over the second face.

Open bend region will close the bend region.

Coplanar faces will automatically select faces that are coplanar to the one selected.

Narrow Corner will attempt to close the gap when using large bend radii.

In the "Gap Distance" we can make the gap in the corner as small as needed. Enter 0.005".

223. – Upon closer inspection of the corners made with the edge flange, we realize that an extra piece of metal is in the bend area. To eliminate it, select the "Edge-Flange1" made before, edit it and check the "**Trim side bends**" option under "Flange Position." Click **OK** to finish. Now all of the corners made with this Edge Flange command are trimmed.

Sheet Metal and Top Down Design

224. – Save the part as *Locker Base*. Add it to a new assembly and locate it at the origin (making it symmetric about the origin). Since we will design the rest of the locker in the context of the assembly using the base as reference we must save the assembly. Save the new assembly as *Full Locker Assembly*.

225. – The next step is to add a new part to the assembly; it will be the locker's body. From the Assembly toolbar select the "**Insert Components**" drop-down menu and select "**New Part**." When asked to select a face or plane to add the new part select the Top face of the "Locker Base."

171

Immediately after selecting the Top face, a new part is added. It's listed with blue in the FeatureManager, the "**Edit Component**" icon is active, the *Locker Base* becomes transparent and a new sketch is automatically added.

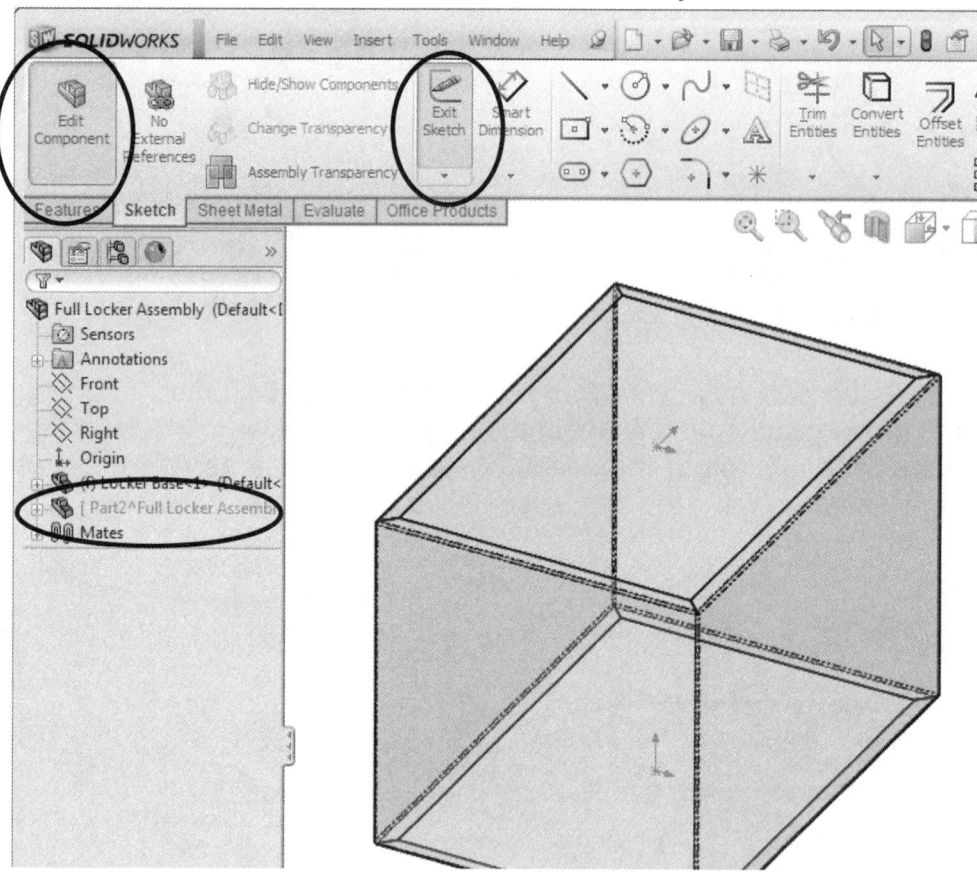

226. – Since we want to make the locker's body the same size as the base, we'll use "**Convert Entities**." In the Feature Manager expand *Locker Base,* "Boss-Extrude1," select "Sketch1" and then click in "**Convert Entities**" from the Sketch toolbar.

 When working with sheet metal parts, it's usually easier to distinguish sketch entities and model edges using "Shaded" view mode.

Sheet Metal and Top Down Design

 Optionally we can show the sketch and select individual lines and convert them.

227. – After converting the sketch edges, extrude it upwards 30″. Switch back to "Shaded with Edges" mode.

228. – When adding features that are not related to other components, we can either continue working in the assembly or open the *Locker* in its own window. To some extent it's really a personal preference; however, when adding references to other component's geometry we have to do it in the context of the assembly. Open the locker's body (the new part) in its own window to convert it into a sheet metal component.

229. – After opening the part, use the Shell command with a 0.03″ thickness and remove the top and bottom faces, which will become the front and back of the locker's body.

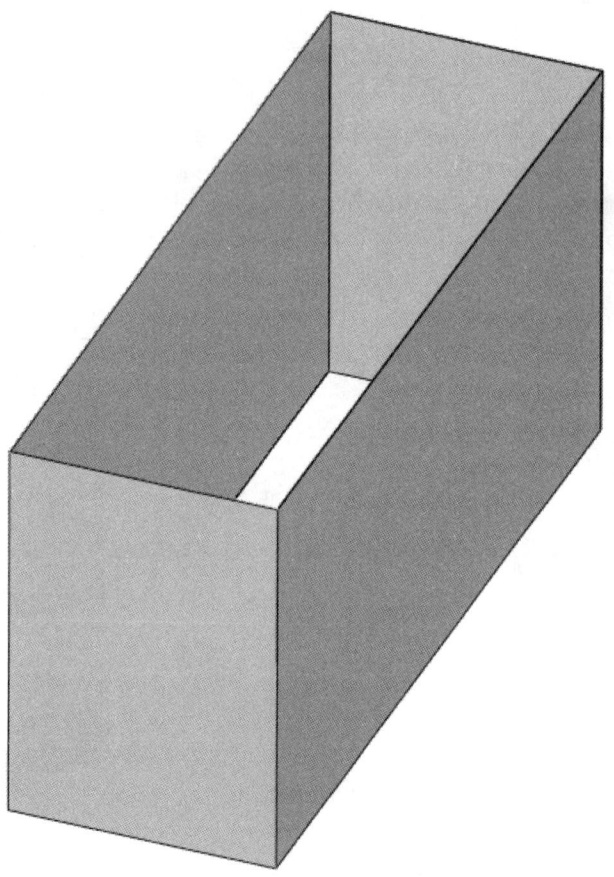

230. – We can convert this model to sheet metal without having to use a shell first like we did before, but we are doing it this way to show a different approach.

From the Sheet Metal toolbar select "**Convert to Sheet Metal**." Select the face on the left as the fixed face; set the thickness to 0.03" and the default bend radius to 0.05". You *may* have to check the "**Reverse Thickness**" checkbox if the inside or outside face was selected. It doesn't really matter which was picked; what is important is that we make sure the material is added to the side we want. Remember, the dimensions in our part are outside dimensions. Zoom in one corner to verify this. Essentially the sheet metal preview must overlap the existing shell thickness. Now we have to define the bends and the rips.

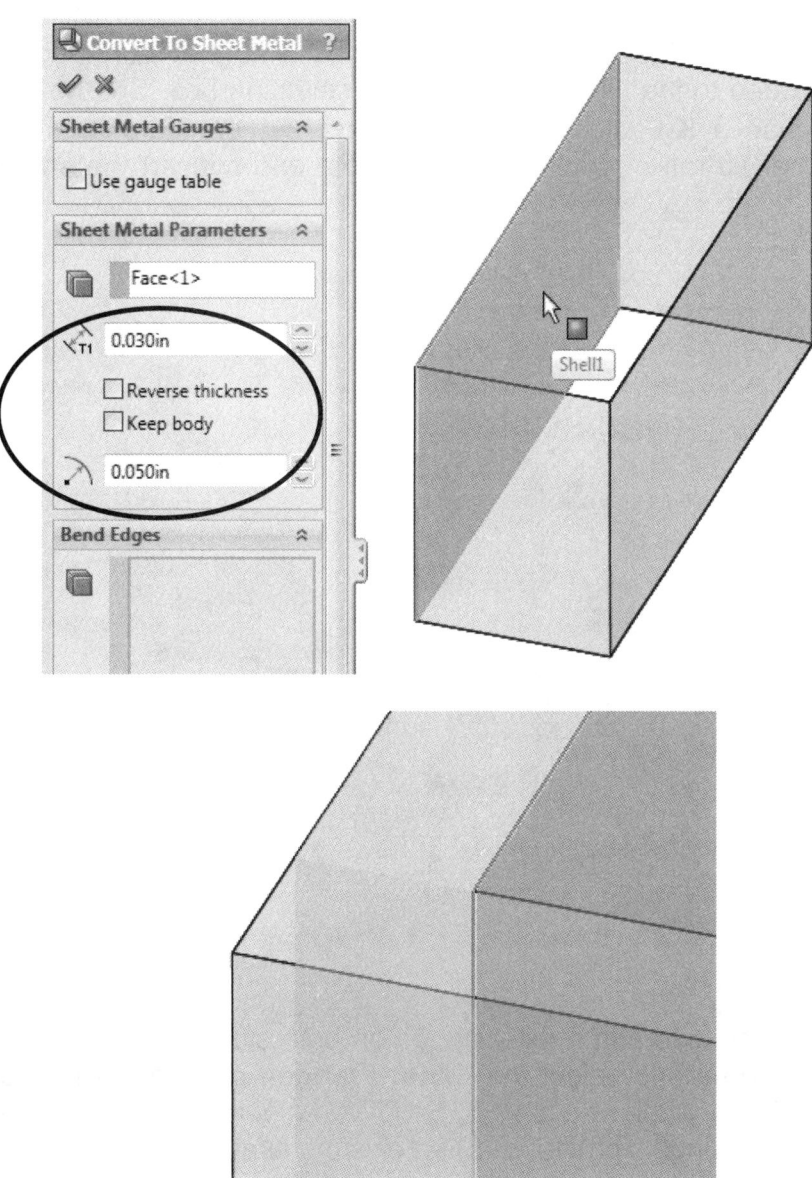

175

When we convert a shelled part to sheet metal, at the time of selecting the "**Bend Edges**" we have to select the edges connected to the face we selected. For example, if we picked the inside face of the shell, we have to select the inside edges; if the outside face was selected, the outside edges have to be selected. If the part is big compared to the shell's thickness, you may have to zoom in to the corners to select the correct edges. If the incorrect edge is selected you'll see the following message:

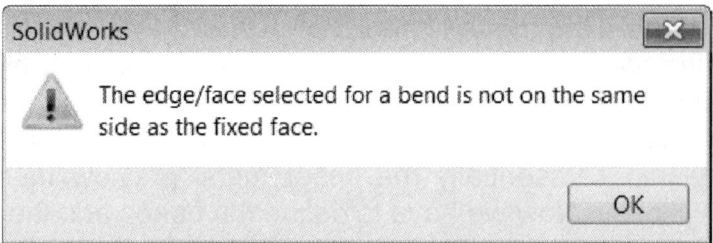

231. – Select three edges to convert to bends and the fourth edge will be automatically added to the "**Rip Edges found**" selection box. Set the default rips gap to 0.01″, use a K-Factor ratio of 0.5, and set the default relief type to "Obround" with a 0.5 ratio. Click **OK** to complete and convert the shell to sheet metal.

232. – The next step is to add a miter flange on both sides of the locker. Zoom in the corner with the rip and select the "**Miter Flange**" icon from the Sheet Metal toolbar. Immediately after selecting it, SolidWorks will ask us for 1) a face or plane to sketch the flange's profile, or 2) an existing sketch with the profile.

Sheet Metal and Top Down Design

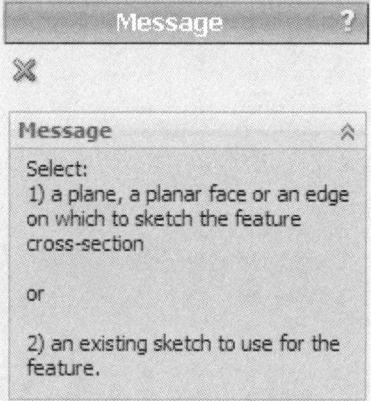

233. – Select the flat face to make the sketch on it, or the edge on top to add a plane perpendicular to it at the end.

Face selection   Edge Selection

Selecting faces is easier using a "**Selection Filter**." Selection filters allow us to select only the type of geometry or element desired. In this case press "**X**" on the keyboard (default filter for faces) to turn it on (press "**X**" again to turn it off). We know the filter is active when the pointer has a small funnel added next to the mouse pointer. The Selection Filters toolbar can be enabled selecting the menu "**View, Toolbars, Selection Filter**," or a right mouse click in any toolbar and selecting "**Selection Filter**," or using the default shortcut "**F5**." In this toolbar you can turn on/off any combination of filters as needed.

234. – Draw the profile for the miter flange as shown. It's a single 0.375" long line.

235. – After we select "**Exit Sketch**" or the "**Miter Flange**" icon the preview is activated. Make the flange with the option "**Material Inside**" and a 0.01" gap distance. Either select the edges on top individually or click on the "**Propagate**" icon to automatically select all the tangent edges connected and click OK to finish.

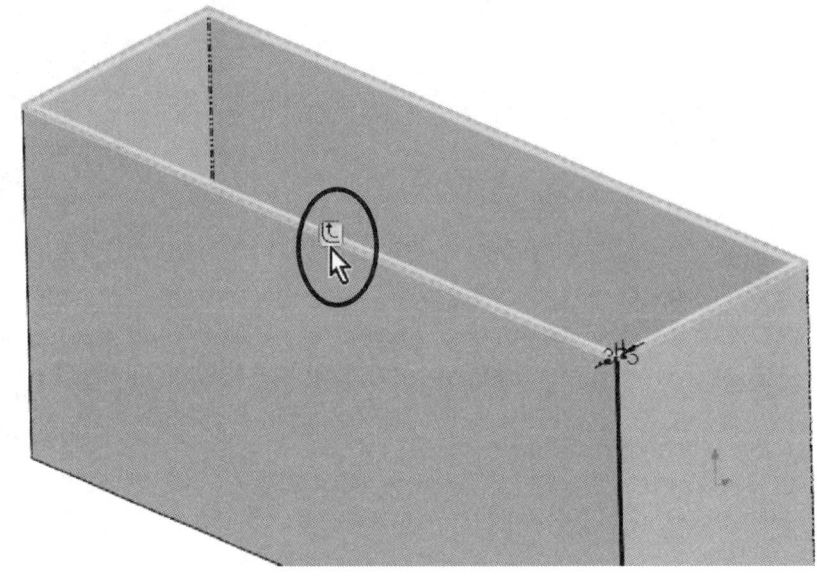

236. – Repeat the Miter Flange command on the other side with the same options. Your part should now look like this:

237. – Switch back to the assembly (if working in the part's window); notice we are still editing the part. Now we need to add a forming tool feature to support shelves inside the locker. Expand the "**Design Library**" and scroll down to "**forming tools, lances**" and find the "**90 degree lance**" library. Drag-and-drop the lance in the right side of the locker; we can press the "Tab" key to flip the lance's direction to go 'into' the locker or "out" of it before releasing the mouse button, or we can do it later in the Property Manager.

238. – After dropping the lance into the side of the locker make sure the preview shows it going *into* the locker, and the bent is on top. Use the "Flip Tool" and rotation angle options if needed. After making sure the rotation is correct select the "Position" tab and dimension its center 3″ from the front and 18″ from the bottom. Click OK to complete it.

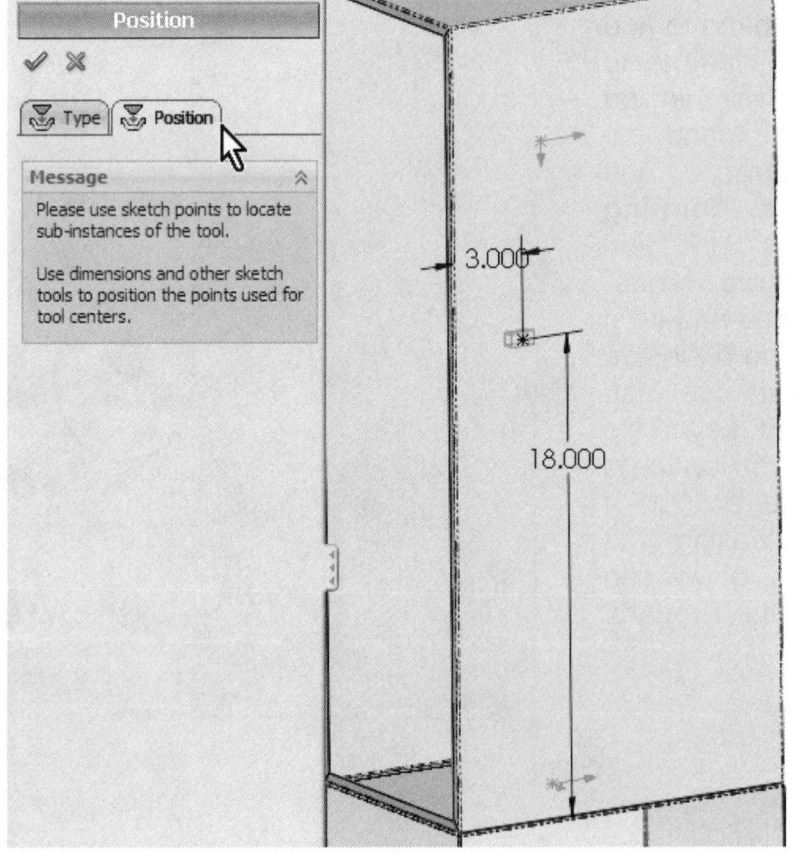

The lance should look like this from inside the locker.

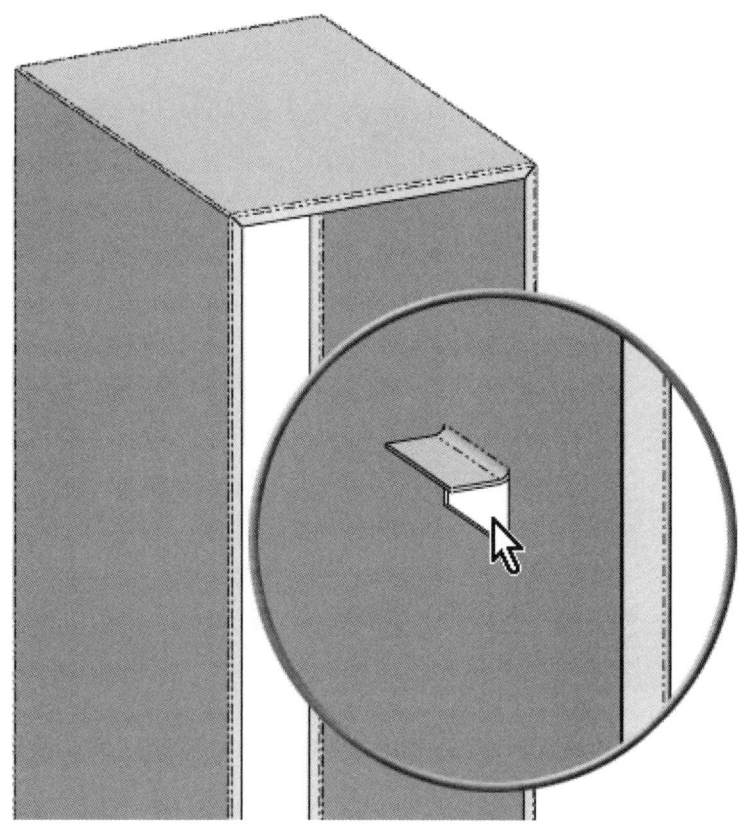

239. – Make a horizontal linear pattern with 3 copies spaced 4″ apart…

240. – ... and then add a vertical linear pattern to copy all 3 instances 8″ up. We'll explain later why we did it this way instead of making the first pattern in two directions. Mirror all lance cuts about the Right plane as shown to add them to the left side.

241. – Rename the internal part as *Locker Body* and save to an external file.

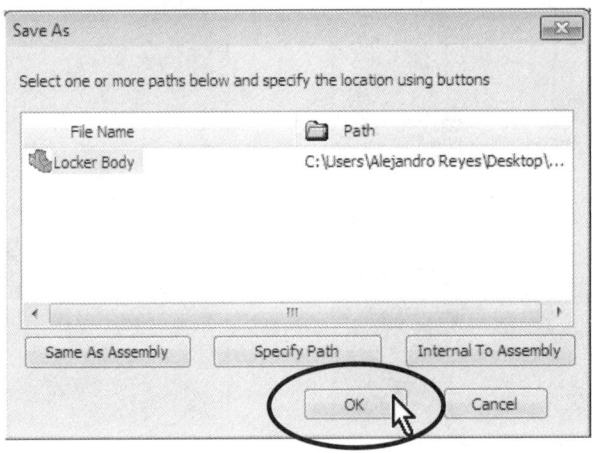

Sheet Metal and Top Down Design

242. – Now that we are done with the locker's body we can turn off "**Edit Component**" and go back to editing the assembly. Next, we'll add a cover in the back and a door.

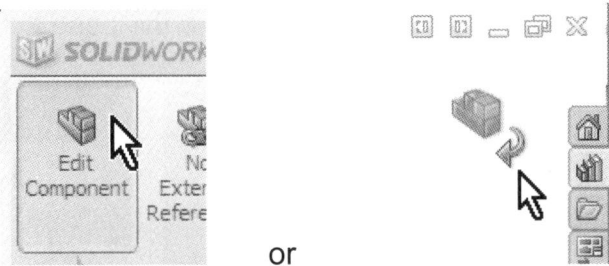

or

243. – The back is a simple sheet metal cover that will be welded or riveted in place. The cover needs to be the same size as the locker's body, and it will also be made in the context of the assembly. Select the "**Insert Components, New Part**" drop down icon and click in the inside face of the back miter flange to locate the back cover.

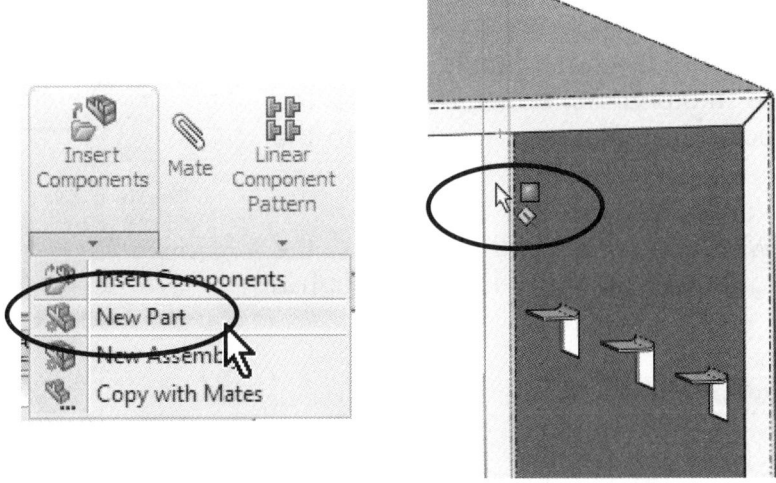

244. – After adding the Back Cover part, the locker's base and body turn transparent; we are editing the new part and a new sketch is ready for us to work on. In this step it is easier to work in an opaque assembly, as it is difficult and/or confusing to select references while the other components are transparent. Select the "Assembly Transparency" drop down icon and select "Opaque."

183

245. – Draw a rectangle starting in one of the lower corners (inside the locker) and finishing in the opposite upper corner. Be sure to capture a Coincident relation to a miter flange vertex. By adding these relations to the miter flange we fully define the sketch and are now ready to make the base flange.

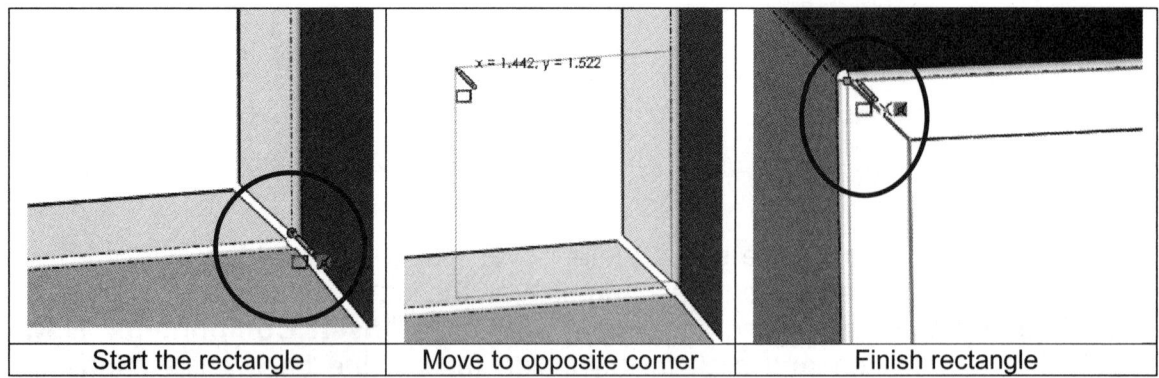

| Start the rectangle | Move to opposite corner | Finish rectangle |

246. – Select "**Base Flange/Tab**" from the Sheet Metal toolbar or the menu "**Insert, Sheet Metal, Base Flange**." Make the base flange 0.03″ thick. Make sure the material is added towards the inside of the locker and does not overlap with the locker's body.

This is a view from above and behind of the locker, showing the inside of the locker through a corner.

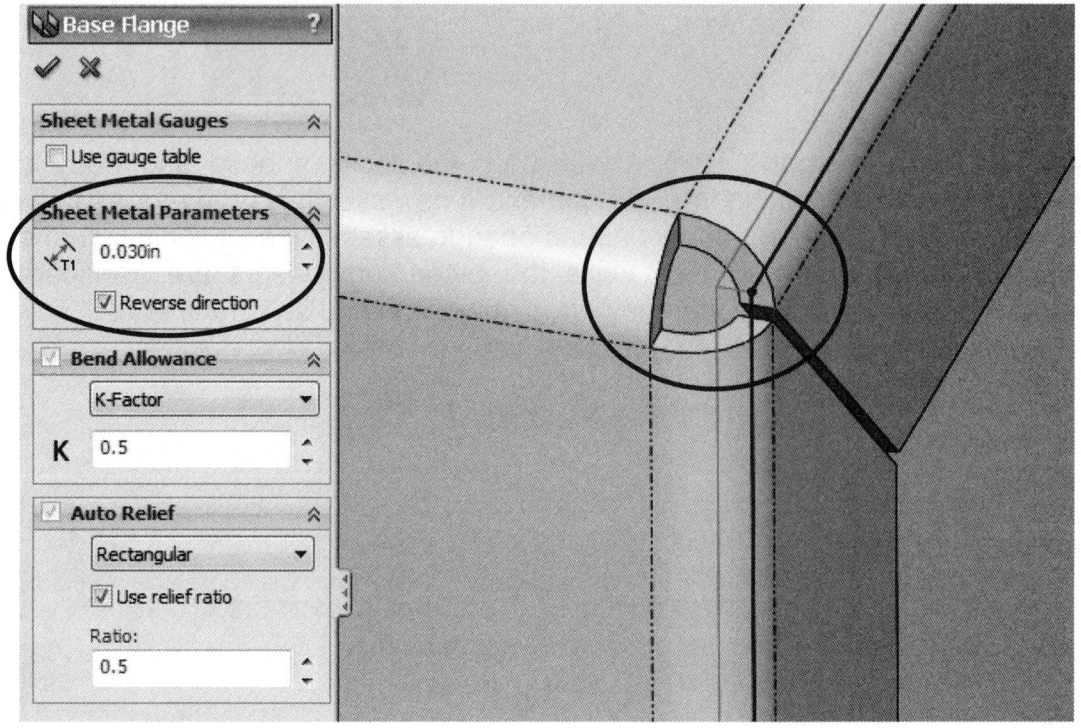

Sheet Metal and Top Down Design

247. – Rename the part "**Locker Back**." Save to an external file and turn off "**Edit Component**" to continue editing the assembly.

248. – The next component to add will be the shelf. Select "**Insert Components, New part**" and select the top face of one of the lower lances we just made to locate it. The magnifying lens was used to zoom into the face to insert the new part.

185

249. – Since we changed the transparency setting to "Opaque" with the previous part, the other components will not become transparent; we are now editing the new part's first sketch. Draw a rectangle starting close to the front right lance and finishing close to the rear left lance as indicated, adding collinear relations to the bend lines and dimensions as indicated to the lances.

Front right lance

Rear left lance

250. – Click in the "**Base Flange/Tab**" command from the Sheet Metal toolbar and make the shelf 0.03″ thick going up, bend radius= 0.015", K-Factor = 0.5 and Rectangular auto relief with a 0.5 ratio.

251. – Since a flat shelf like this is not strong enough, a flange will be added to all edges for reinforcement. Click in the "**Edge Flange**" icon and select all four edges. Immediately after selecting the first edge a preview will be displayed. Click towards the bottom to define the direction of the flange, then select the other three edges. Set the flange length to 0.80", the flange gap to 0.01", and the flange position to "Material Outside."

252. – The flanges we just made interfere with the lances. To eliminate the interferences we'll unfold the side flanges, add cuts to clear the lances and then re-fold them. Select the "**Unfold**" command from the Sheet Metal toolbar; click in the top face of the shelf part to select it as the fixed face.

After selecting the fixed face, select the two side bends (the ones interfering with the lances) to unfold them. SolidWorks will filter your selections to bends automatically. Click **OK** when done.

Sheet Metal and Top Down Design

Unfolded bends

253. – To better visualize the next operation, we'll turn the locker upside down and make the cuts needed in the bottom face of the shelf; the reason for this is that from this angle, we can see the lances that we need to clear. Rotate your locker assembly until you can see the lances in one side.

254. – Create a new sketch in the bottom face. Add dimensions and relations to clear the lances as shown. Make one side of the rectangle coincident to the outside edge of the unfolded flange and the other side collinear to the lance's bend line.

255. – With the sketch fully defined, our next step is to add a Sketch Pattern. Not only can we make feature patterns, we can and also make linear and circular patterns *in the sketch*. Select the menu "**Tools, Sketch Tools, Linear Pattern**" (the icon *may* not be in the Sketch toolbar by default).

Sheet Metal and Top Down Design

The sketch Linear Pattern behaves similar to the Feature Pattern. By default the "**X-axis**" direction is the sketch's horizontal direction (short red arrow) and the "**Y-axis**" direction the vertical (long red arrow). Our pattern will have 3 copies vertically spaced 4 inches apart.

 Pattern directions can be changed by selecting model edges or sketch entities.

Turn on the option "**Add spacing dimension**" to make the spacing dimension visible; otherwise spacing can only be changed by going to the menu "**Tools, Sketch Tools, Edit Linear Pattern**."

Fill in the values for the Y-axis (*or* select an edge for direction in the "Direction 1" options box). Add the rectangle's lines we just made to the "Entities to Pattern" selection box and click **OK** to finish.

If you look closely, the sketch is not fully defined. To fully define it, select the construction line added between the rectangle we drew and the first copy and add a Vertical relation.

191

256. – With the sketch fully defined, we can make a sketch mirror to make all six cuts at the same time, OR make a cut *and then* make a feature mirror. We'll leave the option to the reader. Just remember to use the "Link to thickness" option when making the cut. Our part should now look like this from the bottom (still unfolded):

257. – To finish the part select the "**Fold**" icon from the sheet metal toolbar. Either select both unfolded bends (the selection filter will select bends only) or click in the "**Collect All Bends**" button to add all un-folded bends to the selection list. Click **OK** when done.

258. – The shelf part is complete; finish editing it by clicking on the "**Edit Component**" icon or the confirmation corner. Rename it to *Locker Shelf* and save as an external part. After we are finished, return to editing the assembly by turning off the "**Edit Component**" command.

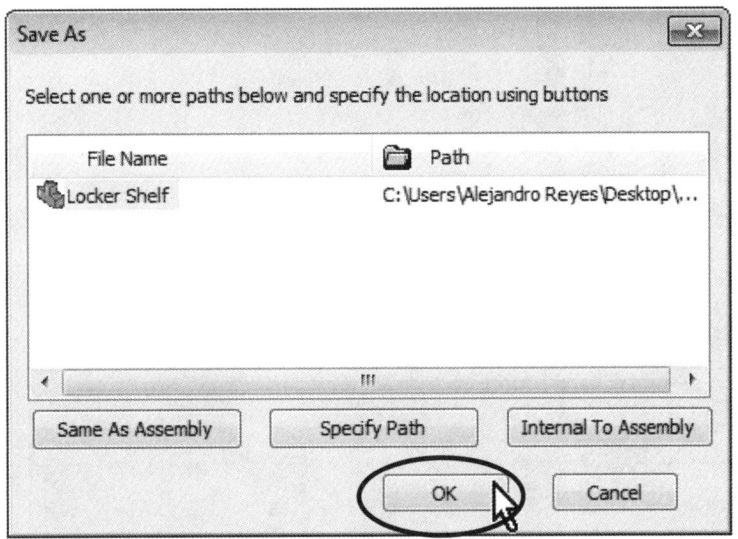

259. – The next step is to add another *Shelf* at the top. We can add it using the "**Insert Component**" command and mating it to the Locker Body or by using a Component Pattern, since parts and assemblies can be patterned in the assembly either linear or circular, just like features in a part; a better option to maintain design intent is to use a "**Feature Driven Pattern**."

In a Feature Driven Pattern a copy of a component (seed) is added in each instance of a patterned feature. This is the reason why we patterned the lances vertically, for example, if we change the vertical lances pattern to 3 copies, we would get 3 shelves in the assembly. While editing the assembly, in the Assembly tab of the CommandManager select "Feature Driven Component Pattern" from the "Linear Component Patter" drop down list or the menu "**Insert, Component Patten, Feature Driven**."

193

260. – In the "**Components to Pattern**" selection box pick the *Locker Shelf* part and for the "**Driving Feature**" select one of the lances in the top position. Turn *on* the "**Propagate component level visual properties**" checkbox to make the patterned copies look like the seed part. Click **OK** to finish.

 This type of pattern is very handy when adding fasteners to an assembly; we can add one fastener to a hole, and use the pattern of holes to add the rest of the fasteners. An advantage is that, if the feature's pattern is changed, the number of fasteners is also updated.

261. – After adding the top shelf, we realize the top space is too small to be useful and we need to change it. Expand the *Locker Body*'s FeatureManager and find the "**90 degree lance**" feature. Double click on it to display its dimensions and change the 18″ height to 14″. Rebuild the model when done to finish. Notice the pattern of shelves updates as expected.

262. – The next thing we need to do is to add a "Hem" to the *Shelf's* front flange. Hems are used to eliminate sharp edges and to reinforce a sheet metal part by folding or rolling the edge. The first thing we need to do is to edit the *Locker Shelf* in the assembly. Select it in the graphics area or FeatureManager and click in the "**Edit Part**" icon. Remember the other parts won't become transparent when editing the *Locker Shelf* because we have the Assembly Transparency setting to "Opaque."

263. – Select the "**Hem**" command from the Sheet Metal toolbar. In the "**Edges**" selection box, pick the front edge of the *Shelf*. A preview will show the hem's direction. Make sure the hem is inside the locker; click on "Reverse Direction" if needed. Besides editing the hem's width, we have the following options:

Material Inside (Notice the selected edge) Applies to all Types		**Bend Outside**. (Notice the selected edge) Applies to all Types	
0.15in		**Closed** Enter hem length. No gap is created.	
0.15in 0.03in		**Open** Enter hem length and gap distance.	
200.00deg 0.02in		**Teardrop** Enter the hem's angle and radius.	
270.00deg 0.02in		**Rolled** Enter the hem's angle and radius.	

Sheet Metal and Top Down Design

264. – For the *Locker Shelf* use a "**Closed**" hem, 0.20" long, and the Material inside option. Click OK to finish the hem.

265. – Turn off "**Edit Component**" and return to editing the assembly. The last component we are adding is the locker's door and it will also be designed in the context of the assembly. Select "**Insert Components, New Part**" and click in the Front face of the *Locker Body* to locate the new part.

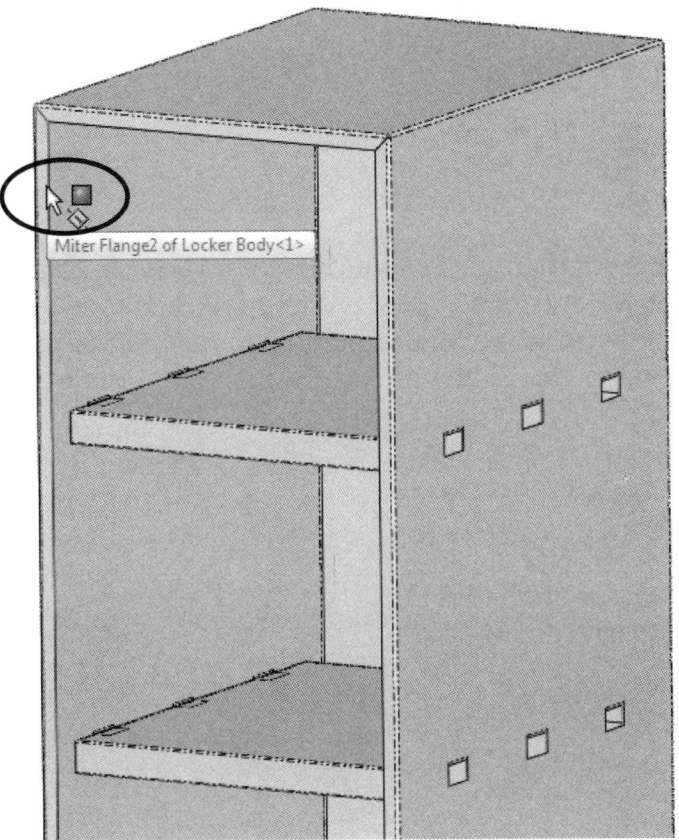

266. – The purpose of adding relations in the context of the assembly is to propagate changes when other components change; however, in the case of the door, we don't want to because we want to be able to open the door and move it. If we capture relations to make the door the same size of the body, when we open the door later, it will be rebuilt and its size will be smaller, fail to rebuild with an error, or produce unexpected results trying to maintain the in-context relations. Notice how the door is smaller when we open it and have in-context relations to define its size.

267. – One thing we can do to prevent capturing external relations is to activate the "**No External References**" option. While this command is activated (it's a toggle) we will not be able to capture automatic (or manual) references to other components. Activate "**No External References**" and draw a rectangle for the door as indicated. Dimension it to match the locker's size and then add a Midpoint relation between the lower rectangle's line and the part's origin to center it about the origin (almost always a good idea). This relation will fully define the sketch.

Sheet Metal and Top Down Design

268. – Extrude the rectangle 0.625" outward. Now we need to convert the part to sheet metal. The next step is to convert the solid door into a sheet metal part. Select the "**Convert to Sheet Metal**" icon to continue.

269. – Select the front of the door to be the fixed face; add the four edges around it in the "**Bend Edges**" selection box. Once the bend edges are selected, the small corner edges will be automatically added to the "**Rip Edges found**" selection box. Set the sheet metal thickness to 0.03" as the rest of the locker, a default bend radius of 0.05", a default gap for rips of 0.02" and a K-Factor of 0.5. Set the "Auto Relief" option to "Tear." Click OK to finish.

270. – After converting to sheet metal, we need to add flanges to the inside of the door. Open the part in its own window and turn it over to see the back (inside).

Sheet Metal and Top Down Design

271. – Select the "**Edge Flange**" command and add all four edges in the back to the "Edge" selection box. Make the flange 0.625″ with a gap distance of 0.01″ and "Material Inside" option.

272. – Switch back to the assembly. Rename the new part as *Locker Door* and save in an external file.

201

273. – Our next step is to add a set of louvers to the door to help ventilate the locker. Since the louver in the SolidWorks Design Library is too small for our design, we'll need to make a new one.

To design a "Forming Tool" library the first thing we need to do is to build the shape of the tool, define a *stopping face*, which is how deep the tool will go into the sheet metal and optionally the face(s) that will be removed (cut) as openings in the part.

Make a new part (outside the assembly), add the following sketch in the Top plane and extrude it 0.375" up. This extrusion will serve as the base for the library.

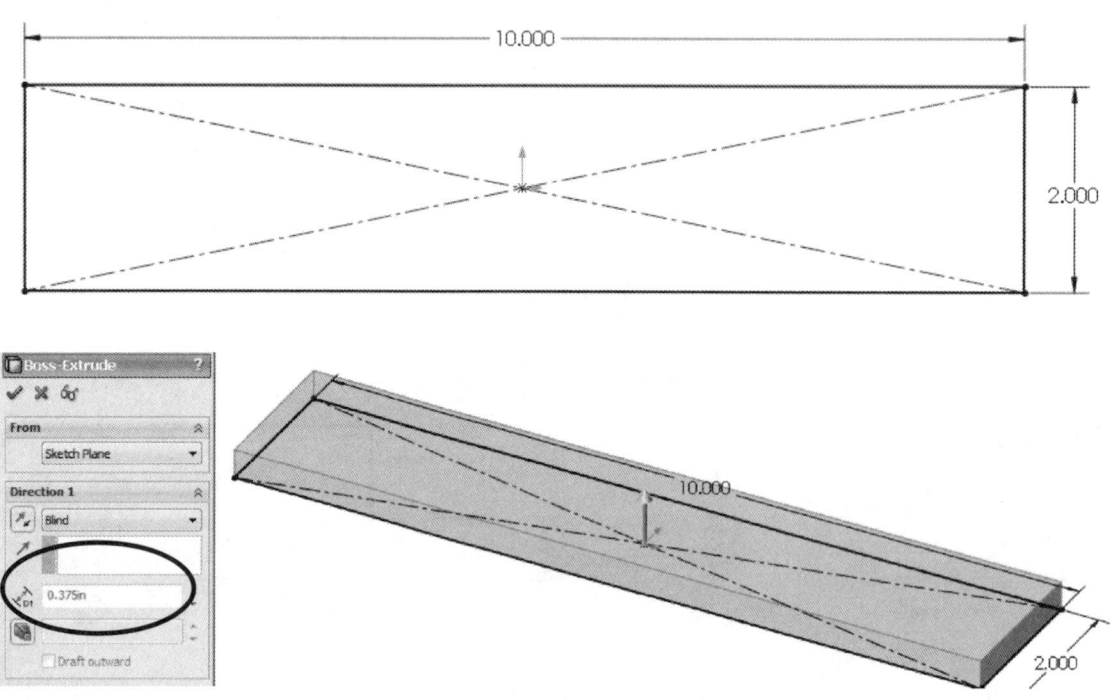

274. – Add the following sketch on top and extrude 0.375." Round the two corners indicated with a 0.625" radius.

Sheet Metal and Top Down Design

275. – Add a second Fillet to the top edge with a 0.25″ radius.

276. – Add a second fillet to the bottom edge with a 0.375" radius; our part now looks like this:

277. – Now we need to remove the base of the part (the first feature). Add a sketch on the top face of the first feature, use "Convert Entities" to project the edges (or draw a square coincident to opposite corners, your choice) and make a "Through All" cut extrude going down to remove the base.

Our Forming Tool now looks like this:

 Cutting the base is not required; in our case we had to do it this way to be able to build the fillet in the bottom for our forming tool.

278. – After the part is complete, select the "**Forming Tool**" icon from the Sheet Metal toolbar or the menu "**Insert, Sheet Metal, Forming Tool**."

Select the bottom face of the part as the "**Stopping Face**." This is the face that will define how deep the tool will go *into* the sheet metal part.

Sheet Metal and Top Down Design

279. – And then select the front flat face in the "**Faces to Remove**" selection box. This is an optional selection, but in our case we want this face to make an opening in the sheet metal part when inserted. Click **OK** when done.

280. – After finishing the Form Tool, SolidWorks automatically changes the face's colors, this is how it knows which are the stopping, forming and open faces.

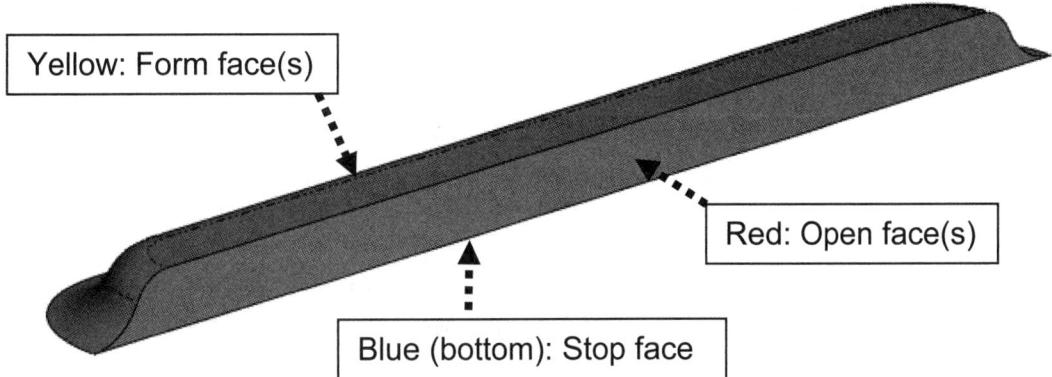

Yellow: Form face(s)

Red: Open face(s)

Blue (bottom): Stop face

After defining the Form Tool, we have to save it to our library. Previously we dragged and dropped the library directly into the Design Library. In this case we'll use a different method. Right mouse click at the top of the FeatureManager and select "Add to Library."

281. – In the "Add to Library" properties, enter '7in Louver' in the "File name:" options, and select the 'louvers' folder. In the "File type:" drop down selection box leave the option as "Part (*.sldprt)."

Now we are ready to use our form tool in our locker's door.

 The form tool feature automatically adds a sketch called "**Orientation Sketch**." This is the sketch that will be used to locate the form tool when it is inserted into a sheet metal part.

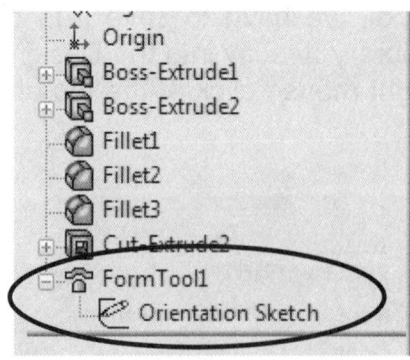

Sheet Metal and Top Down Design

282. – Close the *7in louver* library part and go back to the assembly. Make sure we are still editing the *Locker Door* in context of the assembly to continue. Open the Design Library and drag the new louver to the front of the locker door to insert it.

If the form tool is going into the locker's door click "Flip Tool" to reverse the direction. Also, we may need to rotate it entering a rotation angle to orient the louver correctly.

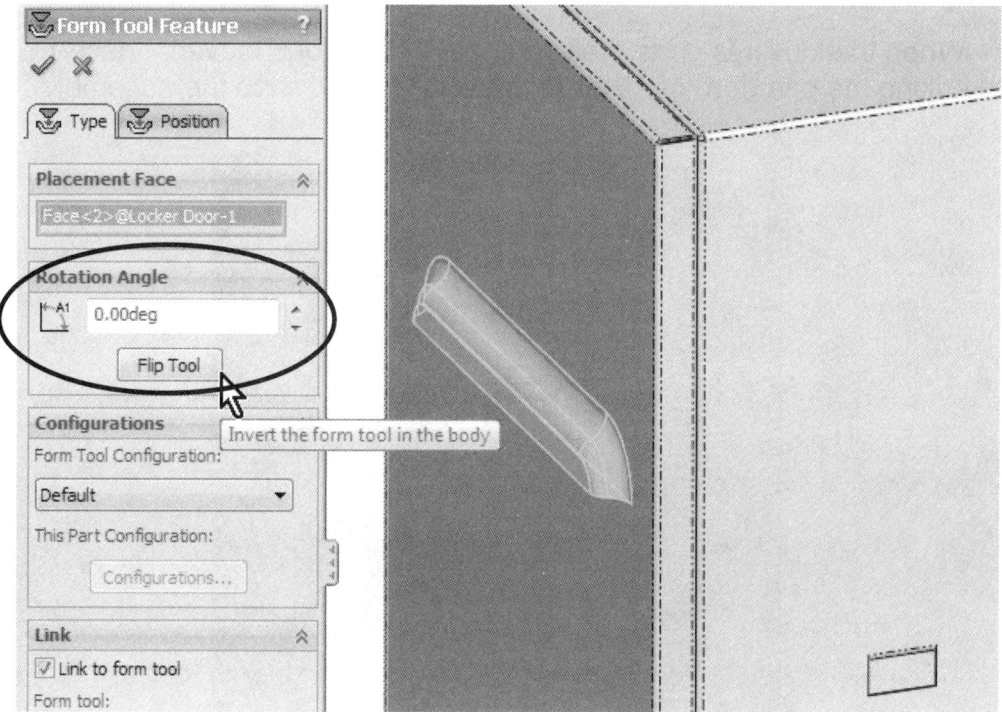

283. – To locate the louver select the "Position" tab. Add a 3" dimension from the louver's center point to the top edge of the door, and a "Vertical" geometric relation between the point and the door's origin to center it. Click OK to finish when done.

284. – When the louver is done make a linear pattern of 6 louvers spaced 1.375″. Finish editing the part (turn off "**Edit Component**") and save the assembly.

Sheet Metal and Top Down Design

285. – After reviewing the assembly in a Left view, we notice that the door protrudes beyond the locker's base. Measuring the difference we can see the *Locker Body* needs to be 0.625" smaller (the thickness of the door) to make the door flush with the base. To correct this we need to edit the first sketch in the *Locker Body* to change its size.

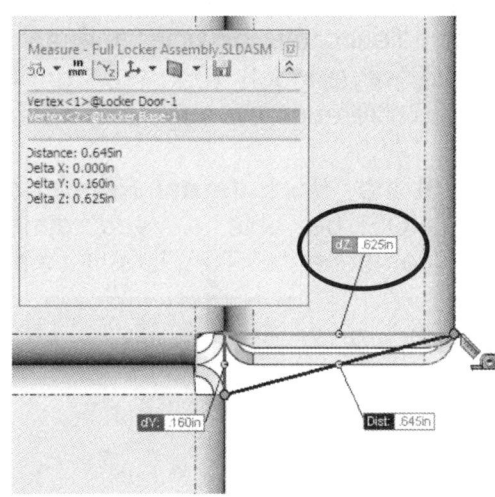

Expand the *Locker Body* Feature Manager and edit the sketch of the "Boss-Extrude1" feature. When we edit a part's sketch in an assembly, the "**Edit Component**" mode is automatically activated.

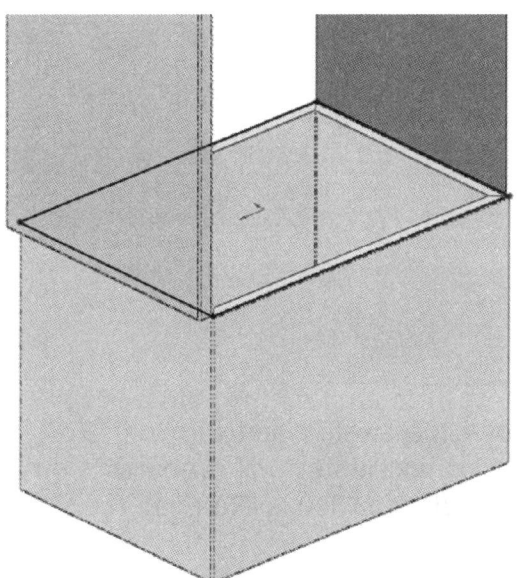

286. – Select the front sketch line and delete the "**On Edge**" relation (created when we use the "**Convert Entities**" command).

209

After deleting this external relation (we know it's external because it is followed by the "**->**" symbol), drag the front line a little to the back and dimension it. (Be sure to reference the edge of the base and not the door to locate it.)

 If the "**No External References**" command is active you will NOT be able to add dimensions (or relations) to other components. Turn it off if it's active.

Close the sketch and turn off "**Edit Component**." All components will rebuild correctly. Your assembly now looks like this:

Sheet Metal and Top Down Design

287. – The last step is to add hinges to the locker to open the door. While editing the assembly, if we try to move the door we get the message:

When we add components in the context of the assembly, an **InPlace** mate is automatically created when we select the face where we want to locate the new part. This mate completely immobilizes the new part, and in order to be able to move it, we have to delete (or suppress) this mate. Expand the FeatureManager for the *Locker Door* part and scroll down to the folder "**Mates in Full Locker Assembly**." This folder contains all the mates referencing the door in this assembly. If you remember, we did not make the door the same size as the body with external relations, but with dimensions. The reason was to be able to move the door using Dynamic assembly motion. If we had added geometric relations in the sketch, after moving the door, its size would have changed and most likely produced undesired results. Delete the **InPlace** mate; click-and-drag to move the door and separate it from the locker. We'll add the hinges in the next step.

211

288. – Download the hinge assembly from our website and add it to the locker assembly (www.mechanicad.com/download.html). Be sure to set the file type to Assembly when adding it.

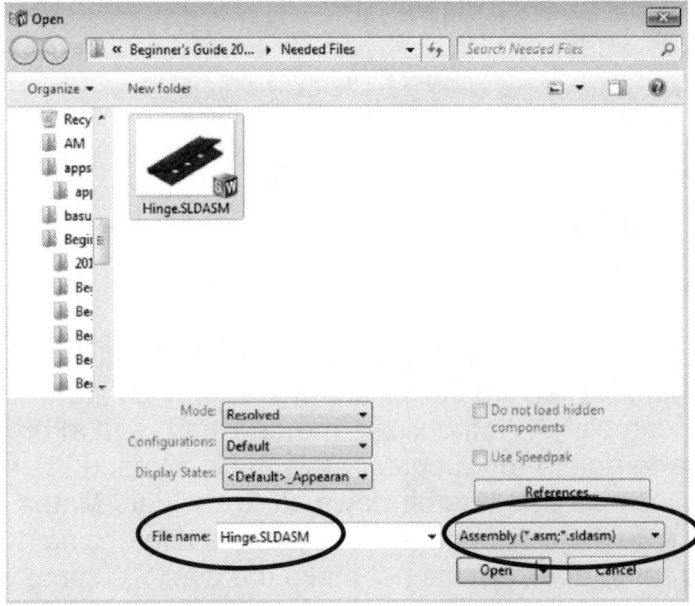

289. – Add a hinge close to the right side of the locker and move the door a little to the left. Mate the *Hinge* Coincident to the front flange of the *Locker Body*.

Sheet Metal and Top Down Design

290. – Add a second mate to make the top of the *Hinge* Coincident to the top face of the upper shelf. Select an edge of the hinge or a face; either works the same.

 To select the smaller faces of the hinge a selection filter can be used. The default shortcut for the faces filter is 'X'. If you use the Selection Filter, don't forget to turn it *off* when done!

291. – And finally make an edge of the *Hinge* Coincident to the outside face of the *Locker Body* (looking from the back).

292. – With the hinge located in place, make a linear pattern and add two more *Hinges* spaced 8 inches apart. Select the menu "**Insert, Component Pattern, Linear Pattern**" or the "**Linear Component Pattern**" from the Assembly toolbar. Use the *Hinge* subassembly as the component to pattern and any vertical edge for the direction.

Sheet Metal and Top Down Design

A component pattern feature is added to the assembly's FeatureManager with the additional two *Hinges*.

293. – Now we have to add mates to locate the door. Rotate the door a little to view the faces to mate. Add a Coincident mate between the inside face of the door and the hinge.

294. – Make the side of the door Coincident to the edge of the hinge (similar to how we mated the hinge to the locker's body).

295. – Finally, add a Coincident mate between the top face of the door and the top face of the locker's body.

296. – When we try to move the door, we get the same **"Fully defined component"** message, and the door cannot be moved. Open the hinge assembly.

297. – When we add mates to assemble components, we are removing degrees of freedom (dof). By default, a component has six degrees of freedom. Three translations along the X, Y and Z axes, and three rotations about the X, Y and Z axes. When a component is under defined, it means that *at least* one dof is not constrained, and it can move. If a part is fully defined, it cannot move or rotate. This is the basis for assembly motion in SolidWorks.

In our hinge assembly one Wing and the Pin have a (-) sign before their names. This means that these parts can move or rotate about *at least* one axis. In this case, both can rotate about the Pin's axis. Since the first Wing is automatically fixed in place (because it was the first part added to the assembly) the other two rotate about it. If we click-and-drag the under defined Wing, it will move as a hinge (as expected) because it was restrained (mated) with one Concentric and one Coincident mate.

298. – If we keep moving the Wing, it will go past through the fixed Wing. This is the normal behavior. We can optionally activate the "**Collision Detection**" to make parts stop when they touch each other. Move the hinge to a position where there is no interference and click in the "**Move Component**" icon in the Assembly toolbar; in the "**Options**" select "**Collision Detection**." By default "**All components**" is selected; as we move any part, SolidWorks will calculate collisions between every part in the assembly.

If the assembly has a small number of components, this is fine (*"small"* varies, from a few to tens or even hundreds depending on the computer's capacity); but if we have a large number of components (and *"large"* also varies..) we can limit the scope of detection by selecting the option "**These components**" and select only the ones we are interested in, greatly enhancing the speed and accuracy of the calculation. With only three parts, "**All components**" should be fast enough in just about any computer. Turn on the "**Stop at collision**" option to prevent a part from going through another, "**Highlight faces**" to visually identify the component faces that are colliding, and "**Sound**" to hear when a collision is detected. Drag the moving wing of the hinge towards the other wing; it will stop when the faces touch each other.

 If we start "**Collision Detection**" with an interference between the components being analyzed, the "Stop at Collision" option will be ignored. The assembly must be set to a non-colliding position to re-activate this option.

Sheet Metal and Top Down Design

299. – Leave the hinge partially open as shown above and switch back to the locker assembly window, where we'll be asked to rebuild it. After selecting "Yes" the hinge will be in the same position we had it in its own assembly. This is one way to move the door, but this is not really the behavior we want.

300. – What we need to do is to propagate the subassembly's motion to the main assembly. By default, subassemblies are calculated as rigid bodies without motion for performance reasons. Select the "**Hinge**" subassembly in the

FeatureManager, click in the "**Component Properties**" icon from the pop-up menu and activate the "**Solve as Flexible**" option. Click **OK** when done.

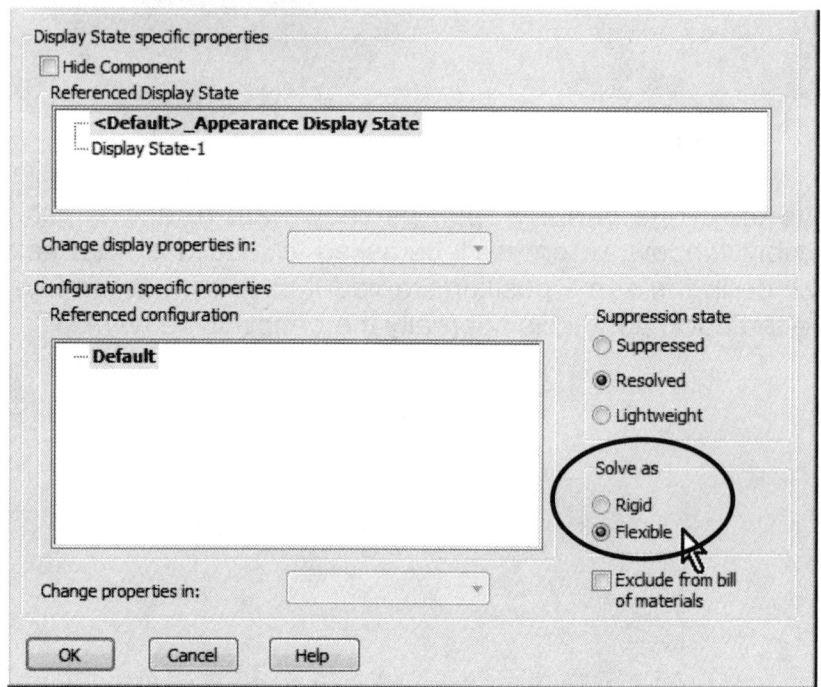

Note the different icon when a subassembly is made flexible.

Rigid sub-assembly   **Flexible sub-assembly**

301. – By making the "hinge" subassembly "Flexible" we can move the door freely. Notice that the lower two patterned hinges are not flexible and when we open the door they remain closed.

220

Sheet Metal and Top Down Design

302. – Make the other two hinges flexible and mate them to the door. We only need to add a Coincident mate to each of the patterned hinges. The assembly may have to be rebuilt to restore assembly motion after making the sub-assemblies flexible.

303. – The last thing to do is to add a series of holes to hold the *Locker Back* with rivets or screws. We can add the holes to one part, and then make the holes in the other part using in-context relations, but that would take too long. In this case, the holes will be added *while* editing the assembly, *not* a part, and will be added to multiple components at the same time using an **Assembly Feature**.

	Most **Assembly Features** remove material, like a post-assembly operation, and in our case would be the equivalent of putting both parts together and drilling through *both* at the same time. Assembly features include:
	Hole Series can make different hole types in the first, middle and last parts like counterbore, countersunk, clearance, threaded, etc.
	Hole Wizard works the same way it works in a part, but for multiple components.
	Simple Hole makes single round holes in multiple components.
	Extruded Cut and **Revolved Cut** work like a cut in a part, but in the assembly through multiple components.
	Fillet and **Chamfer** are used mostly in the weldments environment to prepare mated parts for welding.
	Welded Bead is used to add welds in structural steel, including manufacturing annotations.

304. – Select the "**Hole Wizard**" option from the "**Assembly Features**" drop-down icon. We'll use 1/8" rivets to secure the back to the locker. Turn the locker to see the upper left back corner; select the simple hole, and make it 1/8". Make the hole's end condition "Blind" with a depth of 0.25". (It will be deep enough to go through both parts.)

Select the "Positions" tab and locate a single hole as indicated. We'll make a linear pattern to add the rest. Click **OK** to complete.

Note an additional options box at the bottom titled "**Feature Scope.**" This is where we define which parts will be affected by this feature and if we want the feature to be propagated to the individual parts. If we leave the "**Propagate feature to parts**" option unchecked, the holes will only exist in the assembly and not in the parts. This is useful when making post-assembly operations, like drilling. If the option is checked, the holes will be visible in the parts *and* the assembly like any regular feature, and will be added as an external reference.

A hole is added to both parts. Since the feature was not propagated to the parts (the option "**Propagate feature to part**" is unchecked in the Hole Wizard), opening either part will not show the hole.

Assembly   Part

305. – When assembly features are added, the "**Assembly Features**" drop-down icon is expanded to include feature patterns including linear, circular, table and sketch driven.

Select the "**Linear Pattern**" and make a horizontal pattern with 6 holes spaced 1.625".

306. – Make similar assembly features and patterns in the other three flanges to finish the assembly. (Hint: Edit the Hole Wizard in the top to add a second hole in the bottom flange and pattern both holes together; use the same approach for the sides.) Save and close the assembly.

CHALLENGE EXERCISES:

1: Return the *Locker Body* to be the same size as the base with a collinear relation to the base as originally designed.

2: Change the locker's base dimension to 12" wide x 14" deep x 14" high.

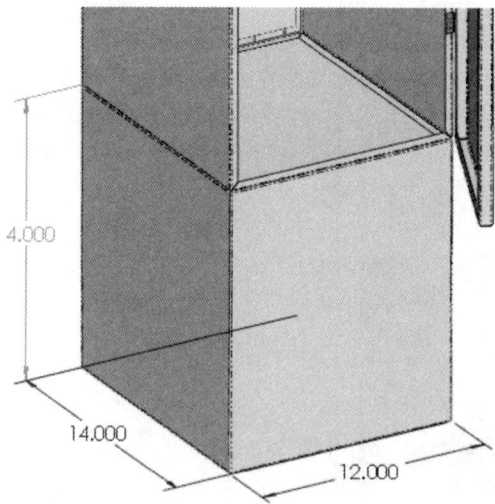

3: Add assembly features using the Hole Wizard to attach the locker's body to the base like we did for the *Locker Back* panel.

Sheet Metal and Top Down Design

4: Add equations in the assembly to make the *Locker Door*'s width 7/8" narrower than the *Locker Base* and the *Locker Door*'s height 7/8" smaller than the *Locker Body*.

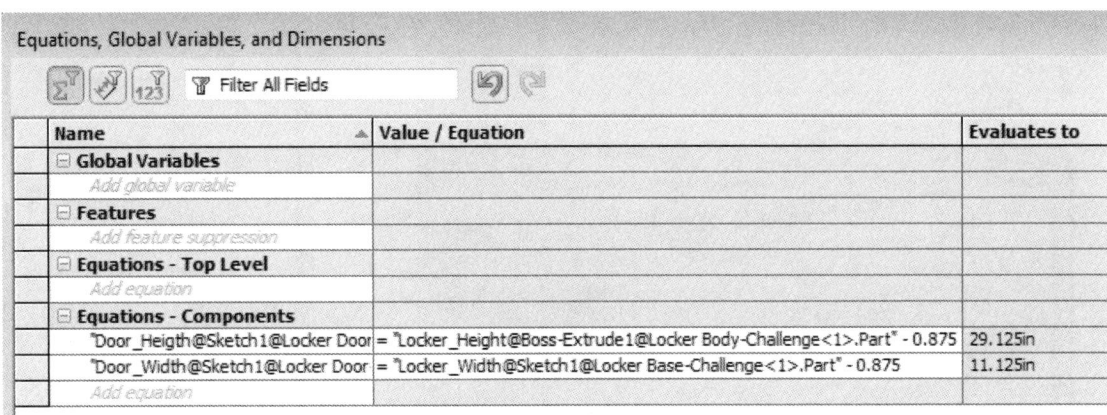

5: Make the *Locker Door* flush with the front face of the *Locker Body*. Modify the front miter flange in the *Locker Body*. Edit the miter flange sketch as shown.

6: Change the *Locker Door* and hinge's mates to make it flush with the front of the *Locker Body*. You will need to add distance mates to center the door.

7: Make detail drawings of all parts including a flat pattern and an assembly drawing with an exploded view and bill of materials.

Extra Credit: Design a suitable lock for the door and incorporate it into the assembly.

Review and Questions:

a) Name the different options available in SolidWorks to calculate sheet metal bend allowances.

b) How is the Relief Ratio calculated (Rectangular and Obround reliefs)?

c) What is and how is the K-factor calculated?

d) Which external reference state will propagate changes immediately in an assembly (In-Context, Out of Context, Broken, Locked)?

e) How can external references be temporarily "frozen"?

f) What does the option "Merge faces" do in a sheet metal component?

g) What is the "Link to thickness" option and what does it do?

h) What is the extension used for library features?

i) What is the option "Flexible" in a subassembly used for?

j) Explain the difference between a Miter Flange and Edge Flange?

Answers:
a.- Bend allowance, Bend Deduction, K-Factor
b.- It's the relation between the sheet metal thickness and the width of the relief.
c.- It's the relation between the distance from the inside bend radius and the neutral plane to the thickness.
d.- In Context.
e.- Locking them using under "List External References."
f.- It eliminates all the bend lines and bend regions in the flat pattern making it a single surface.
g.- It's an option available when adding extrusions and cuts to sheet metal parts to make the extrusion (or cut) the same depth as the sheet metal's thickness.
h.- *.SLDLFP
i.- If a subassembly has mates that permit motion, the motion will be available at the top level assembly.
j.- In an Edge Flange, the width and shape of the flange can be changed but not its profile; in a Miter Flange, only the profile can be edited.

Notes:

3D Sketch and Weldments

A 3D sketch, as its name implies, exists in 3D space and is not limited to a 2D plane. 3D sketches are typically used for guide curves and paths for sweeps and lofts, as "centerlines" for structural profiles (weldments), as references to create auxiliary geometry, etc.

Weldment refers in general to a multi body part that is made from extruded (or swept) profiles along a 2D or a 3D sketch. It is used for designing structures, welded components, tubular parts, etc. and has special features for welding processes and manufacturing annotations like weld types, calculating cut lists of each type and size of material used (very much like a Bill of Materials) and more trade specific tools to fully design and document welded structures.

Notes:

3D Sketch

To learn how to make a 3D sketch, we'll build a tubular frame for a chair. We'll need two sweeps, each using a 3D sketch as a path.

307. – Before making the 3D sketch, we'll make a 2D sketch and an auxiliary plane to help us draw the 3D sketch. Draw a 14″ construction line in the Right plane, and exit the sketch.

308. – Switch to an Isometric view and select the "**Reference Geometry, Plane**" icon. We'll create an auxiliary plane at 20 degrees from the Right plane. Select the "Right" plane in the "**First Reference**" selection box and the sketch line we just drew in the "**Second Reference**" selection box. Make the plane 20 degrees to the left (you may have to "**Flip**" the direction). Click **OK** to finish. This plane will be used later for reference in the 3D Sketch.

309. –The chair will be made from two bent tubular parts, each made with a sweep feature using a 3D sketch path. To make the first path for the tubular frame select the menu "**Insert, 3D Sketch**," or the "**3D Sketch**" icon (not in a toolbar by default). When we start a 3D sketch, notice we are not asked to select a plane and the only difference from a regular sketch is that we get "3DSketch1" in the FeatureManager, status bar and window title.

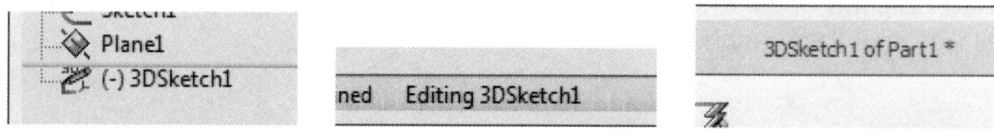

310. – In a 3D sketch we have most of the tools available in a 2D sketch. After selecting the "**Line**" tool, we immediately see a bigger than usual sketch origin, aligned parallel to the "**Front**" plane and an "XY" label is displayed next to the mouse pointer. This is to let us know that, when we draw the line, we'll be working in a 'plane' parallel to the Front plane (XY-plane in the 3D Sketch). Click in the origin to start drawing a line; move towards the right and align it with the 'X' direction. The yellow inference icon is somewhat small, but visible.

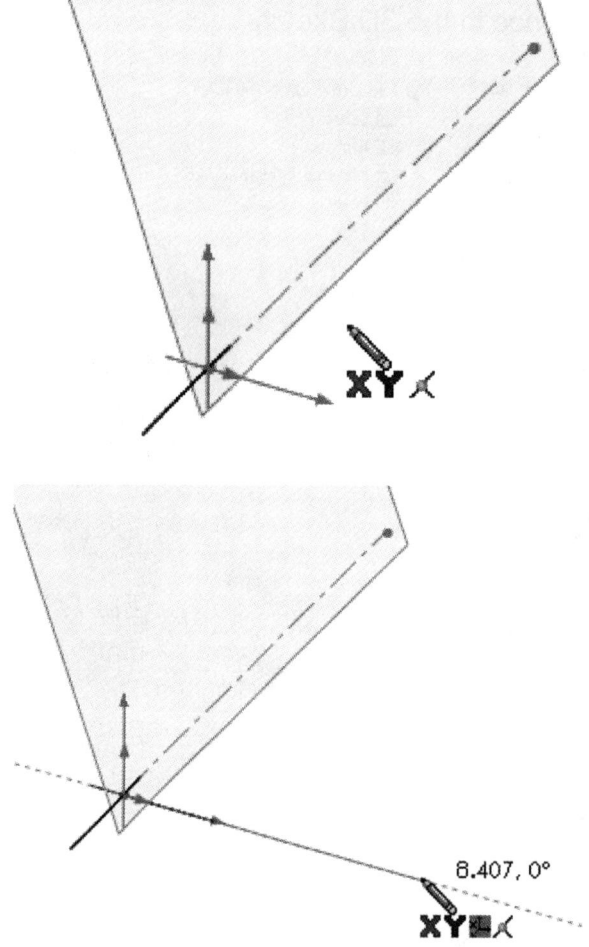

311. – For the second line, go down and right, but still in the XY-plane. Notice the origin moves to the start of the new line to alert us of the plane's orientation we are working on. Repeat the same two lines starting at the other end of the construction sketch; the line tool will snap to the end of the line but will remain in a plane parallel to the XY plane.

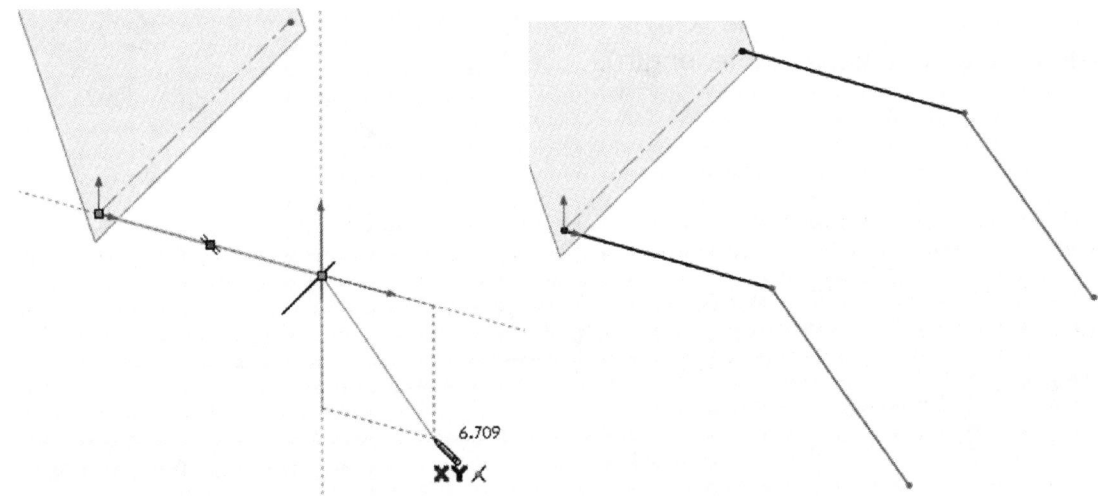

312. – When we work in a 3D sketch, besides the geometric relations we are used to, we have a few more options to help us define a 3D sketch.

Relation:	Between entities:	Result:
Along X	Line or two points	Line or endpoints aligned along the global X axis.
Along Y		Line or endpoints aligned along the global Y axis.
Along Z		Line or endpoints aligned along the global Z axis.
Normal	Line and Plane or flat face	Makes the Line perpendicular to the plane or face.
On Plane	Plane or flat face and Line or point	Makes the line or point Coincident to the plane.
ParallelYZ	Plane or flat face and Line	Makes the selected line parallel to the YZ plane.
ParallelZX		Makes the selected line parallel to the ZX plane.

235

313. – First we need to add the relations we know we need up to this point.

Select both lines along the X axis and add an **Equal** relation (same length).

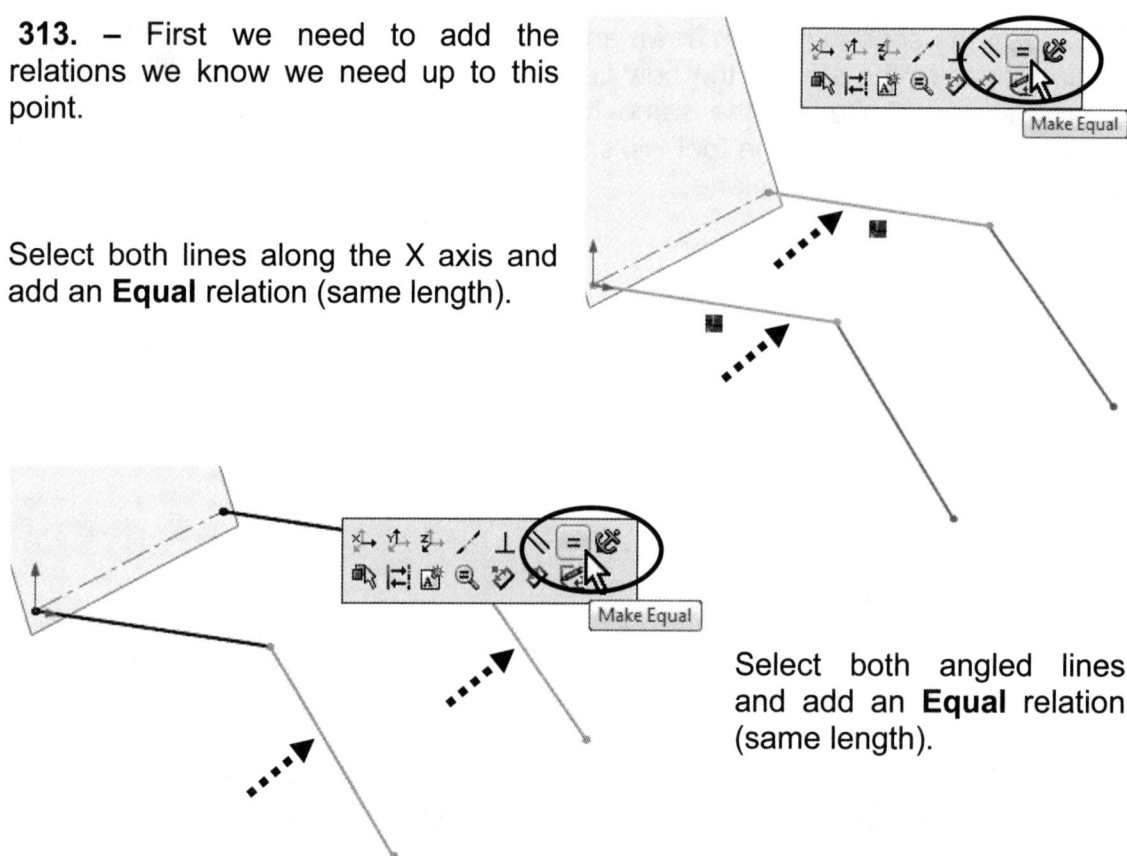

Select both angled lines and add an **Equal** relation (same length).

314. – Add an **On Plane** relation between the first diagonal line and the Front plane. By adding this relation, the line will not 'move' along Z.

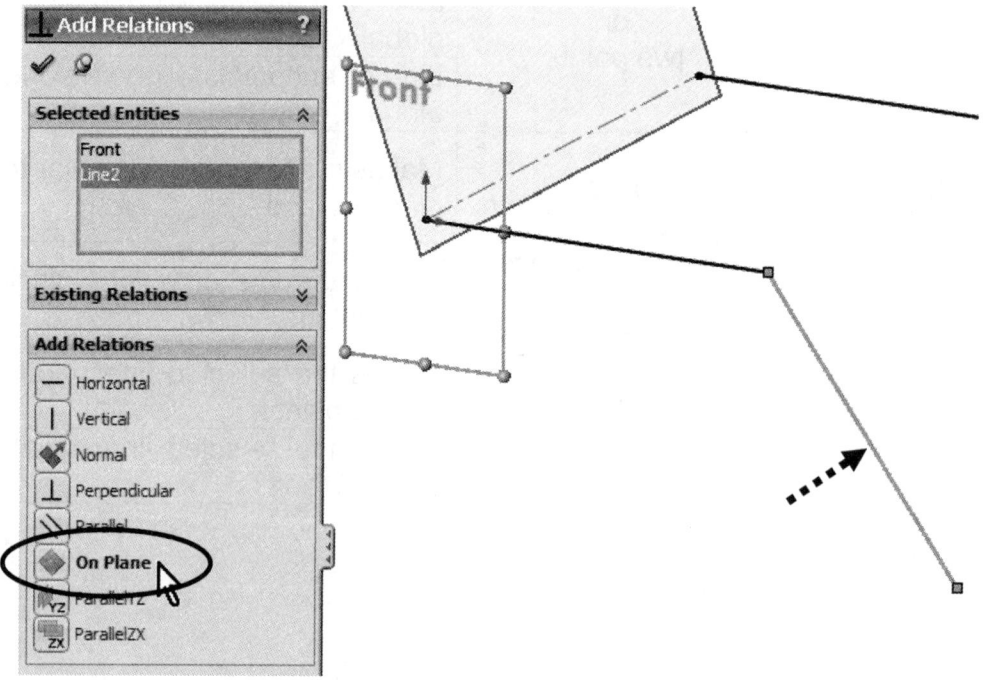

315. – Add a Parallel relation between the two diagonal lines.

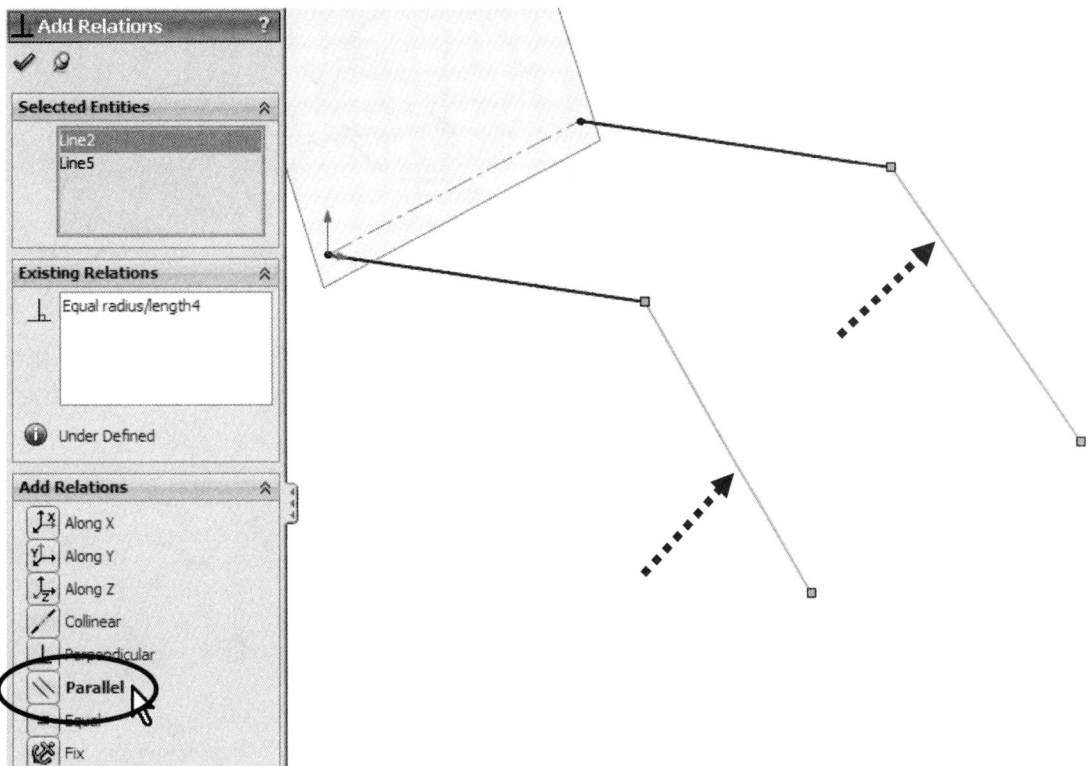

316. – Now add dimensions to the 3D Sketch. The sketch should be fully defined after dimensioning it.

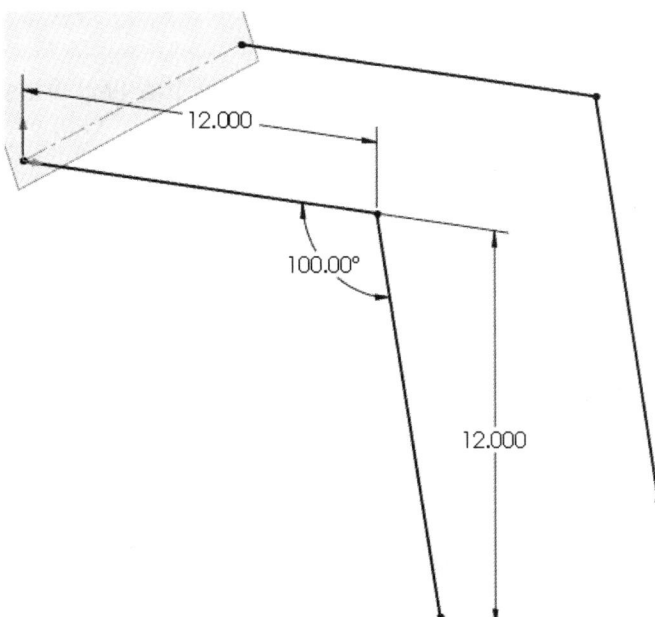

- Dimension the horizontal line 12″ long.

- Add the angular 100° dimension between the two lines.

- Add the vertical dimension between the horizontal line and the endpoint at the bottom. If you select the lower line only, you'll dimension it's length, not the distance from the horizontal.

237

317. – The next step is to add the backrest part of the chair. The plane we added at the beginning will help us align the 3D sketch's X, Y and Z axis directions about it. Select "**Plane1**" and then turn on the **Line** tool. The sketch origin and the local directions will now be temporarily aligned to **Plane1**.

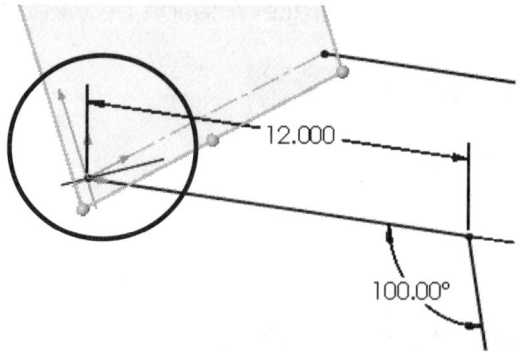

318. – Draw a new line starting at the part's origin going 'up' along "Plane1," then to the 'right' and 'down' ending at the start of the other line to make them Coincident (don't worry if it's not parallel).

319. – Turn off the **Line** tool and add a **Parallel** relation between the two lines aligned with "Plane1."

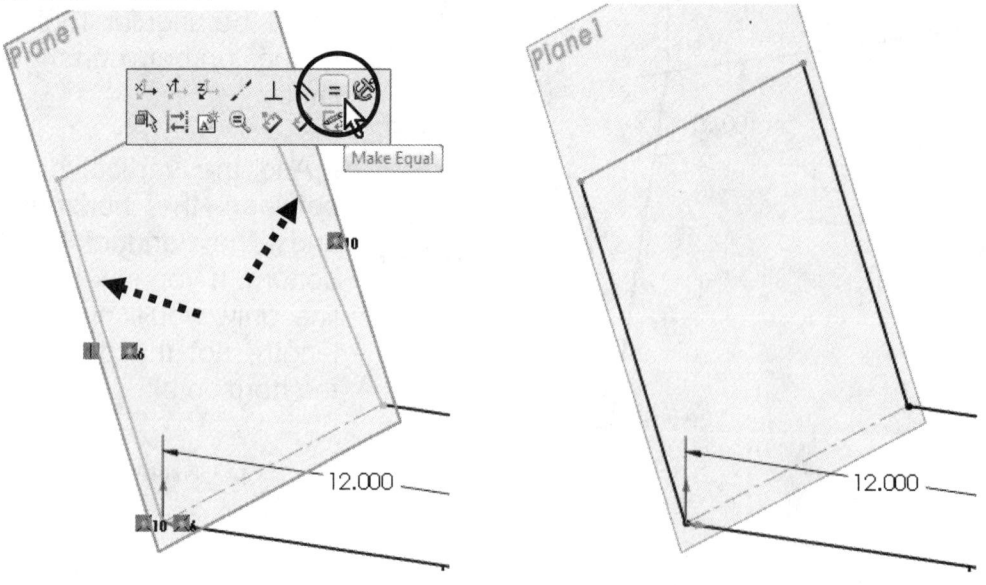

320. – And dimension the length of the backrest 18 inches (its length, not height).

321. – To finish the sketch, select the "Sketch Fillet" tool and round all corners with a 2″ radius. When adding the fillet we are warned about segments with equal relations; keep adding fillets until done. Since we are rounding all segments, they will still be equal at the end. Click Yes to continue when asked.

Click **OK** to finish the sketch fillets and exit the 3D sketch.

239

322. – The next part of the chair will be done similar to the first one. Start a new 3D Sketch (rotate the model as needed for clarity). Draw a line starting close to the origin Coincident to the construction sketch along the X axis. For the second segment we want to go along the Z axis; to change the direction we need to change the working plane orientation to the YZ or XZ plane. To switch the working plane on-the-fly, press the "**Tab**" key (just once; no need to hold it down) to rotate through the other work planes until we see either the YZ or XZ plane next to the mouse pointer. In the second picture we are working in the YZ plane.

323. – After adding the second line press the "**Tab**" key again to switch to the XY work plane and draw the third line parallel to the first one making it coincident to the construction sketch line as shown. The last line will go 'down' at an angle for the rear leg of the chair.

324. – Add a similar line to the other side.

325. – Dimension the lines 0.75″ from the endpoint of the construction sketch, the angle between the two lines and the length of the horizontal as shown.

326. – Now we need to add some relations. Select the endpoints at the bottom of the legs on one side of the chair and add an **Along X** relation; this way we'll make them lie on the same plane and axis.

Repeat the same relation for the end lines on the other side of the chair.

327. – And finally, add an **Along Z** relation between the endpoints of the two lines in the back to fully define the sketch.

328. – To finish the second 3D Sketch, add a 2″ sketch fillet to all corners as we did in the first one. Exit the sketch to finish.

329. – To make the tubes, we need a plane at the endpoint of a leg for the sweep's profile. Add an auxiliary plane Parallel to the Top plane ("First Reference") and Coincident to the endpoint of the chair's leg ("Second Reference").

330. – When the new plane is finished, add a new 2D sketch in it. Be sure to make the circle Coincident to the endpoint of the 3D sketch. Exit the sketch and make a sweep using this last sketch as the "**Profile**" and the first 3D sketch as the "**Path**." Use the "**Thin Feature**" option to make the wall 0.07″ thick with the material added inside.

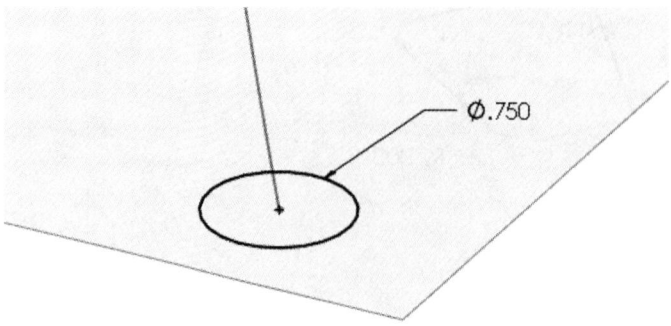

Click **OK** to finish the first tube.

3D Sketch and Weldments

331. – To make the second sweep we need a new profile sketch. Since we want both profiles to be the same, we'll use a function called "**Derived Sketch**" to make the second profile exactly the same as the first one. Using this approach, if the first profile sketch changes, the second one updates, too. To add a derived sketch we have to pre-select the sketch we want to derive *and* the plane/face where we want to put it. Expand the "**Sweep-Thin1**" feature, select the profile sketch, hold down the "**Ctrl**" key and select "**Plane2**" in the FeatureManager or the graphics area. Now, select the menu "**Insert, Derived Sketch**" (if we don't pre-select them, this command is disabled).

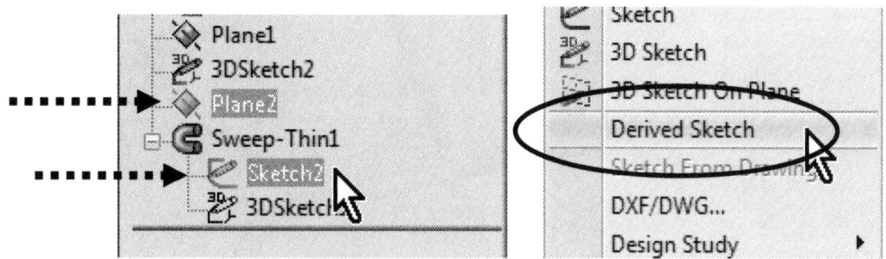

Immediately after selecting "**Derived Sketch**" we are editing the new sketch. Notice that most sketching tools are disabled except dimensioning and relations. In a derived sketch the geometry cannot be modified, it can only be located. The derived sketch will be right on top of the first sketch, drag the circle away from it for clarity.

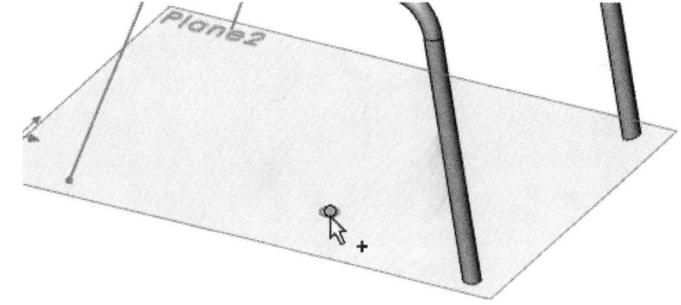

245

The only thing left for us to do is to make the circle coincident to the second 3D sketch. Add a coincident relation between the circle's center and the 3D Sketch endpoint as shown. When done, exit the sketch.

Make the second thin sweep with the same options as the first one and hide planes and sketches.

3D Sketch and Weldments

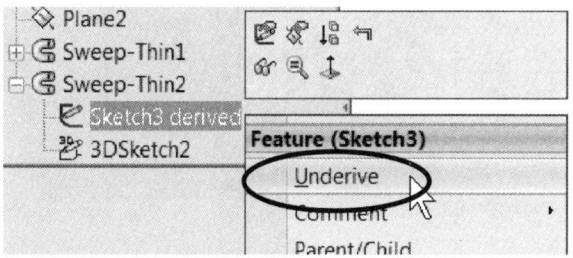

A derived sketch's link to its parent can be broken, or 'underived' from the original by selecting the derived sketch with the right mouse button and selecting "**Underive**" from the pop-up menu, then we can edit the sketch. Underive cannot be undone.

332. –Now that the chair's frame is finished we notice a small problem: the sides of the legs at the end of the sweeps are uneven. To correct this we'll have to extend the legs just enough to go past the 'floor' (*Plane2*) and trim them to size.

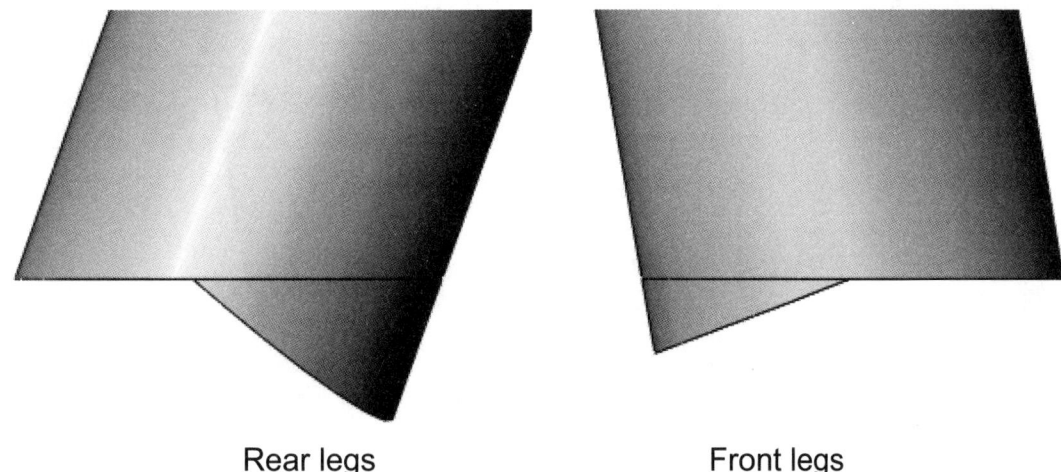

Rear legs   Front legs

Beginner's Guide to SolidWorks 2012 – Level II

333. – Select the flat bottom face at the end of the first sweep, add a new sketch in it and project both circles using "Convert Entities".

Make the first 3D sketch visible and select the "Boss Extrude" command.

After selecting "Boss Extrude," we can see the preview of the extrusion (Back view) is made perpendicular to the sketch plane giving us an undesired result. To correct it, select the "Direction of Extrusion" selection box, and select the (now visible) end of *3DSketch1* to make the extrusion follow that direction. Make the extrusion just long enough to cross *Plane2*. Repeat the extrusion for the second sweep.

334. – After finishing the extrusions we need to cut the excess in the legs. We could draw a sketch and make a "Cut Extrude," but we are going to use a different command. Select the menu "**Insert, Cut, With Surface**." We can use any plane or surface to use as a cutting tool and cut multiple bodies at the same time. Select *Plane2* for the surface, and flip the direction if necessary. "Cut With Surface" will cut everything on the side the arrow is pointing in. Click OK to finish.

Now our chair is correct. Save the part as *Chair Sketch3D* and close.

335. – A different way to make the path to sweep the frame of the chair is by using a "**Projected Curve**." By drawing the desired curve's projections in the Front and Top planes, we can combine them into a 3D curve and use it as a sweep path. Make a new part and add the following sketch in the Front plane. The sketch's origin is at the end of the 18" line. Exit the sketch when done.

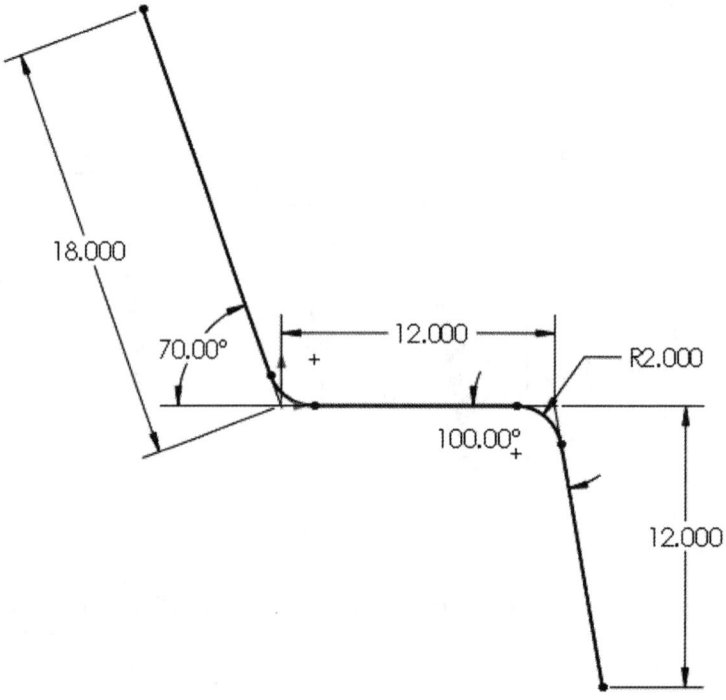

336. – Make a new sketch in the Top plane as shown and exit the sketch when done. Add geometric relations to the previous sketch endpoints to make it exactly the same size. (You may have to rotate the model to select the endpoints.)

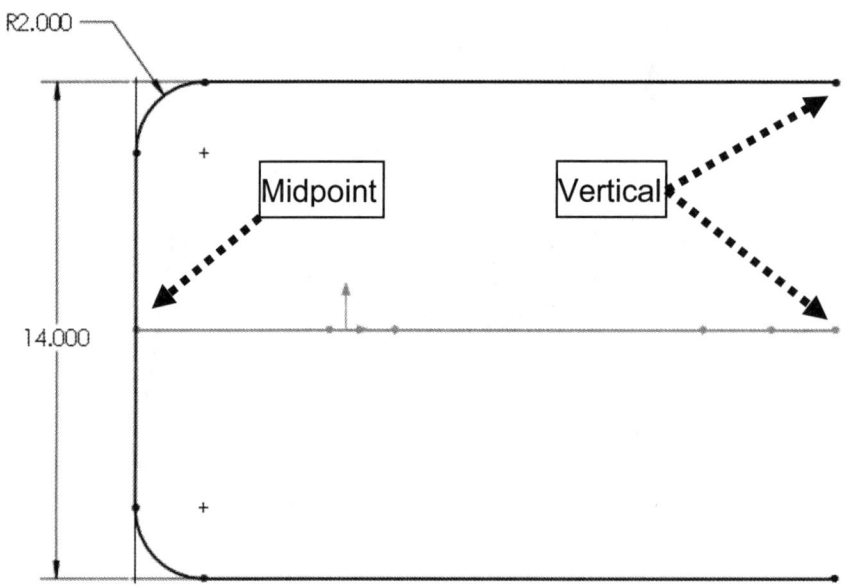

This is what the two sketches look like in an isometric view:

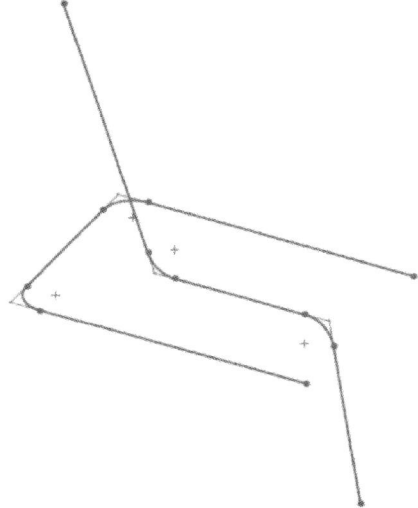

337. – Now, select the "**Projected Curve**" command from the "**Curves**" drop down menu in the Features toolbar or the menu "**Insert, Curve, Projected**."

Select the "Sketch on Sketch" option and pick both sketches previously made. Click **OK** to finish.

251

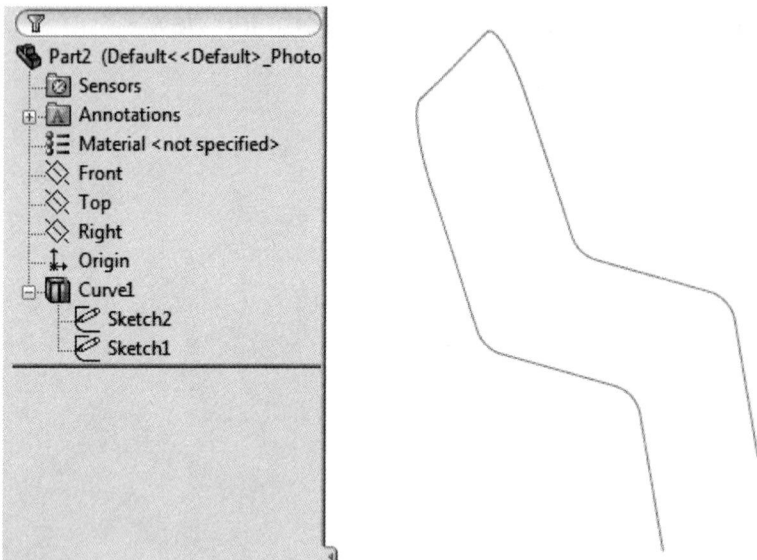

Now we can use the projected curve as a path for the sweep operation.

When projecting curves onto each other the radius may not be correctly projected depending on the angle, as is the case with the curves in the backrest. In this case building the part with a 3D sketch produces a better result. Making this part with a projected curve is a good option to show how making a projected curve and some of its limitations.

CHALLENGE EXERCISE: Create the second curve for the chair's frame using a "Projected Curve" and add the two sweep features.

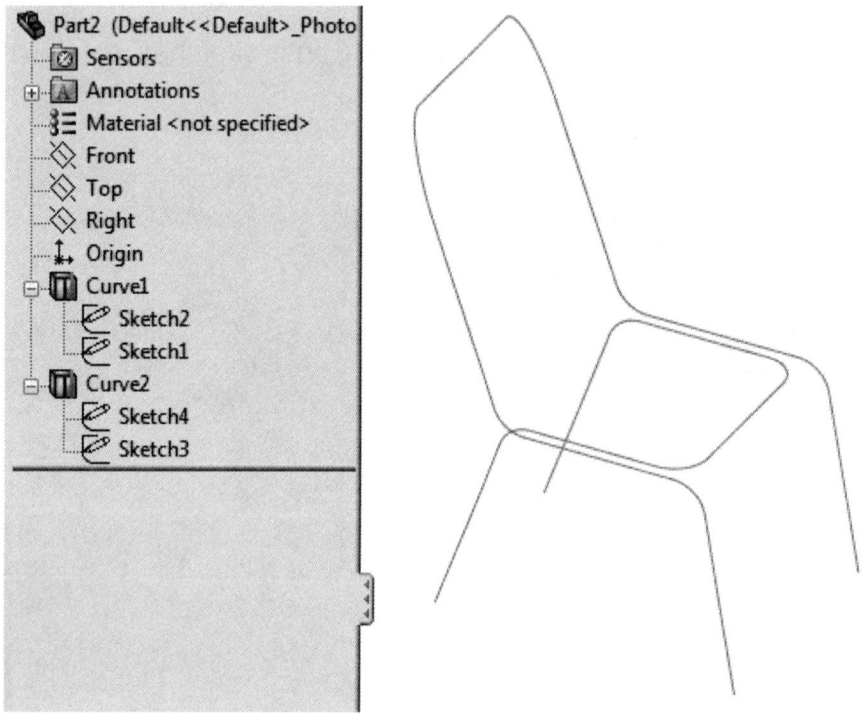

252

3D Sketch and Weldments

 Download a more extensive "Projected Curve" tutorial from our website: http://mechanicad.com/tipstricks.html

Notes:

Weldments

A welded structure can be defined as a part whose elements are long and thin and can be made with standard structural members. The weldments environment in SolidWorks allows us to design welded, modular or similar structures made from constant cross section elements (i.e., round or square tubing) easily, including weld beads, gussets and end caps in a multi body part. Detail drawings of weldments usually include material cut lists with length and cut angles ready for manufacturing.

Besides including a library of structural members in both metric and standard sizes, SolidWorks allows us to add our own structural member profiles to the built-in library.

When we work with weldments, the first thing we need to do is to make one or more 2D and/or 3D sketches that will serve as the structure's 'skeleton,' defining the structure's centerline, inside, or outside dimensions, just like in sheet metal. In a weldments part, each sketch line will be used to locate one element of the structure.

 A weldments part is probably one of the few instances where it's efficient to use a part file instead of an assembly to represent multiple 'parts.'

To learn how to use the weldments environment, we'll make the following conveyor structure using 2″ x 2″ welded steel.

338. – The first thing we need to do is to make a 3D sketch (or a combination of multiple 2D sketches) that will be the *skeleton* for our welded structure. Just as with sheet metal, we need to decide if the sketch dimensions will represent inside, outside or centerline dimensions of the welded structure. In our case, the conveyor's leg dimensions will be at the centerline, and for the top of the structure the dimensions will be outside dimensions; in other words, the width and length of the conveyor are not as important, but the height is. Open a new part and start a 3D sketch (menu "**Insert, 3D Sketch**"). Select the "**Line**" tool and press the "**Tab**" key to switch to the "**YZ**" plane. By default, 3D sketches always start in the "**XY**" plane.

TAB ...   TAB...

 To make the 3D sketch directions easier, the reader will be directed to go along the X, Y and Z axes in the positive or negative directions.

Start the sketch line in the origin using the YZ plane; go up in **Y**, negative **Z**, negative **Y** and stop. Don't worry about the size; we'll dimension it after adding relations.

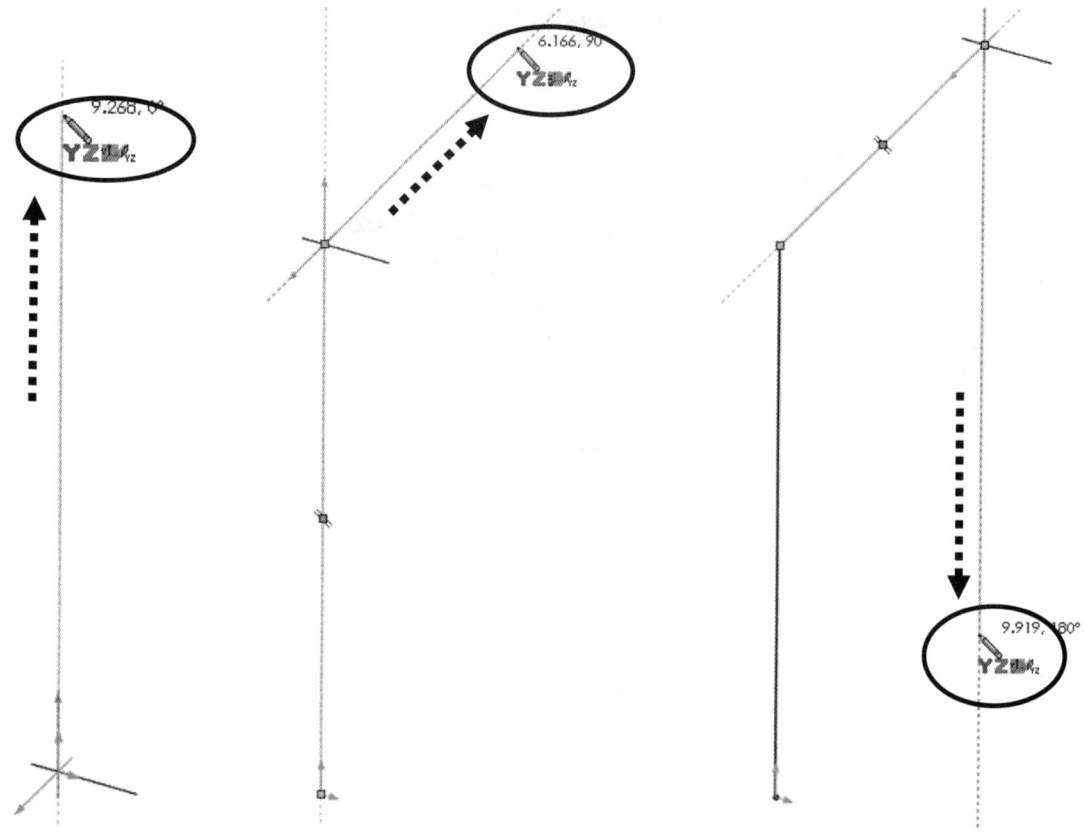

339. – Still with the "Line" tool active, start in the upper left and right corners and draw two lines going in the **X** direction. Press the "**Tab**" key if needed to switch to the **XY** or **XZ** plane; either one works in this case.

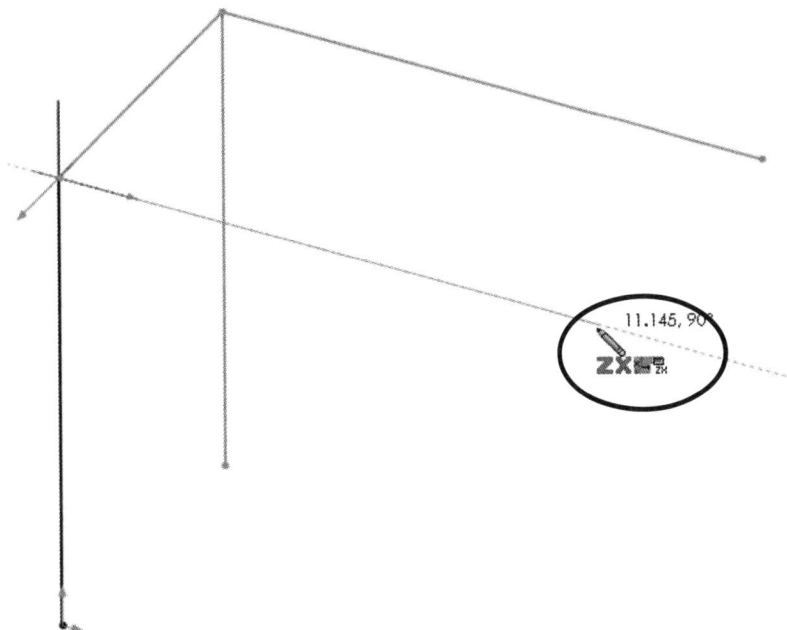

340. – An advantage of working in a 3D sketch is that we can 'snap' to other geometric elements even if they are not in the same plane we are working on. Draw the next four legs, adding **Midpoint** and **Coincident** relations to the two long lines as shown. Switch planes if needed by pressing the "**Tab**" key.

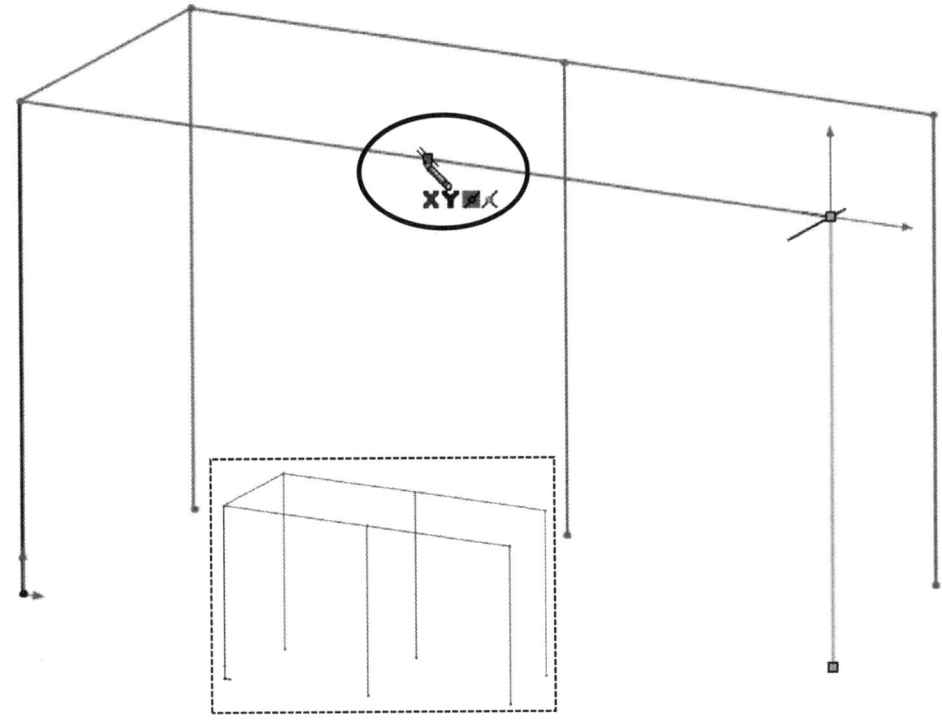

341. – Draw the next two lines along the **Z** direction to complete the geometry. Snap to the endpoints, even if the lines are not exactly along the **Z** direction.

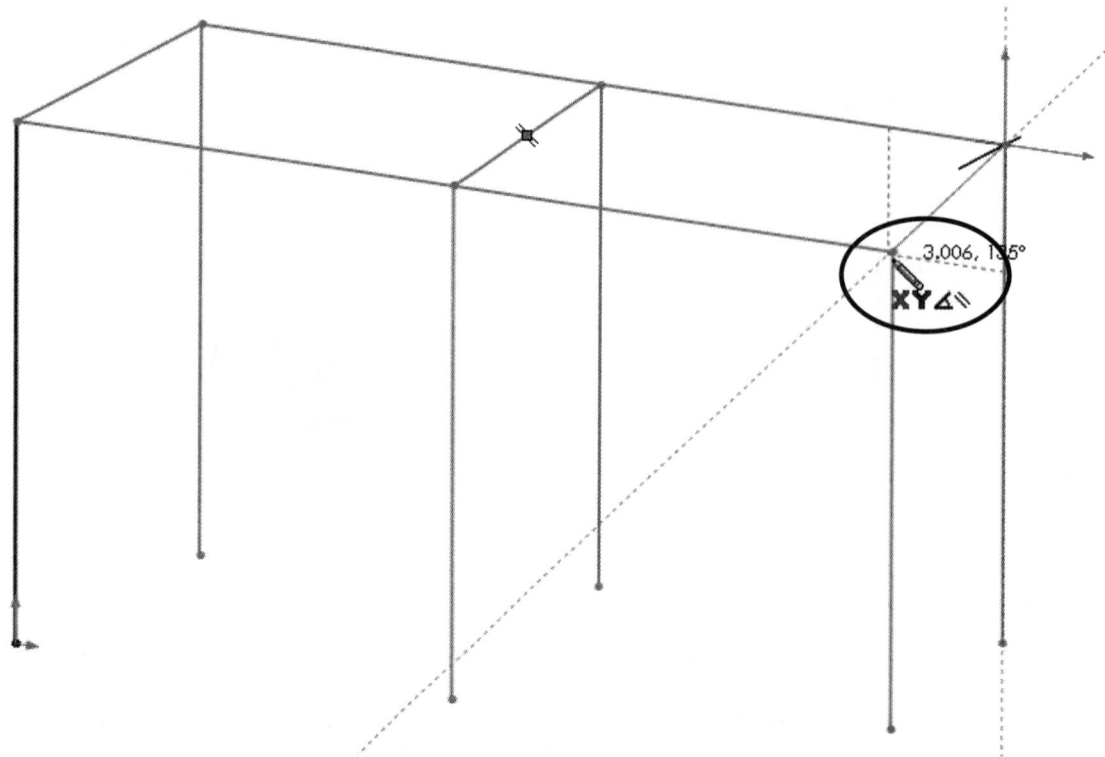

342. – Add **Along X** relations to the three endpoints of the legs on each side, one side at a time, *or* make all six legs **Equal**.

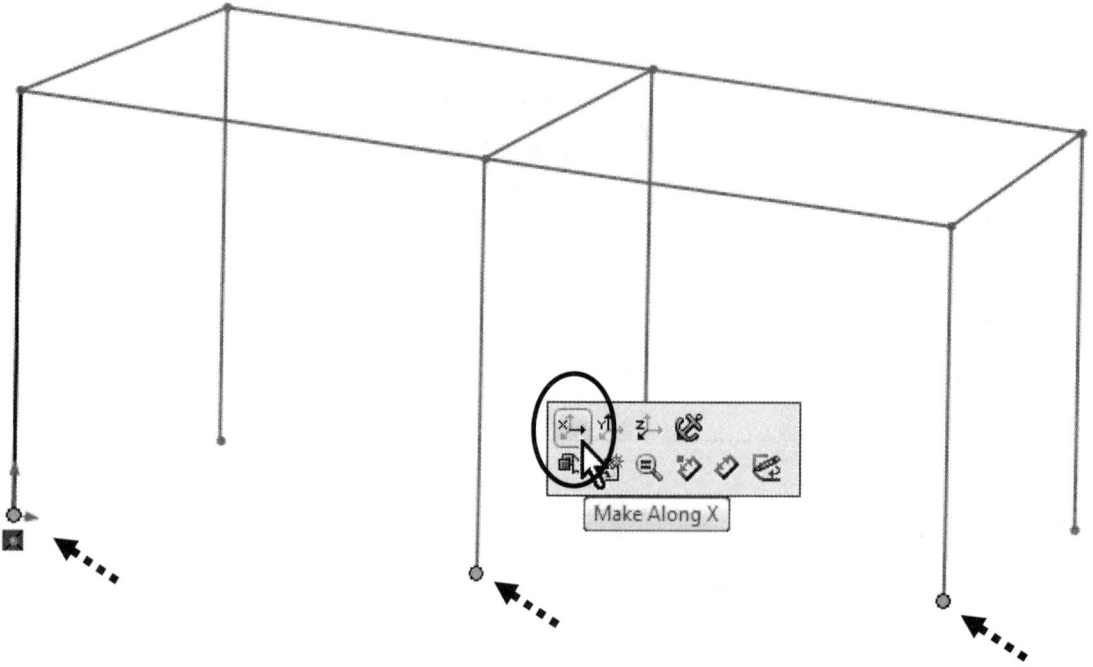

3D Sketch and Weldments

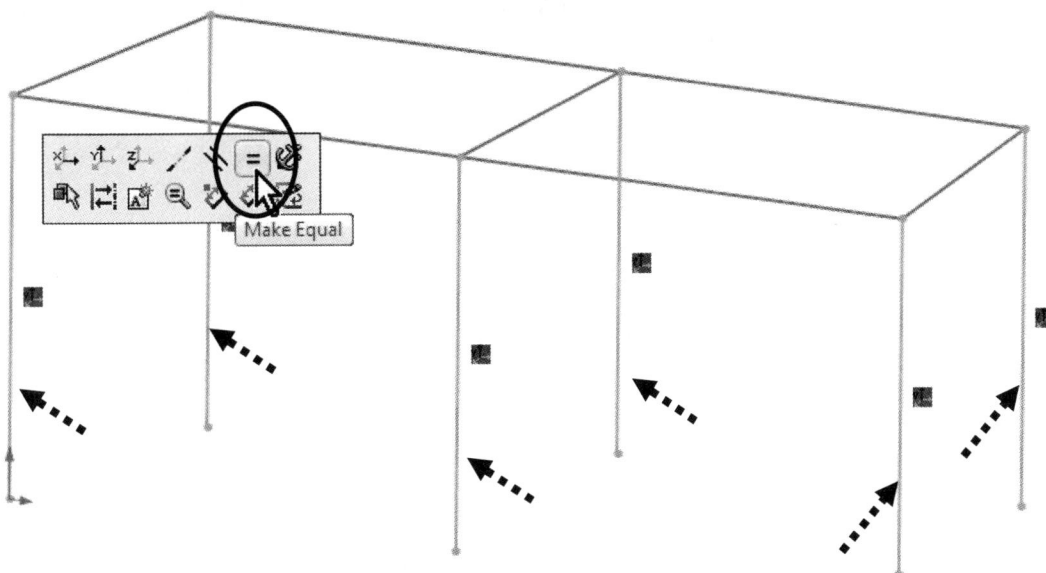

343. – Since we 'snapped' two of the transversal elements to existing endpoints, we need to make them either **Along Z** or **Parallel** to the first one.

344. – Add the following dimensions (we only need one 36″ dimension because we added a **Midpoint** relation to the long line):

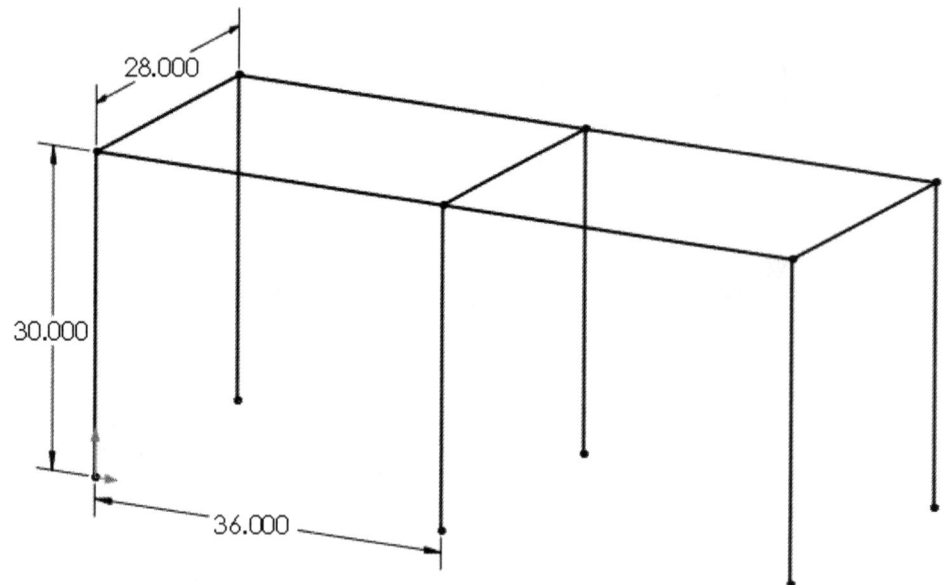

345. – Add corner reinforcements and dimension one as shown. Draw the lines by 'snapping' to the existing lines. Make all the reinforcement lines **Equal**.

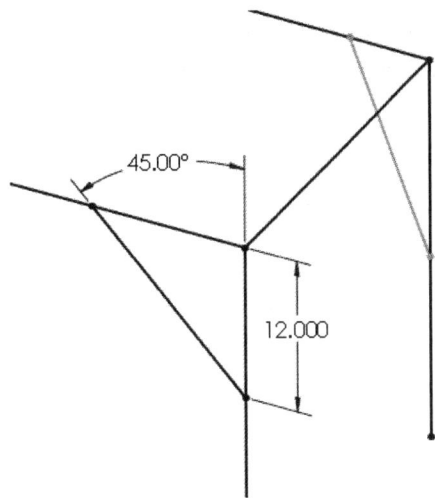

346. – Make the lower three endpoints on one side **Along X**, then the other side, and finally **Along Z** on one end to fully define the sketch.

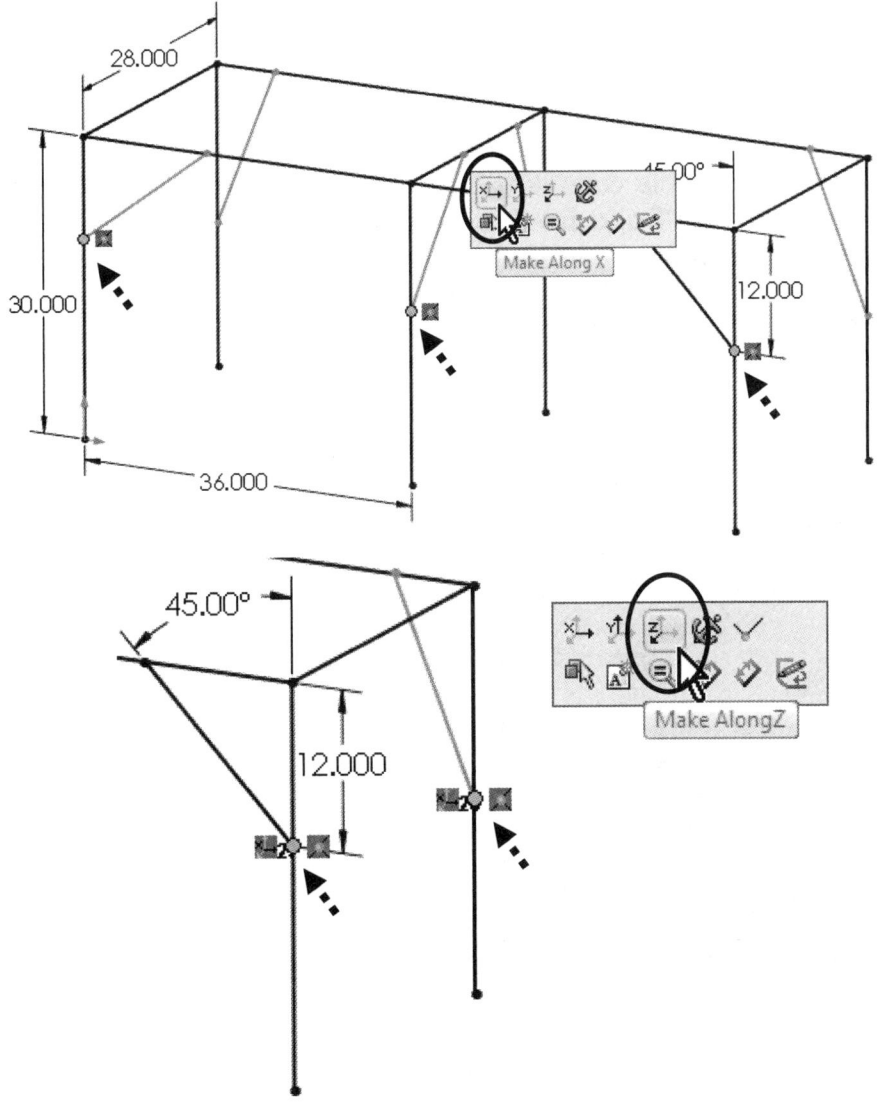

347. – The finished sketch now looks like this. Exit the sketch to continue.

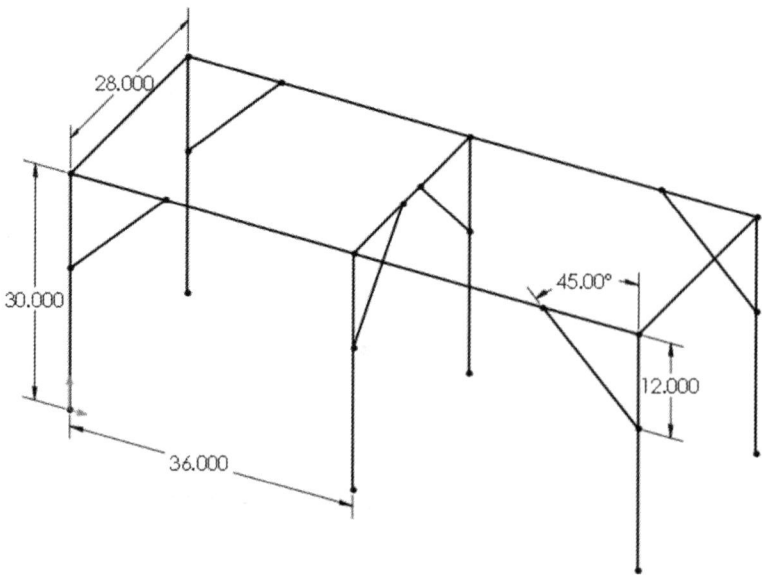

348. – Weldments work similarly to sheet metal in the sense that a special feature is added to the FeatureManager that enables the weldments environment, which in this case is a "**Weldment**" feature and a "**Cut list**" folder that takes the place of "**Solid Bodies**"; the reason for this is because a welded part is essentially a multi body part, where each body represents a structural member. Make sure the weldments toolbar is enabled. Right mouse click in the CommandManager's tabs and activate the "**Weldments**" tab, and/or right mouse click in a toolbar and turn on the Weldments toolbar.

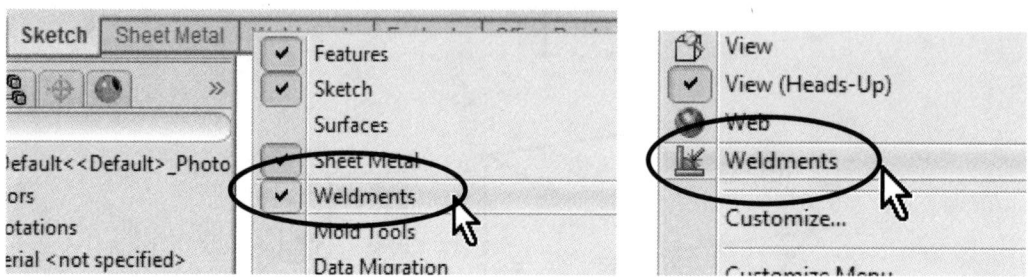

349. – In the Weldments toolbar is a "**Weldment**" icon; selecting it enables the weldments environment in the part but, just as with sheet metal, it is also automatically added when we make the first "**Structural Member**" feature.

3D Sketch and Weldments

To start select the "**Structural Member**" icon. From the "**Selections**" options, select "ansi inch" in "**Standard**," "square tube" in "**Type**" and "2x2x0.25" in "**Size**."

 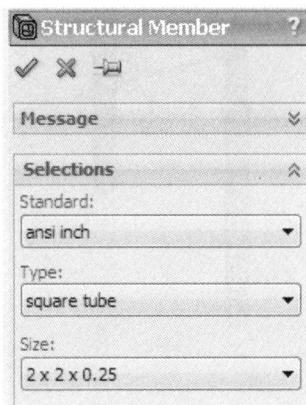

350. – When we add structural members, they are added in groups oriented in the same direction or laying in the same plane. The first group to be added will be the 'legs.' As we start selecting them in the screen, we see a preview of each one with the selected profile centered in each line (we'll talk about locating the profile later). Click OK when finished selecting the legs to create the first group.

351. – Since we'll be adding more members and the legs are just the first group, click in the "**Keep Visible**" option and then **OK** to create them. By doing this we can continue adding more groups.

263

When selecting sketch lines to add Structural Members to a group, remember that the lines in a group can be:
   a) Discontinuous <u>parallel</u> segments in the same or different planes, or
   b) Continuous segments connected by endpoints.

 The idea of having groups is to be able to modify its properties in a single operation, like profile to use, orientation, etc.

352. – The second group will be the four lines that make the outside perimeter at the top. We won' be able to select the cross member in the middle because it's not connected to an endpoint.

353. – Before clicking OK, we need to make a few modifications to how this group will be located about the sketch, and how the corners will be trimmed. Zoom in a corner (the one with the sketch of the member's profile is a good option, but any one works). For this group we'll use the "**End Miter**" corner treatment. By using this option, all the connecting elements in this group will get this treatment. The different options for corner treatments available are:

The preview is translucent; these images are the end result for clarity.

End Miter — End Butt 1 — End Butt 2

 The first distance box after corner treatments is used to specify a gap between the connected segments of the same group, and the second to add a space between one group and the previous. This is usually done to add a space to weld the structural members together.

Also, for "**End Butt**" corner treatments, we can have a simple cut or a coped cut end condition.

Simple Cut — Coped cut

We can change the type of corner treatment individually by clicking in the pink point at the corner of the preview and selecting a different option of corner treatment, including weld gaps.

354. – By default, when adding new structural members, the sketch line pierces the profile's origin automatically. If we remember, the conveyor must have a height of 30"; if we don't change the profile's location, our conveyor will be higher than needed by one half of the profile height.

To do this we have to change the location of the profile to make the element's sketch line pierce the top of the profile instead of its center. At the bottom of the "**Structural Members**" options, click in the "**Locate Profile**" button. The part will zoom into the profile's sketch where we can select the point in the profile's sketch to be coincident to the sketch line. Any vertex or sketch endpoint in the profile can be selected as a pierce point.

355. – Select the top middle point as indicated; the preview will update the profile's location to the desired position. Click **OK** to add the group and continue. Do not worry about the members intersecting each other; we'll trim them as soon as we finish adding the last group.

356. – For the next group, select the middle line, and change the profile's location as we did in the previous step. Click **OK** to continue to the next group.

357. – For the next group, select two reinforcements in one side (since only two are oriented in the same direction, that's why we can only do two at a time). When selected notice the profiles are not correctly aligned. They are in the centerline, but rotated. To rotate the profile and align them correctly to the structure, scroll down to "**Rotation Angle**" and enter "**45**" degrees.

Other options to orient the profile include selecting a line or edge in the "**Alignment**" selection box and aligning the horizontal or vertical axis. We can also mirror the profile horizontally or vertically if needed.

358. – Repeat the same process with the reinforcements on the other side (another group of two) and finally make a group for each of the reinforcements in the center; since they are not parallel to each other or any other member, we can only add one at a time. Close the "Structural Member" command when done. Our structure now looks like this:

 Notice the new "Weldment" feature automatically added to the Feature Manager after inserting the Structural Members.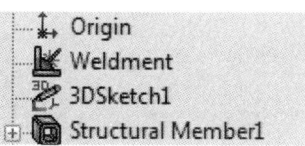

359. – Since the structural members are intersecting each other, the next step is to trim the excess material. From the "**Weldments**" toolbar, select the "**Trim/Extend**" command. We have the option to trim elements with one or more faces/planes, or other bodies. In our example, we'll trim the structural members using a face. Select the "**End Trim**" option to cut the bodies using the selected surface. In the "**Bodies to be Trimmed**" selection box, select two or four elements to trim at a time (we can select all bodies to trim, but the screen will be cluttered with "keep" or "discard" labels).

360. – In the "**Trimming Boundary**" selection box, select the "**Face/Plane**" option and pick the face under any of the top members to use it as the trim boundary. Rotate the model to select the correct face if needed.

361. – After selecting the face, the bodies are 'cut' in the preview and we have to review which bodies we want to keep and which bodies to discard. Check each member being cut. Review the pop up labels of each segment to toggle the "**keep**" or "**discard**" message by clicking in it. The labels can be moved around for clarity. By default, smaller segments are *usually* marked correctly to be discarded. The "discard" elements preview is lighter (almost invisible), making it easier to identify trimmed elements. After reviewing the elements to be discarded, press the "**Keep visible**" button in the "**Trim/Extend**" command and click **OK** to continue trimming the rest of the structure. Trim the top part of the other elements using the same trimming face.

 If we had chosen to trim all the legs at the same time, the screen would have been cluttered with "keep/discard" labels, that's why it was shown with just a few parts. The rest is repetition.

362. – Trim the lower part of the corner reinforcing elements using the faces indicated.

3D Sketch and Weldments

Our structure is now completely trimmed and no bodies intersect each other.

363. – The next step is to add gussets to our structure. Gussets are steel plates used to add strength and support at the intersections of structural components; they can be either bolted or welded. For our example, we'll add gussets to the corners, and weld beads after that. To add the gusset we have to select the faces that will be connected and the gusset's dimensions. Click in the "**Gusset**" icon in the "Weldments" toolbar, select the faces indicated below in the "**Supporting Faces**" selection box and enter the dimensions and location shown (It's easier if we zoom in a corner looking at it from the bottom).

364. – We can make polygonal or triangular gussets. In our example we'll use the triangular option, and dimension it 2" x 2" (measured from the corner).

A chamfer is usually added to allow space for a weld bead. Make the chamfer ('*d5*' and '*d6*') 0.5" x 0.5" (Chamfers can also be defined by one dimension and an angle).

The gusset's thickness can be added on one side, the other side or both sides. We'll make our gusset 0.25" thick mid-plane ("**Both Sides**").

Finally the "**Location**" of the gusset can be set on one side of the face, the center, the other side, or offset from any of them. We'll make ours in the center.

3D Sketch and Weldments

Gusset location options can have all possible combinations of thickness sides, location and even an offset if needed.

365. – Press the "**Keep visible**" icon and add the remaining gussets to the rest of the inside corners that don't have a diagonal member. Click OK to finish when done. SolidWorks remembers the settings, and we only have to select a new set of faces and the gusset is automatically positioned; then we only have to click OK to continue to the next one until we are done. After adding all gussets, our conveyor looks like this (gussets highlighted):

366. – Another feature unique to weldments is the "**End Cap**." An end cap will add a cover to close the open end of a structural member. Rotate the part to look at it from below and zoom at the end of one leg. Click on the "**End Cap**" command in the Command Manager and select the end face of a leg. For our example the end cap's thickness will be set to 0.125". The option **inward** in "Thickness Direction" reduces the element length by the indicated dimension maintaining the original length including the end cap. The "**Offset**" option refers to the distance from the edge of the end cap to the edge of the structural member. It can be set using a ratio of the structural member's thickness or a specified distance turning off the "**Use thickness ratio**." Set the offset ratio to **0.5** (half the structural element's thickness), and activate the option "**Chamfer corners**" with a value of **0.125"**.

3D Sketch and Weldments

 A note about "Thickness direction:" If we make the end cap going '**Outward**', its thickness will be added to the length of the structural member. If we make it '**Inward**', the structural member will be shortened by the end cap's thickness, as in this case.

Select the six legs' end faces to add all end caps with one command (a selection filter for faces is automatically activated while using the command).

 An important detail to keep in mind when working with weldments is that the "**Merge result**" option in all features that add material is turned 'Off' by default. If we add an extrusion (any type) and want it to be merged to one or more bodies, we have to turn the "**Merge result**" option 'On' following multi body part rules.

367. – To complete our structure, we'll add weld beads and the correct welding annotations. Weld beads can be added using a simplified process that is easier to use, lightweight on resources and eliminates certain limitations of versions before 2011, like allowing weld beads in members with gaps and the capability to handle more types of geometry. Some advantages of adding weld beads to our model include automatic creation of weld annotations for drawings, welding symbols for manufacturing, and user-definable welding path. Select the "**Weld Bead**" command from the Weldments toolbar or the menu "**Insert, Weldments, Weld Bead**."

277

368. – Zoom in a corner looking at it from the bottom. There are two ways to add a weld bead: selecting faces or using the Smart Weld Selection Tool. In the first case select the two faces indicated in the inside corner; notice the preview with the intersection of the faces to be welded. Set the weld bead size to **0.25"**. In this case we want the weld to go around the sides, so we'll turn on the "Tangent Propagation" option. Notice the preview goes around the tangency where both bodies touch. It doesn't go all the way around because the body on top is trimmed with a miter cut.

369. – To add a new weld bead on the other side of the leg select the "**New Weld Path**" button, rotate the part, and select the faces shown on the opposite side. Notice the weld bead settings remain the same. If we continue adding all the required weld beads that share the same settings, they will be grouped together.

370. – Click in the "**New Weld Path**" to continue adding the rest of the weld beads. Zoom in the second leg to add weld beads to continue. Instead of selecting faces manually, we'll use a different approach using the **Smart Weld Selection Tool**.

Activate the Smart Weld Selection Tool; notice the mouse pointer changes to a pencil icon.

What we need to do to use this tool is to click-and-drag across the intersection we wish to add a weld bead to, going from one face to the other.

Notice that as we make a new selection, a new 'Weld Path' is automatically added to the list.

371. – Add the rest of the weld beads between all structural members and click OK to finish adding welds. We'll add weld beads to the gussets next.

372. – Right after finishing the 'Weld Beads' the corresponding weld beads and manufacturing annotations are added to each weld.

A new "**Weld Folder**" has been added to the FeatureManager, and under we see the new '0.25in Fillet Weld' including all the weld beads listing the length of each one (useful for cost estimating and manufacturing purposes). Depending on the selections when adding weld beads you may have more or less welds.

 To turn off the cosmetic weld beads right mouse click in the "Weld Folder" and select "Hide Cosmetic Welds." To hide the welding annotations, right mouse click in the "Annotations" folder and turn off "Display Annotations."

373. – To add the weld beads to the gussets, we'll use a different option. Select the "**Weld Bead**" command from the Weldments toolbar and zoom in one of the gussets (annotations have been turned off for clarity). Select the two faces indicated to weld the gusset to the structural element; make the bead size **0.125"** and in this case select the option "**Both sides**" under "**Settings**." Notice a new weld bead is added to the opposite side of the gusset, saving us time (similarly, if we select "**All around**," the entire loop is selected).

 When adding weld beads using the Smart Weld Selection Tool, click and drag <u>starting in an unselected face</u>; otherwise it will get unselected and you'll have to re-select again to add a weld bead.

In these pictures it's easier to see that the reason why we added the chamfer in the gusset is to allow the weld bead to pass through it. Weld Bead options include defining a starting offset and bead length, and an intermittent (optionally staggered) weld bead.

374. – Add weld beads to all gussets using the same settings. Click OK to finish.

Every time weld beads are added, the part's annotations are displayed again. Turn them off to avoid a busy screen.

375. – Now that we have completed the welded structure, SolidWorks automates the creation of the 'cut list' by grouping structural members of the same type and size together. If we expand the "**Cut list**" folder in the FeatureManager, we'll see a long list of solid bodies. To group them make a right mouse click in the "**Cut list**" folder and select "**Update**" from the pop-up menu.

If desired, the "Cut-List-Item" folders can be reordered; the reason to do this is because this is the order in which they will be listed when we import the cut list into the drawing. A good idea is to reorder the elements by type and size, and leave the gussets and end caps at the end. To reorder the items, simply drag-and-drop them up or down as needed.

376. – Save the part as *Weldments Table* and make a new drawing with an isometric view; shaded with edges view mode and tangent edges removed will work fine for this example. Import the model dimensions to this view.

377. – Select the isometric view and from the right mouse click menu, select "**Tables, Weldment Cut List**," or from the menu "**Insert, Tables, Weldment Cut List**." Accept the defaults for the table and click OK. Locate it in the upper right corner. Adjust the view's scale if needed.

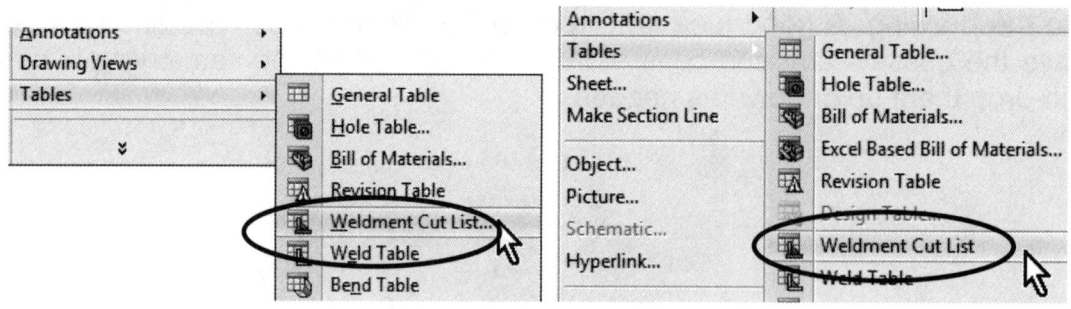

ITEM NO.	QTY.	DESCRIPTION	LENGTH
1	2	TUBE, SQUARE 2.00 X 2.00 X .25	74
2	2	TUBE, SQUARE 2.00 X 2.00 X .25	30
3	1	TUBE, SQUARE 2.00 X 2.00 X .25	26
4	6	TUBE, SQUARE 2.00 X 2.00 X .25	27.88
5	6	TUBE, SQUARE 2.00 X 2.00 X .25	14.73
6	12		
7	6		

The rows without description in the list correspond to the gussets and end caps. For SolidWorks to fill in the correct information we have to go back to the part file; in the "**Cut list**" select the corresponding folder with a right mouse click and select "**Properties**." In the "**Cut List Summary**" tab we can see all the properties for each group of elements, or we can select the "**Properties Summary**" tab to see a list of properties with the values of each group. Fill in the appropriate descriptions for the groups missing one. Click OK to complete.

 You *may* have to fill in the "MATERIAL" property of some cut list items for the table to update correctly in the drawing.

378. – While in the part, expand the "**Weld Folder**"; right mouse click in each of the "Fillet Weld" items and select "Properties" from the pop-up menu.

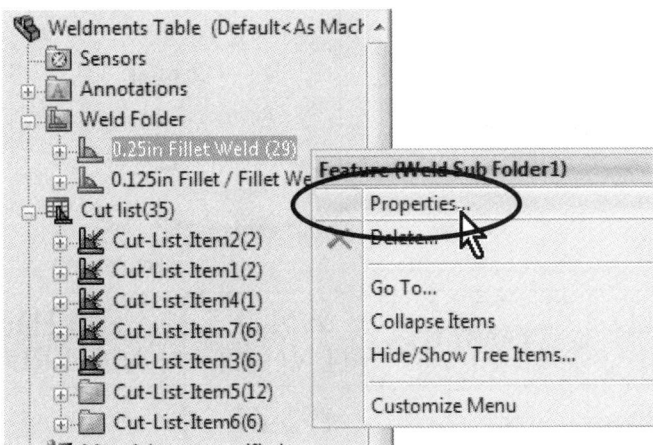

285

379. – In the **Fillet Weld** properties we can fill in additional properties like material, process, weight per unit length, cost, welding time per unit length and number of passes. We are also provided with the total number of welds, total weld length, mass, cost and time. This information is not required, but is useful if we add weld tables to our weldment drawing.

380. – Go back to the drawing. Our cut list will be updated and now we can add a **Weld Table**. Right mouse click in the isometric view; from the pop-up menu, select "**Tables, Weld Table**." Turn on the "**Combine same weld type**" option and click OK to locate the table in the drawing. Change the table's font and size as needed.

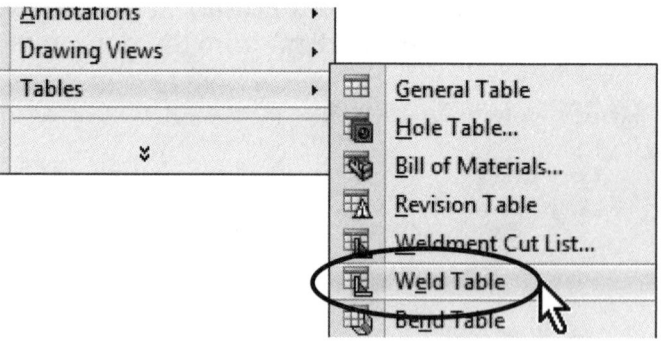

ITEM NO.	WELD SIZE	SYMBOL	WELD LENGTH	WELD MATERIAL	QTY.
1	0.25	◸	193.61	Steel	1
2	0.125	◸	144	Steel	1

381. – Add the identification balloons to identify each structural element using the "**Auto Balloon**" function. Select the "**AutoBalloon**" command from the Annotation toolbar, or the menu "**Insert, Annotations, Auto Balloons.**" In the "Balloon Layout" options select "**Faces**" to attach balloons to the structural members' faces. Under "Balloon Settings" select the "**Circular Split Line**" style, and pick "**Quantity**" in the "**Lower text**" selection list. Arrange the balloons as needed.

In the "**Balloon text**" or "**Lower text**" selection lists, we have the option to select "**Custom Properties**"; if we do, a new selection list is revealed where we can select any property including weldment cut list properties.

382. – To identify the welds, select the "**Weld Symbol**" command from the Annotation toolbar or the menu "**Insert, Annotations, Weld Symbol**."

In the Weld Symbol properties window we can add all the necessary specifications for the welding instruction sheet, or we can click in the Weld Beads and the symbol is automatically filled. Click to select a weld bead, locate the symbol in the sheet and repeat as needed.

When adding more Weld Symbols, the last type used is remembered. When a different weld bead is selected, the symbol is updated to reflect the currently selected bead. Close the Weld Symbol properties window when done adding welding annotations.

383. – Save the finished drawing and close.

384. – To review more weldments options, make the following (2D) sketch in the Top plane. The center of the arc is coincident to the origin; this will save us from making an auxiliary plane for the next step. We can only use circular arcs and straight lines for weldments. Exit the sketch when finished.

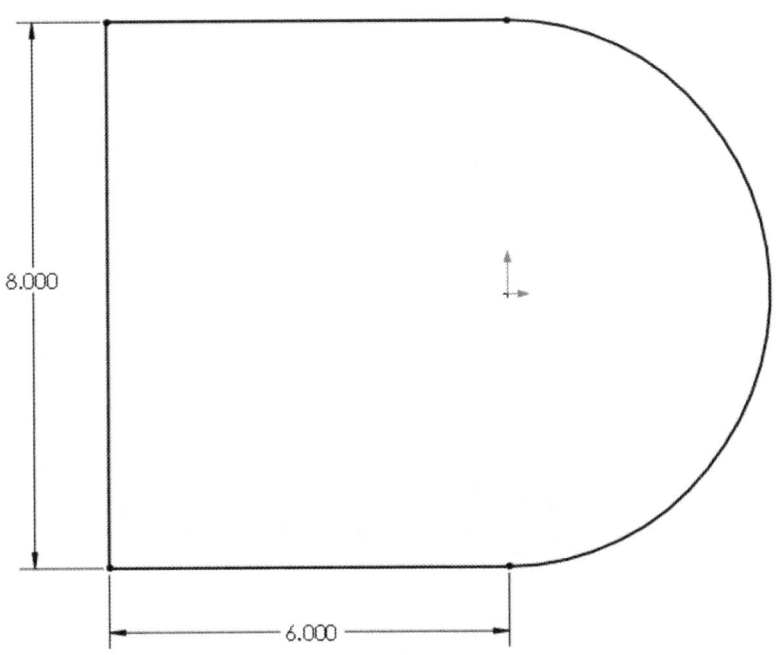

385. – Switch to an isometric view and add the following sketch in the Right plane and exit when done.

💡 As an alternative (or challenge), make a 3D sketch including the lines from the two sketches. When we work with weldments it makes no difference if we use 2D or 3D sketches.

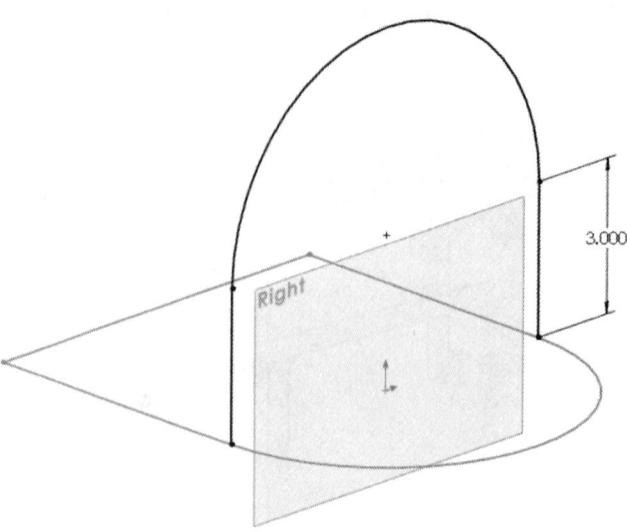

386. – Select the "**Structural Member**" icon from the Weldments toolbar. Select the "ansi inch" standard, "pipe" type and "0.5 sch 40" size. Pick the lines indicated in the preview.

For "**Corner treatment**" instead of applying a global option, we'll manually select the treatment for each connection. When using circular arcs in the structure, we have the option to either merge the arc member to adjacent segments globally by checking the option "**Merge arc segment bodies**" or on an individual basis.

290

387. – Click on the point in the corner and select the following corner treatments:

 The option "**Set corner specific weld gaps**" will add the indicated gap between the connecting elements for welding.

388. – In the case of the joint between a straight line and an arc, changing the corner treatment gives us the option to merge the segments into a single element. In our example we'll leave this option unchecked.

389. – Add the rest of the structural elements using the same structural member with the same settings. Click OK to complete. Save the part as *Welded Frame*.

390. – Now select the "**Trim/Extend**" command to trim overlapping elements. Select the "**End Trim**" corner type option. Select the vertical elements in the "**Bodies to be Trimmed**" selection box. In "**Trimming Boundary**" use the option "**Bodies**" and select the straight and curved members. Make sure the trimmed segments are correctly marked "**keep**" or "**discard**." Click OK to complete.

 After the structural members are completed we can hide the sketch(s) used.

391. – Right mouse click in the "**Cut list**" folder and select "**Update**" from the menu to group elements together. Remember that we can preview the cut list by selecting "**Properties**" from the cut list item's right mouse menu.

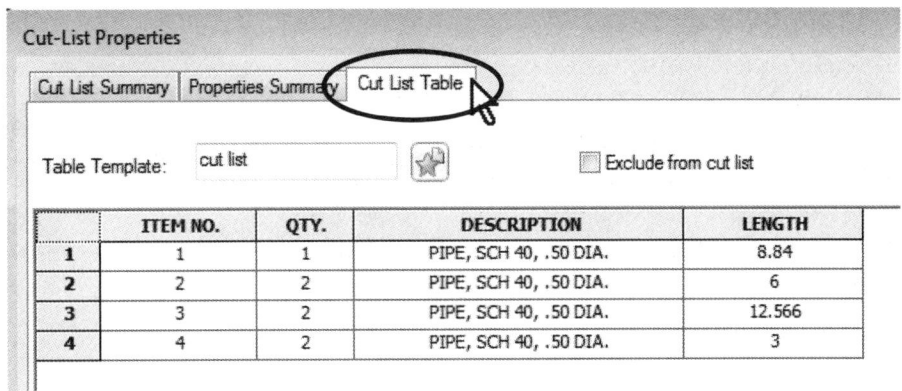

392. – When working with multi body parts (like weldments), we can save each body to a new part file and/or make a new assembly with those parts at the same time. To save a single body as a new part we can select it from the "Cut-List-Item" folder or the graphics area with the right mouse button and select "**Insert into new part...**" from the pop-up menu. But….

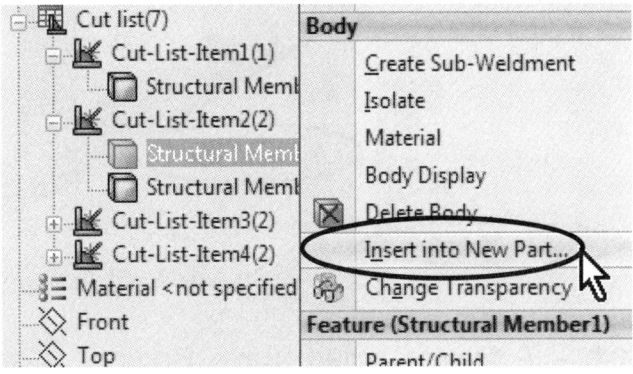

…what we want to do is to save all of the bodies, each to a part, *and* make an assembly at the same time using those parts. Right mouse click in the "**Cut list**" folder and select "**Save Bodies**."

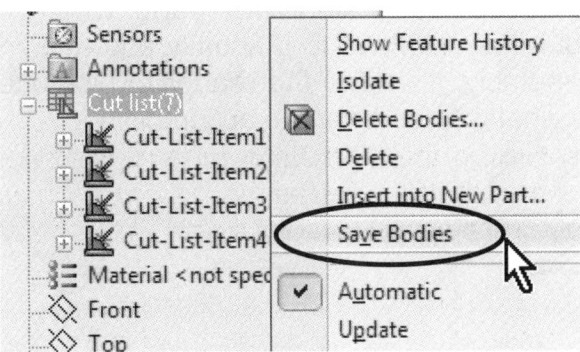

393. – In the "**Save Bodies**" command, we can select one or more bodies to be saved to a part. In our example we'll name them 'Body 1' to 'Body 7' by clicking in the label attached to each body or double-clicking in the row for each body. The option "**Consume cut bodies**" removes the bodies from the part after saving to an external file. We'll leave this option unchecked. Since we also want to make a new assembly, select the "**Browse...**" button in the "**Create Assembly**" option box and name it *Welded Frame Assembly*. Click OK to finish.

394. – A feature called "**Save Bodies**" is added to the FeatureManager; a new part file is generated for each body saved as well as the new assembly which is already open. Switch to the new assembly window just made. An inconvenience of making an assembly from bodies using this technique is that all the parts will be automatically "fixed" in the assembly, and identical parts are given different names. We could skip duplicate parts when saving the bodies, but then we have to manually add and mate them to the assembly. It's up to the reader to pick one approach over the other, depending on what we need/want to accomplish.

294

3D Sketch and Weldments

 The bodies saved to a part have an external reference to the original welded part. In this case, the reference status is "In context" because the *Welded Frame* part is open and loaded in memory.

395. – Opening one of the assembly parts shows the only feature is a saved body from a multi body part, listed as "**Stock-*part-name***." From this point on, we can add more features to a part if needed, and these changes will be reflected in the assembly, but not in the original multi body part.

 If we add a feature to the welded <u>multi body part</u>, like a cut across multiple bodies, the changes will be propagated to the externally saved parts only if the feature is added BEFORE the "**Save Bodies**" feature. To add a feature before the "Save Bodies" feature we have to raise the Roll Back before it.

295

Notes:

3D Sketch and Weldments

Structural Member Libraries

A word about structural profile members: SolidWorks includes a small number of profiles pre-loaded in the "**Structural Member**" library. To add more profiles we have to make a new part, draw the desired sketch profile and save the sketch as a library feature part in the folder designated for structural members.

396. – Make the following sketch in a new part. We can use any plane. Units are in millimeters (mm). Don't forget the sketch points in the middle of each side; the reason to add these points is to use them location points to position the profile in the weldment. Exit the sketch when done.

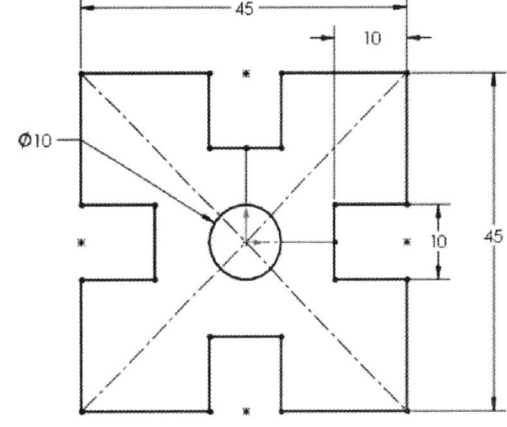

397. – Pre-select the sketch in the FeatureManager and save the file as a Library Feature Part (Lib Feat Part *.sldlfp). The default folder for weldments profiles is "*<SW_Install_Folder>***data****weldment profiles**." The folders in this location reflect the standard and types of libraries available. Here we can select a Standard and Type to save our library, or if desired we can create our own library folder. Save the library as "**45 x 45**" in the folder:
 "*<SW_Install_Folder>*\data\weldment profiles\iso\square tube." Now this profile is available for structural members.

And now we can use our structural member library in our designs.

398. – To add more weldments profile library folders, go to the menu "**Tools, Options**." Under the System Options tab, select "**File Locations**" and pick "**Weldment Profiles**" from the drop down list. The folders we add will be listed under "Standard" in the Structural Members command.

 SolidWorks Toolbox has a considerably larger list of profiles, but unfortunately they cannot be used directly in weldments. They would have to be converted to library features first, following the procedure we just followed.

298

3D Sketch and Weldments

Review and Questions:

a) Name three geometric relations available in a 3D sketch that are not available in a 2D sketch.

b) Describe how to create a Derived sketch.

c) What is the difference between using a 2D or a 3D sketch for weldments?

d) Name the conditions to be able to select multiple sketch segments at the same time for a structural member group.

e) Can multiple gussets and end caps be added at the same time?

f) How can we generate a cut list to include the structural member's type, length and cut angles?

g) If welded part bodies are saved to an assembly, are identical bodies saved as a unique file or different files?

Answers:
a - Along X, Y, Z, On-Plane, Normal, ParallelYZ, ParallelZX.
b - Pre-select the sketch to derive and the plane/face to place the derived sketch and click in the menu "Insert, Derived sketch."
c - None. They both work the same.
d - They must be parallel or continuous connected by an endpoint.
e - Gusset's have to be added one at a time, end caps can be added multiple at a time.
f - Right mouse click in the "Cut list" folder and select "Update." Then import the Cut List table to a drawing.
g - Each body, even identical ones, are each saved to a different file always.

Surfacing and Mold Tools

Notes:

Surface Modeling

So far we have been working with single and multi body solid parts, and now we'll start working also with surfaces. By including surfaces in our models, we are able to create increasingly complex designs that would otherwise be very difficult to model with solids. Working with both solids and surfaces is called 'hybrid modeling', as we incorporate both solid and surface bodies in the same model. When we work in a hybrid model, the surfaces are usually used as support geometry, as stopping or trimming boundaries for solids and/or other surfaces, etc.

Background and a little history: The first computer models used for design (over 40 years ago) were wireframe models capable of defining the edges of a part and had severe limitations, especially when it came to defining a three dimensional surface, as it could only be approximated using a mesh of lines with little detail. Think of a wireframe model as a 'stick figure'. A wireframe model is basically what we are able to do now with a 3D sketch – just lines.

Some years later, surface models were developed that allowed more definition of a component, including curved faces and were a huge improvement over the wireframe models, but still had limitations when it came to calculate a part's volume, weight, etc. When we talk about a surface model, think of a parade's floating balloon. It has the surfaces (fabric) and the wireframe (stitches), and is essentially hollow. Similarly, it's safe to say that a surface model *may* have imperfections, like faces not matching correctly creating gaps (think of the balloon with an opening at a corner) or overlapping faces. This would create a problem if we wanted to calculate volume, weight, etc., or use it for manufacturing.

Later, in the 1980's (give or take a few years...), solid models became available, but (just like surface modelers) were difficult to use, required special training and were available in high end (read 'expensive') workstations. A design station's cost, complete with hardware and software, would be in the tens of thousands of dollars, affordable only by big corporations or government agencies, and design tools were greatly improved, producing better results faster, making it easier to integrate with computer numerical controlled (CNC) manufacturing.

Some years later (circa 1990's), solid modelers became available in the Windows operating system, making them considerably more affordable to mainstream designers, and being native Windows applications made them easier to learn and use. These solid modelers incorporate many of the advantages surface and solid models offer, including better integration with manufacturing, analysis, animation and many other downstream applications.

At present, with the advances in technology making computers faster than ever before (and continuing to get faster every day), we are able to take advantage of it and create bigger, ever more complex designs in record time, helping us bring product designs faster to market.

A word about hybrid modeling: It is not uncommon to see that dedicated surface modelers can generate superior and better looking surfaces for automotive, aerospace and consumer product design than many solid modelers (like SolidWorks), and they can also make changes easier and faster maintaining the intended shape. This makes creating highly complex surfaces easier. With that said, it is common in those industries to generate the complex surfaces in one software package and then import them into solid modelers to complete the rest of the design process.

When we talk about surface modeling, we are referring to creating models using mainly surfaces, or the 'skins' of parts, and afterwards converting them into a solid or using them to build solids. The tools available include almost all the solid features like extruded, revolved, swept and lofted surface…

plus a few more specific to surface modeling, most of which will be covered in this lesson.

To start modeling with surfaces, we'll make a hair dryer using a few simple surfaces and then we'll convert them into a solid model. After finishing, we'll split the model to make a file for each of the different parts to practice and learn more about multi body parts.

 If the Surfaces toolbar is not visible, activate it by right mouse clicking in a CommandManager's tab, and selecting "**Surfaces**," and/or the menu

"**View, Toolbars, Surfaces**."

399. – To save time and focus on the surfacing functionality, download the file *Hair Drier.sldprt* from www.mechanicad.com/download.html and open it. It has a number of pre-made sketches and planes.

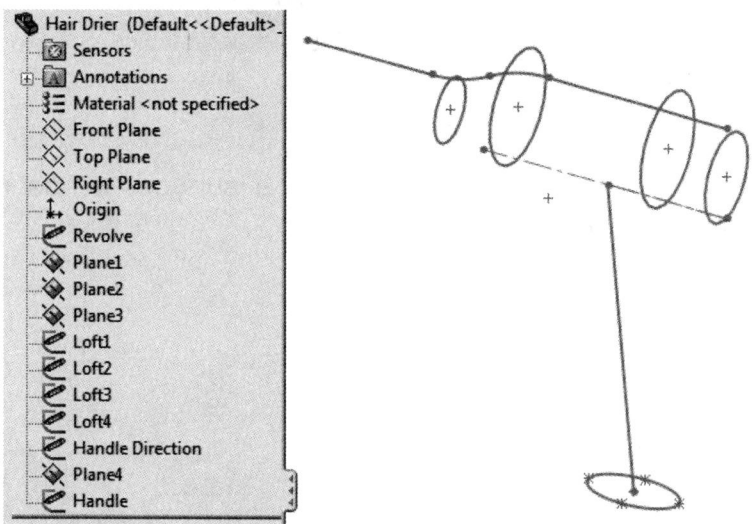

400. – The first feature will be a revolved surface. Select the sketch named *Revolve* in the FeatureManager and click on the "**Revolved Surface**" command, or the menu "**Insert, Surface, Revolve**." The sketch's centerline is automatically selected.

The revolved surface will be made 360 degrees. Click OK to complete it.

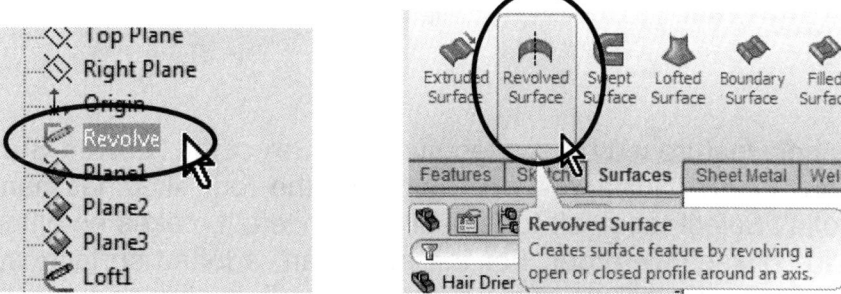

305

As opposed to when we work with solids, when the first surface body is created a "**Surface Bodies**" folder is immediately added to the FeatureManager.

The 'Surface-Revolve1' we just made is only a surface. It has no thickness, volume or mass; it's only a surface.

401. – The next feature will be a lofted surface. Select the "**Lofted Surface**" icon or the menu "**Insert, Surface, Loft**," and pick the four sketches named 'Loft1' through 'Loft4'. Select them left to right or right to left, it makes no difference; just pick them in consecutive order. For the most part, a lofted surface works like a solid body loft; we can include guide curves, centerline, start and end constraints. Leave the rest of the loft options to their default value for this example and click OK to complete it.

Surfacing and Mold Tools

After the loft we have two surface bodies. Note that surfaces do not 'merge' automatically as solids do; they simply intersect each other but remain separate bodies.

 The main difference between a lofted surface and a solid body loft is that in a lofted surface we can use open *or* closed sketches, curves, edges, etc., to create irregular, complex surfaces.

402. – The next feature will be the handle. We'll make an extruded surface with a draft along a defined direction. Select the sketch named 'Handle' in the FeatureManager and click in the "**Extruded Surface**" icon, or the menu "**Insert, Surface, Extrude**."

307

The end condition for the extrusion will be up to the revolved surface. Select the "**Up to Surface**" end condition and select the revolved surface. By default, extrusions are made normal to the sketch plane, but in this case we'll use a little used option to make the extrusion along a defined direction. That direction will be defined by the sketch called *'Handle Direction'*. Right under the end condition selection list is the "**Direction of Extrusion**" selection box. Click inside to activate it and select the sketch line shown.

 The "**Direction of Extrusion**" option is also available for extruded boss and cuts in solid bodies.

403. – Another option we'll use in the extrusion is the option to add a draft as we extrude. Adding a draft makes the body (surface or solid) grow out or shrink in with a defined angle. To turn the draft option on, click in the "**Draft On/Off**" icon; the angle box will be activated as well as the "**Draft outward**" checkbox. For our example, enter a **3 degrees** angle and check the "**Draft outward**" checkbox.

308

Surfacing and Mold Tools

Now we have three surface bodies. You can hide the *Handle Direction* sketch; we will not need it anymore.

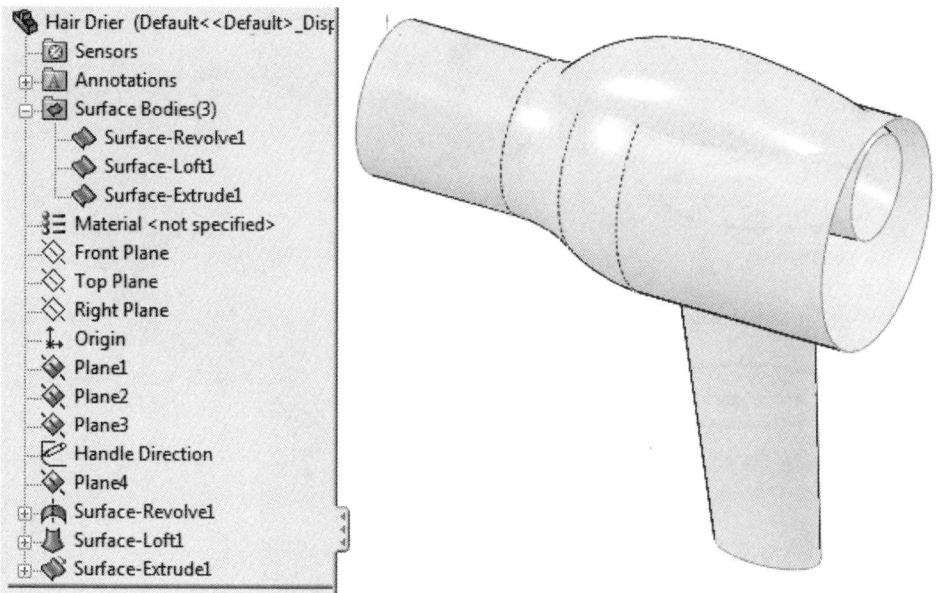

404. – The next step is to trim the surfaces to make them match exactly. By trimming the surfaces, we are looking to make all surfaces touch each other at the edges only, with the ultimate goal to form a single, closed, continuous surface that will be converted into a solid body. There are several ways to trim surfaces. We can use other surfaces, planes, or a sketch as a trimming tool. First, trim the revolved surface with the handle.

Select the "**Trim Surface**" icon from the CommandManager, or the menu "**Insert, Surface, Trim**." Under "**Trim Type**" select "**Standard**"; this means that we'll use a trim tool (Sketch, Plane or Surface) to cut *other* surfaces; add the handle surface under the "**Trim tool**" selection box.

405. – Select the "**Keep selections**" option and in the "**pieces to keep**" selection box, pick the revolved surface anywhere but the area where it meets the handle surface, as this is the part we want to keep after trimming.

Alternatively, if we use the "**Remove selections**" option, we have to select the elliptical surface inside to remove it. Use either approach and click OK to complete.

Trimming surfaces using this approach only cuts one surface. In the next step we'll see how to mutually trim two surfaces.

Surfacing and Mold Tools

 When we use a sketch as a trim tool, the surface is trimmed by projecting the sketch normal to its plane onto the surface. To understand it better, think of the sketch being extruded as a surface with the "Through All" end condition in both directions first, and then used as a trimming surface.

This is the result of trimming the first surface, and we still have three surface bodies.

406. – For the next feature, we'll trim two surfaces at the same time. This means that we'll select two (or more) surfaces, and they will be cut at their intersection(s); then we can select which bodies we want to keep or delete. Select the "**Trim Surface**" command, and use the option "**Mutual Trim**." In the "**Surfaces**" selection box, pick the revolved and lofted surfaces. With the "**Keep selections**" option chosen, and them in the "Keep selections" box select the outside faces for both. They will change color when selected. Click OK to finish.

311

When we trim two surfaces using the "**Mutual Trim**" option, the resulting surfaces are merged into a single surface.

Our resulting model now looks like this:

 If we had selected the "**Remove Selections**" option, we would have selected the inside faces instead.

407. – Since we need to make a fully closed volume before we can convert it into a solid, we'll need to close the openings with surfaces. We have a couple of options to close them. For the opening at the bottom of the handle, we'll make a flat surface. Select the "**Planar Surface**" command from the Command Manager or the menu "**Insert, Surface, Planar**."

To make a planar surface, we can select a set of closed edges or a closed sketch. Turn the model over and select the edge at the bottom of the handle and click OK to finish.

312

Surfacing and Mold Tools

We added a new surface, and now have three surface bodies again.

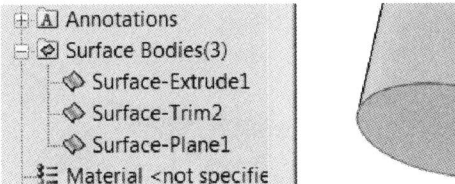

Edges that are connected to other surfaces are colored black (default setting) and open surface edges that are not 'connected' to other surface bodies are a different color. Surface bodies may have touching edges, but are not necessarily connected, think of it as two pieces of fabric aligned, but not stitched together.

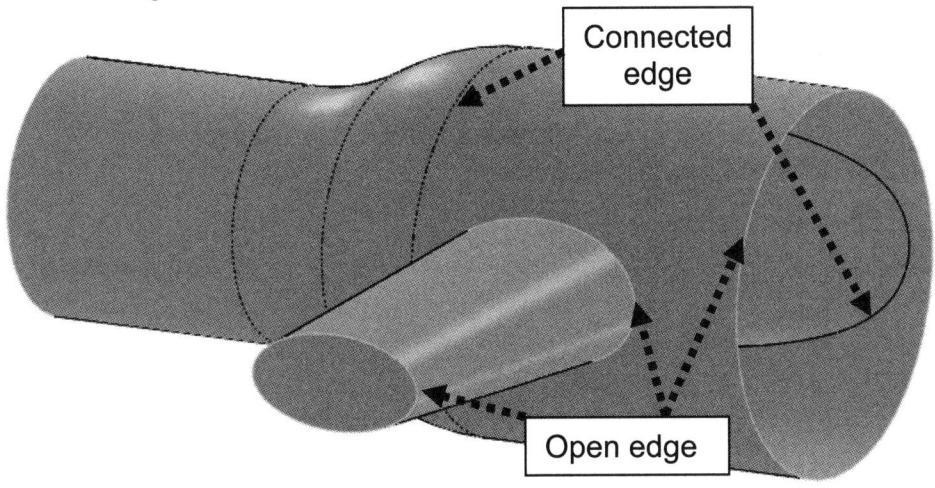

408. – For the front of the hair drier we'll use a different command. Select the "**Filled Surface**" command from the Command-Manager or the menu "**Insert, Surface, Fill**." This command is more flexible than the planar surface; it allows us to use planar or non-planar sketches, edges or curves, make the new surface tangent to adjacent faces, or constrain the surface to one or more curves giving us more control over the resulting surface. For the first part of this command we'll add the open edge in front of the hair drier to the "**Patch Boundary**" selection box. In the "**Curvature Control**" selection list pick "**Contact**." Using this option, the new surface is made to only touch the selected edges. Click OK to complete this surface.

313

The Fill Surface command has an option to merge the resulting surface to other surfaces; we'll use the default setting, unchecked.

This is our fourth surface in the model.

409. – The only place left to close in our model is the back of the hair drier. Before we close it, we need to add two sketches that will be used in a "**Filled Surface**" command. Select the Front plane and add the following sketch. Use a **3 Point Arc** or a **Centerpoint Arc**. Be sure to add "Pierce" relations between the endpoints of the arc and the surface's edge. Exit the sketch when done.

Surfacing and Mold Tools

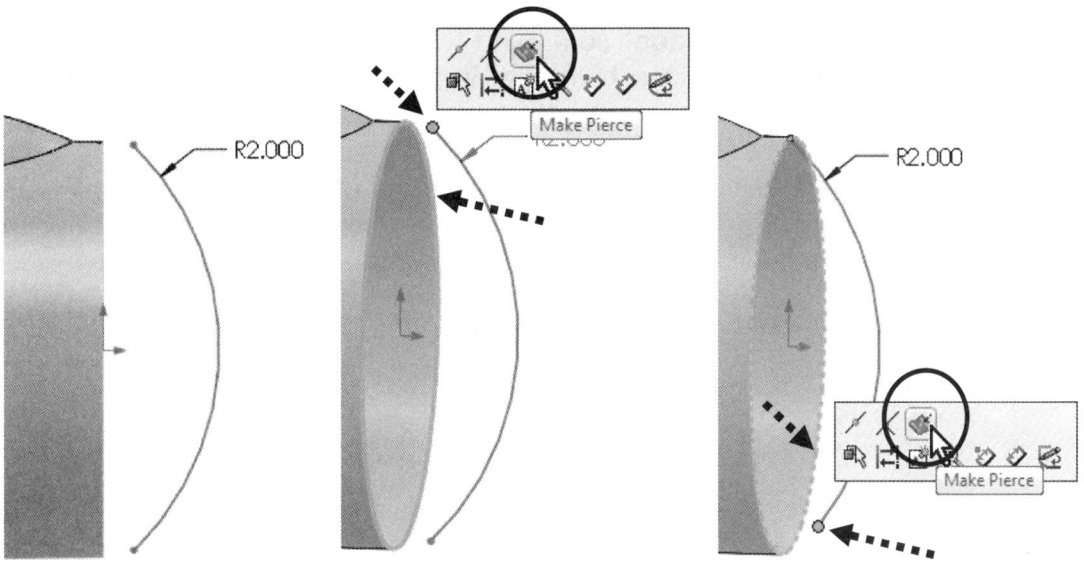

410. – Add a new sketch in the Top plane with a similar arc and add "Pierce" relations to the surface edge on both sides as we just did.

To make the arc coincident to the previous sketch, add a "**Sketch Point**" to its midpoint, and then a "**Pierce**" relation between the point and the previous sketch. Exit the sketch when done.

411. – Select the "**Filled Surface**" command from the Surfaces toolbar. Select the open edge in the back of the hair drier in the "**Patch Boundary**" selection box, and in the "**Constraint Curves**" selection box both of the sketches we just made. The surface will conform to the curves and match exactly with the edge. Since we are adding constraint curves, changing the curvature control will make no difference in this case. Be sure to check the option "**Merge result**" at the bottom; this way the new surface will be merged with the revolved surface.

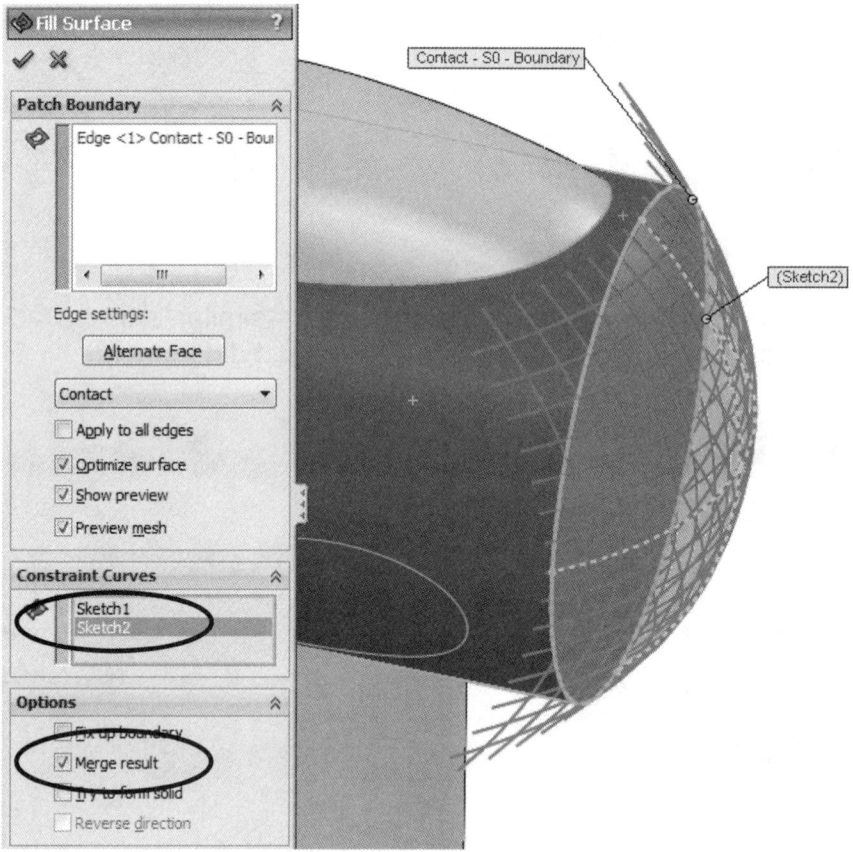

It would now appear that we have a closed surface to convert into a solid, but we need to do one more step before, and that is to merge all four surface bodies into a single surface using the "**Knit Surface**" command. Note the open edges color.

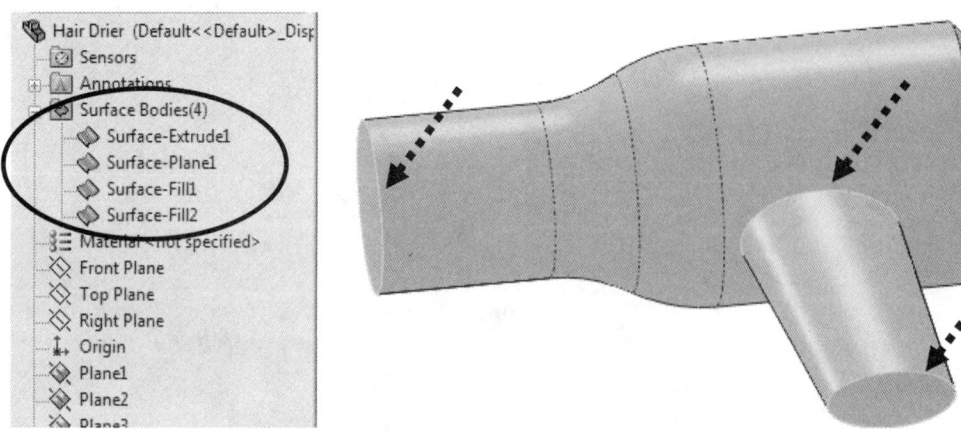

Surfacing and Mold Tools

There are basically two ways to convert the surfaces to solid models:
a) We can thicken an open or closed surface, giving the surface a specified thickness.
b) We can convert a surface into a solid if the surface body is a single body defining a closed volume.

 When we refer to a *closed surface*, we are talking about a *water tight* surface. In other words, it has to be a completely enclosed volume, like a balloon.

412. – We'll show both ways to form a solid. The first option will be to thicken a surface. To merge the necessary surfaces into a single surface body, select the "**Knit Surface**" command in the Surfaces toolbar, or the menu "**Insert, Surfaces, Knit.**"

For our hair drier we will ultimately leave the front open, so we'll knit the other three surfaces into one. In the graphics area, select the handle, the flat surface at the bottom of the handle, and the second surface fill. In this case, the "**Merge entities**" option will not make any difference. Click OK to finish.

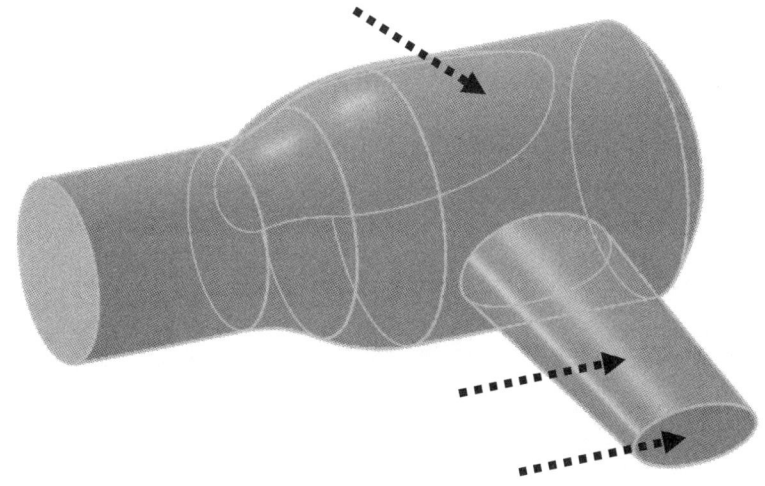

317

Now our model has two surface bodies.

Things to keep in mind when knitting surfaces:

- Surfaces must be touching at the edges.
- Surfaces must not overlap.
- Surfaces knitted will be absorbed into a new surface body.
- If the surfaces selected form a closed volume, they can be turned into a solid body that will absorb the surface bodies.

413. – Before thickening the surface, we want to add fillets to our hair drier. We can add fillets to a surface the same way we do to a solid body. Select the "**Fillet**" command and add a 0.25 inch fillet to the back of the drier and a 0.125 inch fillet at the bottom of the handle.

Surfacing and Mold Tools

414. – For the top of the drier, add a 1 inch fillet. Make sure the "**Tangent propagation**" option is turned on.

415. – For the last fillet, if we use a regular fillet with constant radius, we get a fillet that covers a large surface. Select the "**Fillet**" command again, but in this case select "**Face Fillet**" in the "**Fillet Type**" option and pick the two faces indicated, one in each selection box. We may need to click on the "**Reverse Face Normal**" option to make the arrows in the faces point to each other in order for the Fillet command to work. Make the fillet 1″ radius.

In the "**Fillet Options**" section select the "**Constant width**" option; notice the difference in the fillet's preview. The option "Trim and attach" must be selected to correctly trim and merge the surfaces and the newly created fillet. Click OK to finish.

416. – Now we are ready to convert the knitted surface body into a solid. Hide the "**Surface-Fill1**" body to see the effect of thickening the surface better. Select it in the graphics area or the FeatureManager and click in the "**Hide**" icon.

417. – The first method to make a solid is to thicken a surface. Select the "**Thicken**" command in the Surfaces toolbar, or the menu "**Insert, Boss/Base, Thicken**." In "**Surfaces to Thicken**," select the surface '*Fillet4*'. When we thicken a surface we can add material to one side, the other, or 'mid plane' (in both directions). For our example, we'll make the surface 0.1" thick inside to keep our model dimensions as outside dimensions. Notice the preview when we change the side to thicken. Click OK to finish.

Surfacing and Mold Tools

Now we have a solid body.

418. – To show the second method to convert surfaces to solids, delete the '**Thicken1**' feature, and show the surface that we had hidden before.

419. – With the surface visible, select the "**Knit Surfaces**" command, and select both surfaces. When the surfaces knitted form a closed volume, the option "**Try to form a solid**" is enabled. Check this option and click OK to finish. Now we don't have any surface bodies and our model is a solid body.

From this point on we can treat our model as a regular solid body; we don't have any surface bodies left and only one solid body. Make a 0.1″ thick Shell feature removing the front face of the hair drier to complete the model.

Choosing an option to convert surfaces to solid depends on many different factors; sometimes one method fails and we have to use a different approach. A common reason for errors is when a face overlaps with another after thickening. If we change the fillet at the bottom of the handle to a 0.5" radius, the "Thicken" command will fail. In this case we would add the fillets *after* thickening the surfaces.

Master Model

When making a design that is made of multiple parts that need to maintain an overall shape when assembled, like our hair drier, we use a technique called *Master Model*, where we start with a part that has the general shape and size of the complete assembly, and it's later split into individual components. The master model has all the features that are common to all the components (usually the outside shape), then it's split and the bodies are saved to individual parts. And from this point on each part is finished with the features unique to each one.

The first body we are going to split from the hair drier's master model will become the back cover. To split a solid into multiple bodies we can use a plane, a surface that crosses the entire model or an open or closed sketch.

420. – Add a sketch in the Front plane and draw a line 0.125" to the left of the origin as shown. When using an open sketch to split a model, the sketch *must* cross the model, and the split will be made by projecting the sketch normal to the sketch plane.

421. – While editing the sketch select the **"Split"** command from the menu **"Insert, Features, Split"**. The current sketch will be added to the **"Trim Tools"** selection box. Click in the **"Cut Part"** button to divide the body.

422. – After cutting the part we have two bodies listed in the "**Resulting Bodies**" list. With this split operation we'll make the back cover. Select its body and double click in <None> to give the new file a name. Save this body as *Hair Drier Cover*.

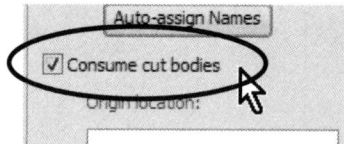

Before finishing the "**Split**" command, turn on the "**Consume cut bodies**" option. By doing this the body we are saving will be deleted from the master file. Click OK to finish.

A "Split" feature is added to the FeatureManager, the master model is now cut, and the cut body is added to a new part file with a single feature.

Surfacing and Mold Tools

423. – The next split feature will cut the remaining body in two parts using the Front plane of the part. Select the "**Split**" command again; select the Front plane in the "**Trim Tools**" selection box and cut the part. Save both bodies and name them *Hair Drier Left* and *Hair Drier Right*. Check the "**Consume cut bodies**" option and click OK to finish.

 The "Split" command can use multiple surfaces, planes or sketches at the same time to cut a part.

After completing the second "Split" command, there are no more bodies in our master part and the two bodies have been added to new files. It is not necessary to use the "Consume bodies" option; the split bodies can remain in the master part, just be aware that features added *after* the bodies are split and saved will not propagate to the split bodies' parts. We used this option to show the reader its effect. Likewise, we don't have to save to an external part; the split bodies can remain in the master.

325

From this point on we can add more features to each part and then add them to an assembly to finish our design.

Surfacing and Mold Tools

 When *re-assembling* components from a split part, we can add them to the assembly's origin and they will be fixed in the same place they were in the part before they were split.

CHALLENGE EXERCISE:

Using the hair drier files, add the following features. Select the best place to add them: in the master file before splitting the part *or* in the split bodies (after saving them to a part). Remember, to add features before the split feature we have to roll back the FeatureManager.

Hint: Features present in more than one part can be added in the master file; features unique to each part can be added in the master file or the split part.

- Add vents to the back cover and sides (this is your chance to be creative ☺).
- Add a lip and cut extrusion to assemble the left and right sides, and between both halves and the back cover.

- Add cutouts for a switch and power cord.

For the next example, we'll design a bucket using surfaces and, at the end, convert to a solid model. The process followed here to build the bucket is not the most efficient way to build a bucket, but it will show the reader how to use several surfacing tools using a simple model.

424. – Make a new part and add the following sketch in the Front plane. Don't forget the vertical centerline at the origin.

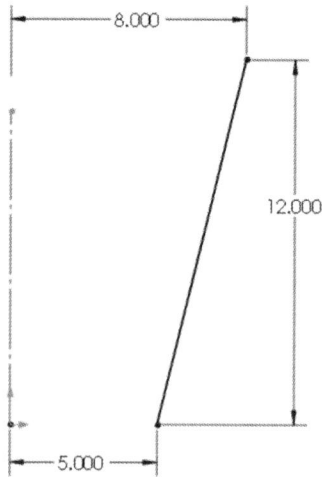

425. – Select the "**Revolved Surface**" command from the Surfaces toolbar, or from the menu "**Insert, Surface, Revolved**." Make the revolved surface 360 degrees. The surface will be revolved about the centerline.

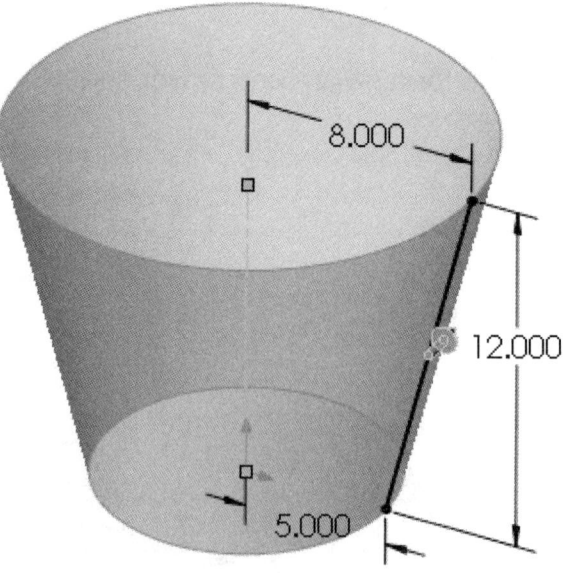

328

Surfacing and Mold Tools

426. – Add the following sketch in the Front plane and make a second revolved surface. The top of the line is horizontal with the top edge of the first surface.

427. – After creating both surfaces we have to trim them. Select the "**Trim Surface**" command from the Surfaces toolbar, or the menu "**Insert, Surface, Trim.**" In this step we'll use the "**Mutual**" trim option; this means that both surfaces will work as a trim surface. In the "**Surfaces**" selection box, pick both surfaces. Activate the "**Keep selections**" option and select the main body of the bucket and the outside face of the second surface. Notice how the surfaces change color to preview the part of the surface that is kept. Click OK to finish.

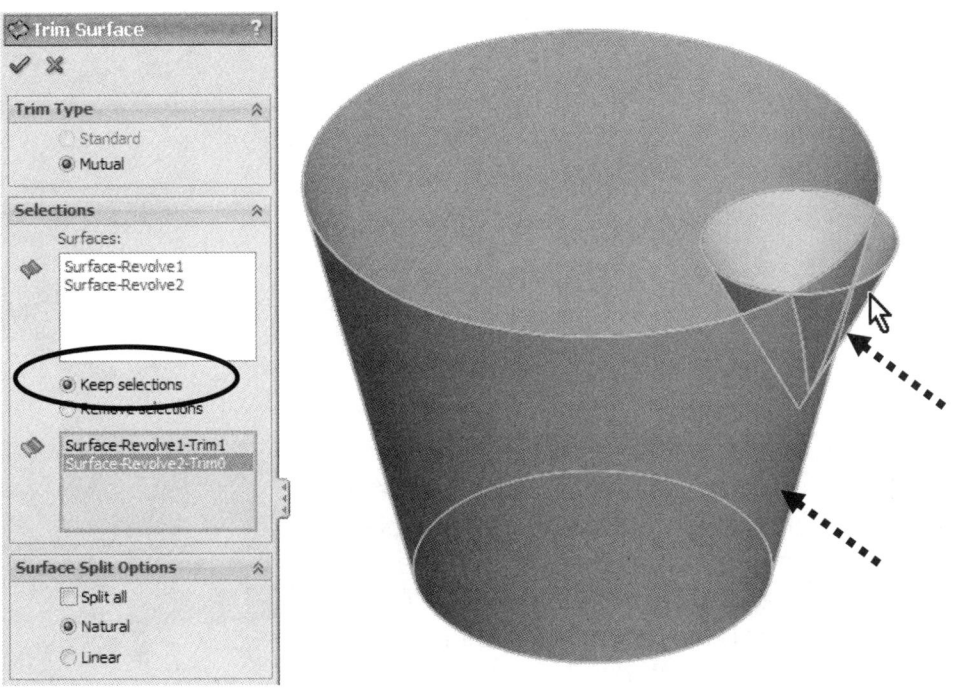

329

The resulting trimmed surfaces are merged into a single surface body. By default open surfaces have a light blue color on the open edges. Note in our surface the upper and lower open edges of the surface are blue and the edge where we the trimmed surfaces meet is black.

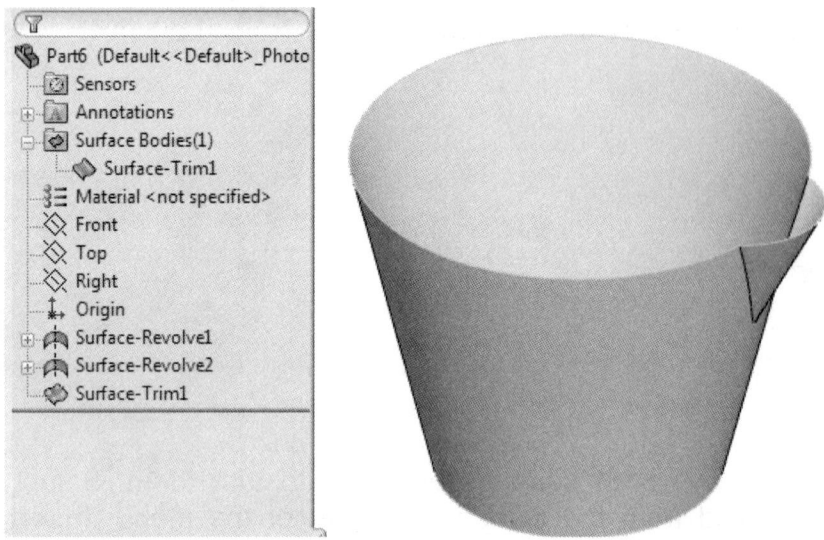

428. – Now we'll fillet the edge where both surfaces meet. Select the "**Fillet**" command, and add a 1″ radius fillet.

429. – We need to add a lip to the top of the bucket, but instead of creating a plane at the top of the bucket and making a sketch for the planar surface, we'll make a planar surface with the open edge, extend it and trim it. Select the "**Planar Surface**" icon from the Surfaces toolbar or the menu "**Insert, Surface, Planar**."

330

Surfacing and Mold Tools

430. – To make a planar surface, we need to select a sketch that defines a closed area, or a closed loop of edges. To select the top edges (which are all tangent to each other), right mouse click on one edge and select the option "**Select Tangency.**" This option automatically selects all tangent edges, which in our case are all the edges needed. The preview of the flat surface will be automatically shown covering the bucket. Click OK to complete it.

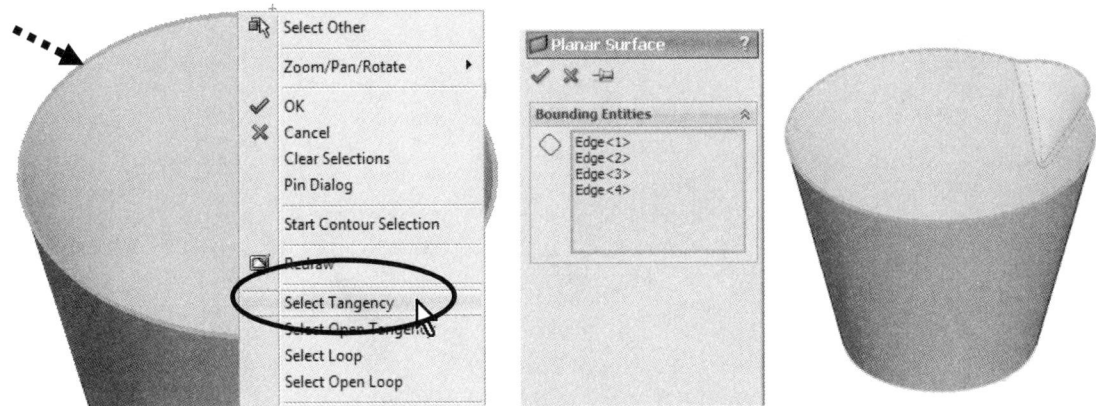

431. – The planar surface we just made will be an intermediate step. What we'll do now is make this surface bigger to build the lip at the top of the bucket, and then we'll fillet and trim the surfaces at the same time. Select the command "**Extend Surface**" from the "Surfaces" toolbar, or the menu "**Insert, Surface, Extend.**" The "**Extend Surface**" command helps us to make a surface bigger, extending its edges by a given distance, up to a point or another surface. In case of a curved surface, we can extend its edges continuing the same surface, or linearly. Select the planar surface we just made and enter a distance of 0.875". Since this is a flat surface, using the "Same surface" or "Linear" option makes no difference. Make sure the preview is going out and click OK to complete the surface.

331

432. – Click in the "**Fillet**" command and select the "**Face fillet**" type. Enter a 0.375″ radius and select the planar face in the "**Face set 1**" and the bucket's body in the "**Face set 2**" selection boxes. If a fillet preview is not visible, click on the "**Reverse Face Normal**" buttons next to the selection boxes to make both arrows point towards each other. Under "Fillet Options" make sure the "**Trim and attach**" option is selected; this option will trim the unused surfaces and knit the fillet with the other surfaces automatically. Click OK to complete.

After completing the fillet, the inside face is trimmed, the fillet is blended along the perimeter of the bucket, and all surfaces are merged into a single body.

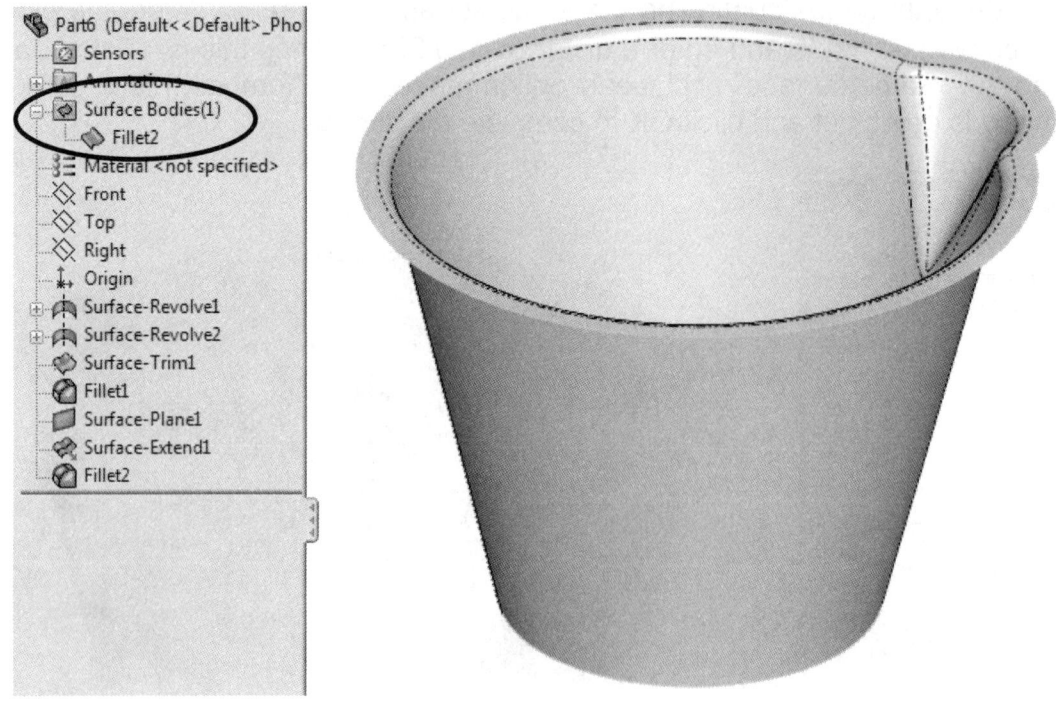

433. – Add a new planar surface at the bottom of the bucket using the "**Planar Surface**" command and selecting the round edge. We'll have two surface bodies after this command.

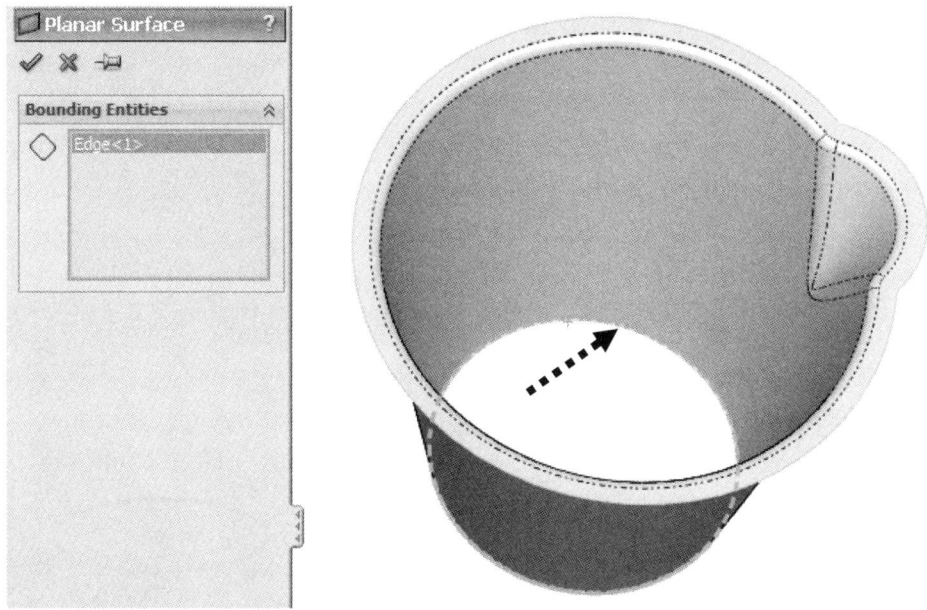

434. – Add a 0.625" face fillet between the bucket and the bottom surface we just made using the same settings we used for the fillet at the top to trim and merge the surfaces. Note the arrows are pointing towards each other.

Now the bucket's surface is complete.

435. – To convert the surface to a solid, select the "**Thicken**" command from the Surfaces toolbar, or the menu "**Insert, Boss/Base, Thicken**."

Make the surface 0.125″ thick, going *inside* the bucket; click OK to finish.

 Now our part is a single solid body (no "Solid Bodies" or "Surface Bodies" folder). The surface body was absorbed by the "**Thicken**" command.

Surfacing and Mold Tools

436. – To complete the bucket's design, we'll add a couple of attachment points for a handle. To make the first extrusion we'll use the "**Extrude From**" option. Switch to a Front view and make the following sketch in the Front plane. Notice the sketch is in the middle of the part.

437. – Select the "**Extruded Boss**" command. In the "**From**" selection box, pick "**Offset**" and type **8.25"**. In the "**Direction 1**" option box, reverse the direction if needed to point towards the bucket and select "**Up To Next**". Clear the "**Merge result**" checkbox, we'll model this feature as a multi body part. Click OK to finish.

Now we have two solid bodies listed under the "Solid Bodies" folder in the FeatureManager.

335

438. – Add a new sketch in the front face of the boss we just made with a concentric circle 0.625" in diameter. Make an Extruded Cut with a "**Through All**" option. Before finishing the cut extrude, under the "**Feature Scope**" options, clear the "**Auto-select**" checkbox and select the body made in the previous step, as we only want to affect this solid body with the cut and not the entire bucket. We could have added the hole in the extrusion, but chose to show how to do it this way instead to expand on multi body operations. Click OK to finish.

439. – In the next step we'll make a mirror of this body to have two attachment points for the bucket's handle. Select the "**Mirror**" command, and using the Front plane as the mirror plane, select the "**Cut-Extrude1**" body to be mirrored in the "**Bodies to Mirror**" selection box. Do not merge the bodies at this time; we'll do that in the next step. Click OK to finish. Notice that selecting the "Bodies to Mirror" selection box automatically hides the features and faces to mirror boxes.

Surfacing and Mold Tools

440. – At this point we have 3 solid bodies, and now we need to combine them into a single one. Select the menu "**Insert, Features, Combine**" or select all three bodies in the "Solid Bodies" folder and right mouse click to select the "**Combine**" option.

441. – Select "**Add**" under the "**Operation Type**" options and click OK to complete. This will merge all three bodies into one.

442. – The last step is to add a 0.25" fillet to the bosses. We can select the face of the bucket or the two edges.

337

443. – Save the part as *Bucket* and close it; we'll use it later to make a mold. Our finished part looks like this:

More about Surfaces

When modeling more complex shapes, we may have to resort to surfaces in order to create auxiliary geometry as support for our models in the form of trim surfaces, start or end conditions for extrusions and cuts, to generate guide curves, etc. In the next model, we'll use a couple of surfaces to generate a curve that will be used for a sweep. Look at the following image of a sword's grip.

At first glance it seems to be a simple enough model; but when we think about it, the groove in the grip is going in a spiral around an uneven surface, which makes for an interesting challenge and which we are going to show in the next few steps.

444. – The first thing we are going to do is to define the profile of the grip. Start a new part and make the following sketch in the Front plane. The vertical and horizontal lines are centerlines (construction geometry), and the top is an arc.

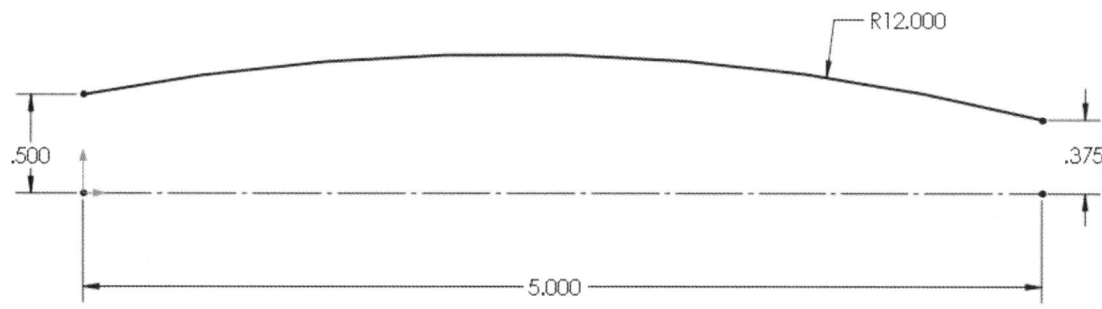

445. – Select the "**Revolved Surface**" command and make a 360 deg. revolved surface.

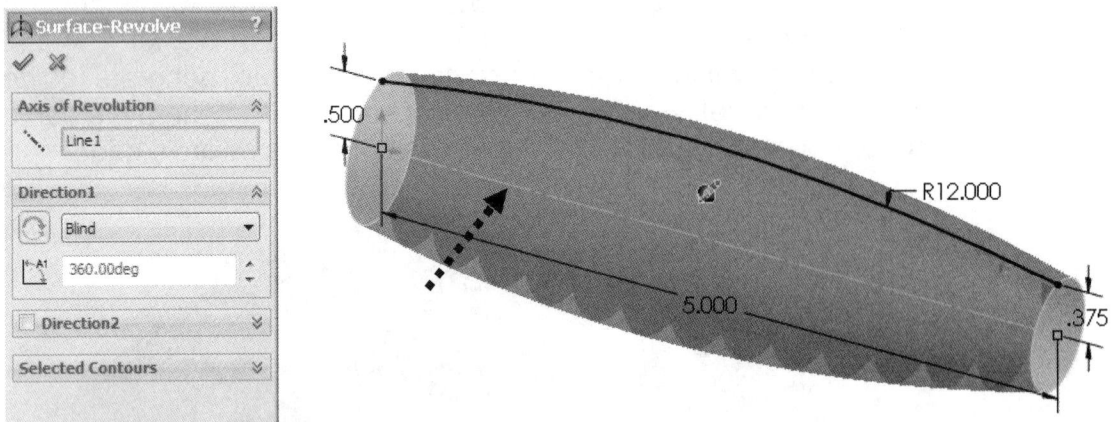

446. – For the next step, we'll make a swept surface that will twist along a path. The purpose of this surface will be to create an intersection with the revolved surface; we'll trim the surface and the resulting edge will be the path for a sweep cut. Make the following new sketch in the Front plane and exit the sketch when done. It's a single horizontal line; this will be our path. Make the sketch longer than the part to make sure the surfaces intersect along the full length of the grip.

447. – Make a second sketch in the Front plane; this time it will be a vertical line as shown. Be sure to make this line higher than the revolved surface. Exit the sketch when done.

448. – Select the "**Swept Surface**" command from the Surfaces toolbar or the menu "**Insert, Surface, Sweep**." Select the vertical line sketch as the Profile, and the horizontal line sketch as the Path. Under the "**Surface Sweep**" options select "**Twist Along Path**" under the "Orientation/Twist" selection list, and in the "Define by:" selection list pick "**Turns**"; enter a value of **4**. The Profile sketch will twist along the length of the Path sketch 4 turns. Click OK to finish.

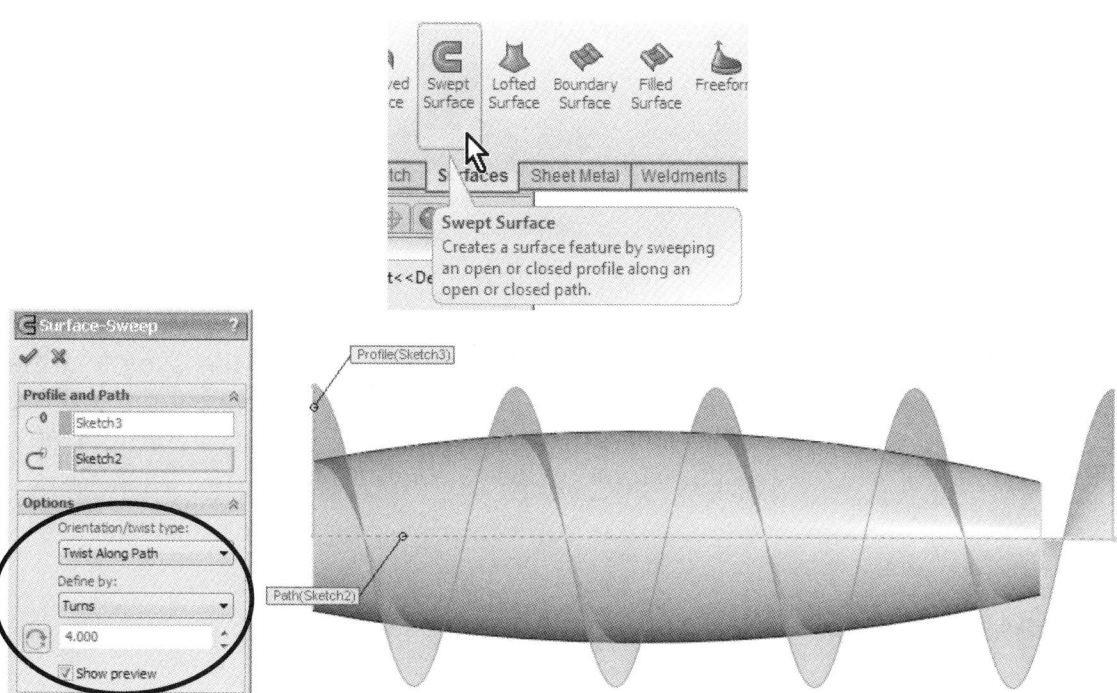

449. – What we are interested in is the curve along the intersection of both surfaces, so we'll trim the swept surface with the revolved surface, and use the edge as a path for a swept cut. Select the "**Trim Surface**" command; using the "Standard" trim type, select the revolved surface in the "**Trim tool**" selection box, activate the "Keep selections" option, and select the outside of the swept surface to keep it. Click OK to finish.

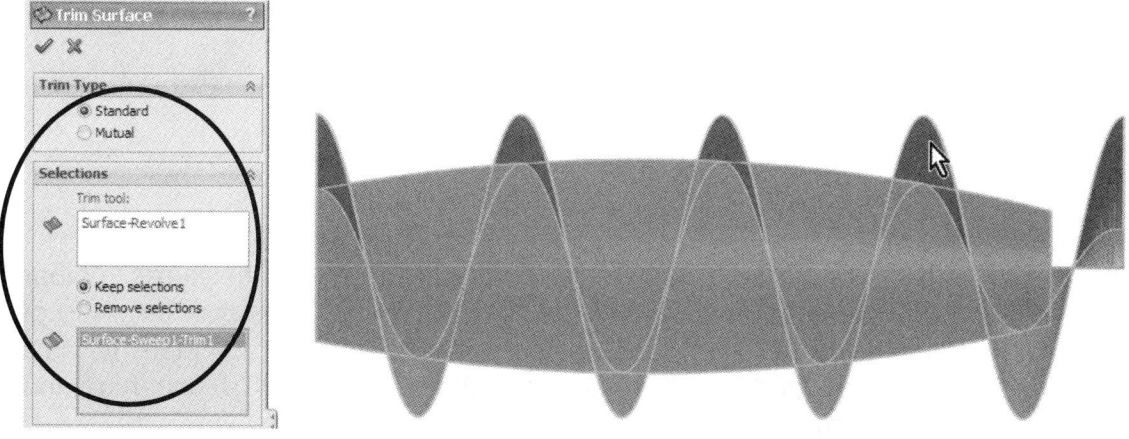

341

Select the revolved surface in the graphics area (or the FeatureManager's "Surface Bodies" folder) and hide it.

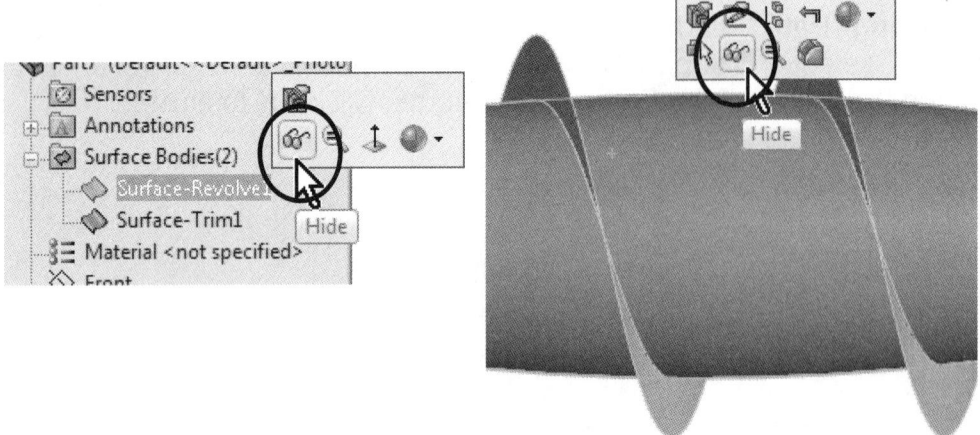

450. – Now we need to make a solid body for the grip. Show the sketch in the "Surface-Revolve1" and start a new sketch in the Front plane. Select the top line in the revolved surface sketch, use "**Convert Entities**" to project it into our new sketch and complete the sketch to form a closed contour.

451. – Select the "**Revolved Boss/Base**" command from the Features toolbar (this will be a solid feature), and select the horizontal line to use as the Axis of Revolution to make the revolved feature about it. Click OK to complete it. Now we have a solid body and two surface bodies in our part. We can hide the revolved surface sketch when done.

342

Surfacing and Mold Tools

452. – After completing the solid we need to make the profile for a Sweep Cut. Add a new sketch in the Front plane, close to the left of the swept surface, and draw it as shown. Draw an equilateral triangle (hint: make all three lines equal) and add the two construction lines as indicated, then add a "Pierce" relation between the endpoint of the horizontal construction line and the swept surface edge. Exit the sketch when done.

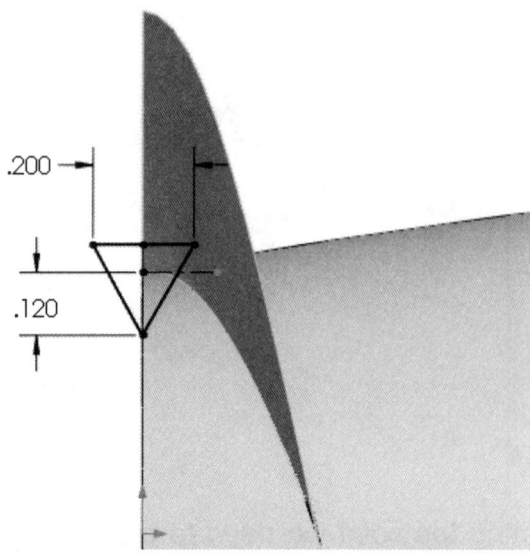

453. – Select the "**Swept Cut**" command from the Features toolbar or the menu "**Insert, Cut, Sweep**," and select the triangular sketch for the Profile and the inside edge of the trimmed surface for the Path. In the "**Options**" box, select "**Follow Path**" in "Orientation/Twist type:" and "**All Faces**" in "Path alignment type:." Turn off the "**Align with end faces**" option and click OK to finish.

Surfacing and Mold Tools

454. – Hide the trimmed surface to view the resulting cut in the solid body.

455. – Add a 0.035" radius fillet at the bottom of the swept cut

456. – Add a 0.075" radius fillet to the two outer edges of the swept cut.

457. – Add a guard and pummel to the grip using a revolved boss. Add a new sketch in the Front plane and make a revolved boss. The Revolved Boss is overlapping the ends of the spiral cut to cover the ends.

Save the file as *Sword Grip* and close it.

CHALLENGE EXERCISE:
Add a hand guard and a blade to the sword grip to finish your sword. Here are just a few suggestions:

Review and Questions:

a) What is the thickness of a surface?

b) When two surfaces intersect each other, they merge. True or False.

c) The option to make an extrusion along a specified direction is available **only** when extruding a surface. True or False.

d) Name two types of elements that can be used to trim a surface.

e) When we trim two surfaces using the "Mutual Trim" option, how many surface bodies do we end up with?

f) Name two types of geometry that can be used to create a planar surface.

g) Which of the following is a requirement to knit two or more surfaces:
   A - Surfaces must be touching at the edges.
   B - Surfaces must be open.
   C - Surfaces must be closed.

h) When thickening a surface, the option "Try to form a solid" can be used if:
   A - The surface is open.
   B - The surface is closed.
   C - The surface is a loft.

i) Name two elements that can be used to split a part into multiple bodies.

Answers:
a - Zero, it has no thickness.
b - False. When two surfaces intersect they need to be trimmed and knitted to be merged.
c - False. This option is available with any extrusion or cut feature, either solid or surface.
d - Another surface, a Plane or a sketch that will project onto the surface.
e - One, the mutually trimmed surfaces are merged automatically.
f - A closed 2D sketch or a group of closed edges on a plane.
g - A. Surfaces cannot be knitted if they are not touching at the edges.
h - B. When thickening a closed surface the option "Try to form a solid" will be enabled.
i - A Plane, a surface or sketch that extends past the solid body.

Notes:

Mold Tools

After completing a part its common practice to design a mold for it if the part is going to be made by plastic injection or forge. Mold making is a manufacturing specialty where experience plays as big a role as preparation and study, and it's not an easy trade to master.

When designing a mold, a large number of factors must be taken into consideration, including: the shape and size of the part, the material to be used (plastic, resin, metal, etc.), the process, the tooling necessary to make the mold, etc. In other words, it's a complicated process.

The purpose of this chapter is not to teach the mold making trade, as that by itself is enough to fill several books and there would still be much more to learn. The intent is to show the user the tools available in SolidWorks for mold making, understand how to use them and briefly touch on design considerations that can affect manufacturing of a molded part, like draft and parting line selection.

Be aware that a complete mold design includes a large number of components starting with a mold base; from there we have to design cooling lines, runners, gates, add hardware components (springs, nuts, bolts, ejection pins, dowels, O-rings, slides, lifters, etc.). Our focus in this chapter will be limited to showing how to create the core and cavity, side cores and inserts. Many times these are the most difficult tasks; adding the rest of the components and design elements to a complete mold design is just what we were talking about.

In this chapter we'll learn how to make molds for a few of the parts we have previously made and a couple others where we'll learn different techniques. This will give the reader a good idea of what needs to be done and, more importantly, how these techniques can be used in different situations. More complex parts will require additional steps, multi part molds, inserts, sliders and such, but that's precisely where the skill and knowledge of the designer comes into play. We are only showing how to use the most common tools available for that purpose.

Notes:

458. – We'll start by making a simple two part mold for a business card holder. Download the file *Card Holder* from mechanicad.com/download.html and open it.

459. – One of the most critical and important details when making a mold is to know if we can get it out of the mold. The first thing we need to do is to make a **"Draft Analysis."** A draft analysis will tell us if we have the required draft in the 'vertical' faces to eject the part from the mold. By 'vertical' we are referring to the faces parallel to the direction the part will separate from the mold or 'direction of pull'. Picture it this way: when we make a cake or a pie, the mold's vertical walls have an inclination, or **"Draft"** angle, to facilitate releasing the cake from the mold. If the walls were truly vertical, it would be very difficult to get the cake out of the mold in one piece. Even worse would be to have the walls inclined inside; this is a condition known as a negative draft, and the cake would never come out complete without breaking the part or the mold.

Pull   Positive Draft   No Draft   Negative Draft

The required draft to easily separate the part from the mold will vary depending on the part's size, the material to be used, whether the part has texture or not, the process used, etc. What we know for sure is that we <u>always</u> want to have a positive draft and as much as possible. If our part's design forces us to have a negative draft in one or more faces, we have to use a different approach, like a multi part mold, side cores or a combination of both. Later in this lesson we'll cover how to deal with this situation.

460. – To start, make sure the "**Mold Tools**" toolbar is open in the Command-Manager. (Right mouse click in a tab and select "**Mold Tools**" or turn on the **Mold Tools** toolbar.)

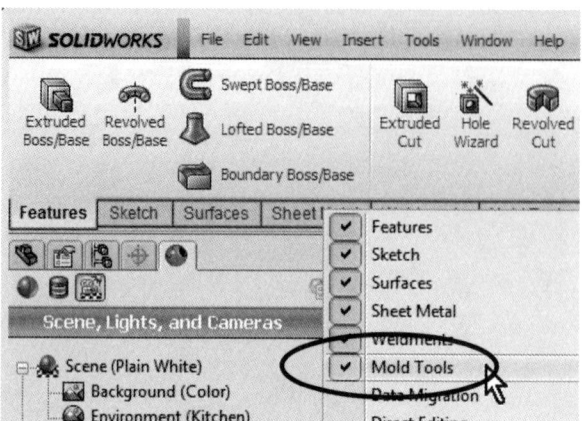

461. – In the Mold Tools toolbar we have some commands available in other toolbars, for example, from Features, Surfaces, Evaluate tools and a few mold specific tools.

 When we design a mold, surfaces are used to create the Core and Cavity. A Core is defined as the 'male' half of the mold, and the Cavity as the 'female' half of the mold. Some molds only have either a core or a cavity.

462. – The first step is to analyze our part to make sure we have at least 3 degrees of draft in the vertical walls. This is an arbitrary value that we'll use for our example. Select the "**Draft Analysis**" command from the Mold Tools toolbar or from the menu "**View, Display, Draft Analysis**."

 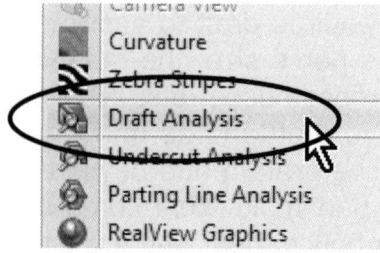

Surfacing and Mold Tools

For the "Draft Analysis" tool we have to select a face or plane <u>perpendicular</u> to the desired direction of pull or an edge along the direction of pull. In our case, we'll use the bottom of the *Card Holder* for our direction of pull (we could also use the Top plane). Enter **3 degrees** in the "Draft Angle" value box. Immediately after selecting the direction of pull direction, the part is color coded to let us know which faces have the required draft and which ones don't. Our part's faces are colored with:

Green	Positive draft, indicated by the arrow direction
Yellow	Faces with less than the required draft angle
Red	Faces with negative draft

 Note that as we move the mouse around the part, the angle to the direction of pull is displayed next to the mouse pointer.

"**Positive**" and "**Negative**" are only telling us what side of the mold a face will be made with, and the direction can be reversed using the "**Reverse Direction**" icon next to the "**Direction of Pull**" selection box. When we have a Core and Cavity mold, "Positive" faces will be on one side, "Negative" faces will be on the other. In our case the green faces will be made in the Cavity, and the red faces in the Core. What we are interested in are the yellow faces that need to be given a draft to properly release from the mold, and these are the ones that have to be modified to be either "Positive" (green) or "Negative" (red). Once we have identified the faces that need to be given a draft, cancel the "Draft Analysis" tool. If we click OK, the draft analysis colors remain visible and we can see which faces need to be modified as we edit the part. The first feature to be modified will be the 'Boss-Extrude1'. Select it in the FeatureManager or the graphics area and edit it.

 To turn off the Draft Analysis view, click on its icon again; it works as a toggle.

463. – In "Direction 1," activate the "**Draft On/Off**" option and enter **3 degrees**. You will see the faces in the preview 'leaning in' the part. Click OK to complete.

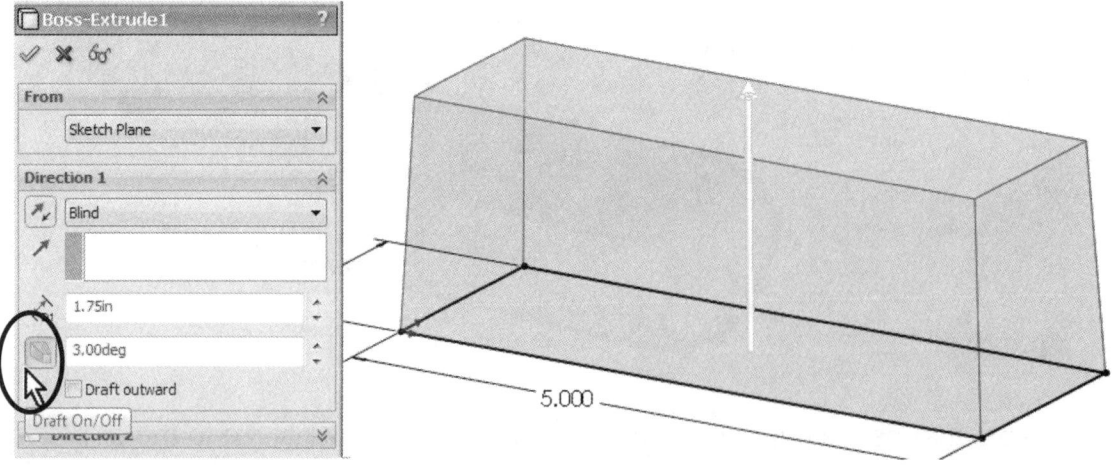

DRAFT ANALYSIS VIEW: After completing this change make a Draft Analysis again; we can see that only a few faces still require draft and are still yellow, some in the top (Cavity side) and some in the bottom (Core side).

464. – Since not all faces can be given a draft at the time a feature is created, we may have to add it as a secondary operation. To add a draft to the remaining faces that need it, we'll use the "**Draft**" command. Faces to be drafted must not be connected to a fillet or the draft will fail. Analyzing our model, we can see that we have a few operations, then fillets and a shell at the end to make the part hollow. What we need to do is to 'rollback' the model just before the 'Fillet2' feature to be able to add the

draft. Since the part is shelled at the end, fixing the faces in the top (Cavity side) will also take care of the faces in the bottom (Core side). Select the 'Fillet2' feature; from the pop-up menu select "Rollback." By doing this we go *'back in time'* in the FeatureManager, to right before the fillets and the shell are created. By doing this, we are able to add a new feature at this position in the Feature-Manager and when we are finished we can "Roll Forward" to finish building the part, essentially un-suppressing the remaining features. Notice the Rollback bar is now located just below the 'Cut-Extrude2' feature and the remaining features are grayed out below it ('Suppressed').

465. – Select the "**Draft**" command from the Command Manager or the menu "**Insert, Features, Draft**." The "**Draft**" command is available in the Features or Mold Tools toolbars. (To make selection easier, the "Draft Analysis" view is off.)

The faces we need to draft are the inside area, where business cards will be placed.

In the "**Draft**" command, select "**Neutral Plane**" in the "Type of Draft" selection box. The "Neutral Plane" is a reference flat face or plane that will be used to measure the draft against. This is also where the faces to be drafted will start to *'incline'*; think of it as a hinge where the face starts to move. Select the bottom face of the cavity as the "Neutral Plane" and enter **3 degrees** in the "Draft Angle" value box. Notice the arrow in the corner of the selected face is pointing up; this is the "**Direction of Pull**" we want.

Surfacing and Mold Tools

The draft's "Direction of Pull" can be reversed using the "Reverse Direction" icon next to the "Neutral Plane" selection box. Reversing the direction of pull would invert the direction of the draft.

466. – Add the four vertical faces in the "Faces to Draft" selection box and click OK to finish. Notice the faces moving after completing the draft. Make sure the draft direction arrow is pointing up.

Top view before the draft…

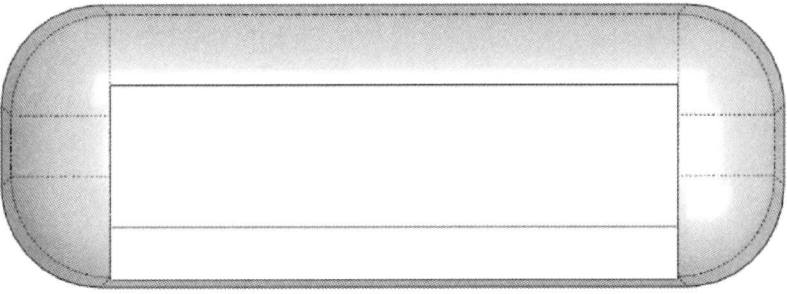

… and after the draft.

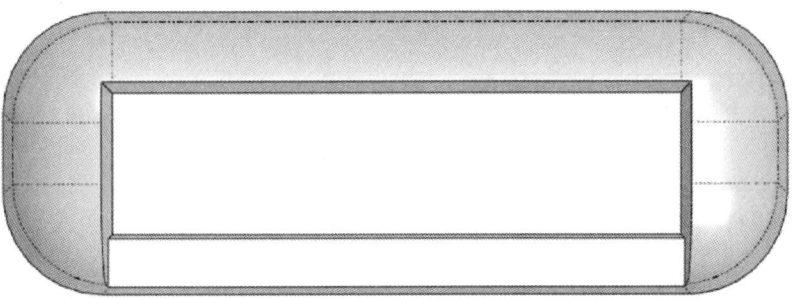

More information about the "Neutral Plane":

The plane we select as the "Neutral Plane" will define how the drafted faces will be inclined. Look at the following images and the neutral plane selections. In all cases the "Direction of Pull" is pointing up.

The difference between the different "Neutral Plane" selections is that the faces to be drafted are projected to the "Neutral Plane" and at this point is where they will be 'hinged' and start to incline.

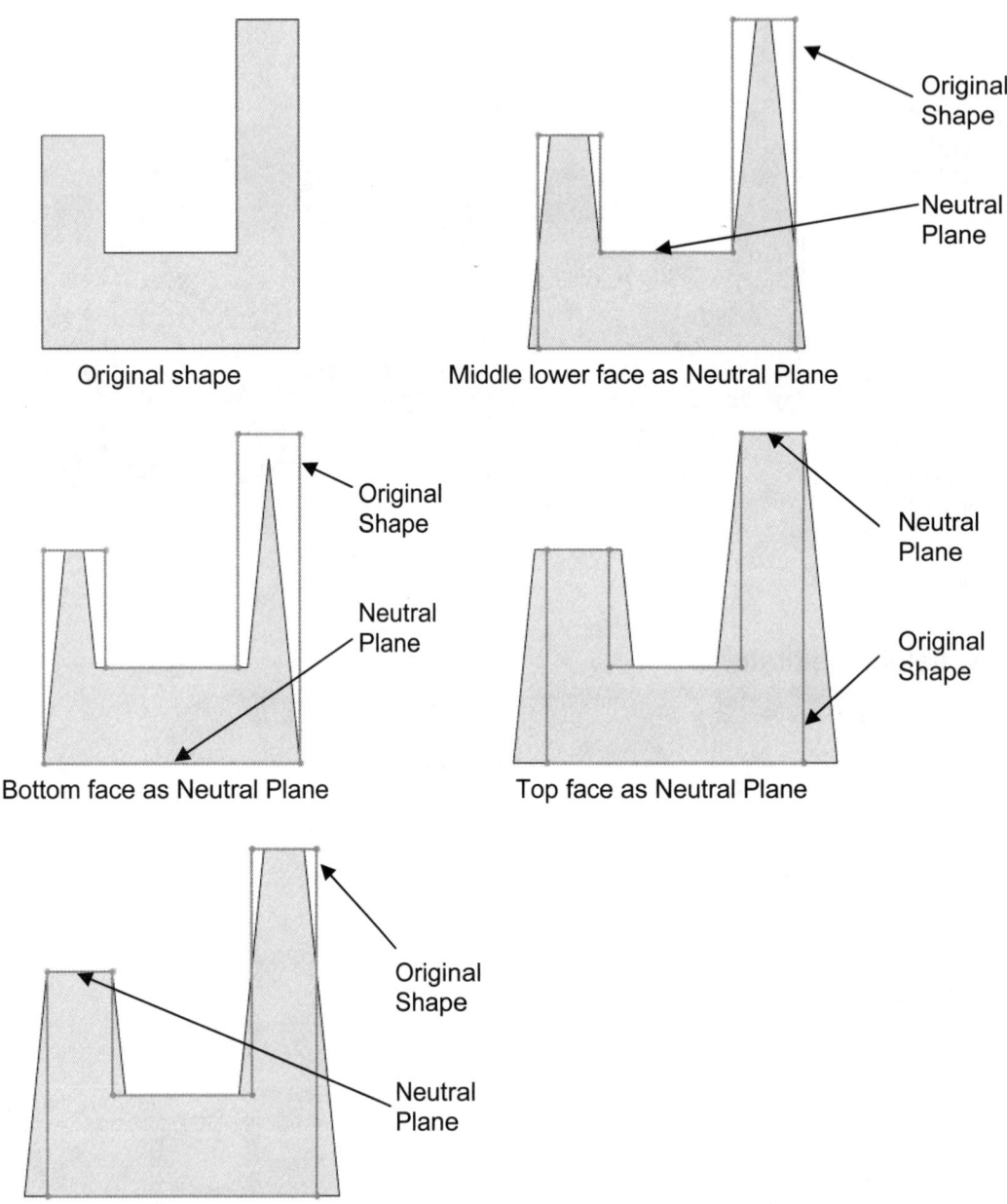

Depending on the desired result, we may have to make multiple "Draft" features with different "Neutral Plane" selections.

Surfacing and Mold Tools

467. – Now back to our part. Select the "Rollback bar" and drag it all the way to the bottom. If you get an error message, close it for now.

468. – By changing the faces of the model we get an error in the 'Fillet2' feature. The error is caused because this fillet cannot find edges that were eliminated after we added the draft feature. To fix this error, edit the fillet and reselect the missing edges.

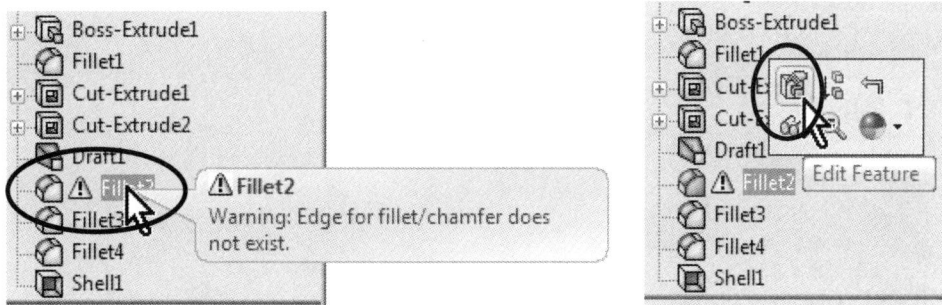

Notice the edges that are missing are highlighted with a faint red dotted line. Erase the missing edges in the selection box and click OK when done to finish.

469. – Use the "**Draft Analysis**" view again and verify all faces have the required three degrees of draft to continue. One side is now completely green ("Positive" draft), the other side is completely red ("Negative" draft) and no yellow faces. Click Cancel to continue (if we press OK we'll keep the "Draft Analysis" view colors).

Surfacing and Mold Tools

470. – When we make a mold for a plastic part, the design part is usually scaled up to compensate for part shrinkage in the mold when the melted plastic solidifies. To scale the part, select the "**Scale**" command in the Mold Tools toolbar or the menu "**Insert, Features, Scale**."

471. – Scale the part about the "**Centroid**" using a scaling factor of **1.03**; this will make the part 3% bigger to compensate for mold shrinkage. Click OK to complete. Notice the part is slightly bigger when complete and a "Scale" feature is added to the FeatureManager.

See the difference? Roll back and forward the 'Scale' feature to see the change. Subtle, but visible.

 Shrinkage values vary depending on the material used and the part's geometry. If a part is elongated, it may shrink differently along one axis than the other. In that case a non "Uniform scaling" option is used.

361

472. – After scaling the part, we are ready to make the mold. The process to make a mold in SolidWorks is:

- Define a Parting Line.
- Create Shut-off Surfaces to close holes in the part (If needed).
- Create a Parting Surface to split the mold.
- Make a Tooling Split to generate the Core and Cavity.
- Make additional side cores and inserts (If needed).

473. – A **parting line** is formed by the edges where the two halves of the mold meet. An easy way to identify the parting line is using the "Draft Analysis." In simple terms, the parting line will be the edges where the faces with "Positive" draft (green) meet the faces with "Negative" draft (red). In simple two piece molds (a single core and cavity) like this, the parting line is usually automatically found and selected. Select the "**Parting Line**" command from the Mold Tools toolbar or the menu "**Insert, Molds, Parting Line**." The command works similar to the "Draft Analysis," with the addition of some options and a selection box. In the Mold Parameters selection options, select a plane or flat face for a "Direction of Pull" (like we did with the "Draft Analysis"). Select the same flat face inside the *Card Holder* or the Top plane (your choice); set the draft angle to **3 degrees** and press the "**Draft Analysis**" button.

Make sure the "**Use for Core/Cavity Split**" option is checked. This option will automatically generate surfaces for Core and Cavity (we'll see them later). In the "Parting Line" selection box the edges that make up the parting line are already selected, and the message "The parting line is complete" is highlighted in green at the top. Click OK to finish.

Surfacing and Mold Tools

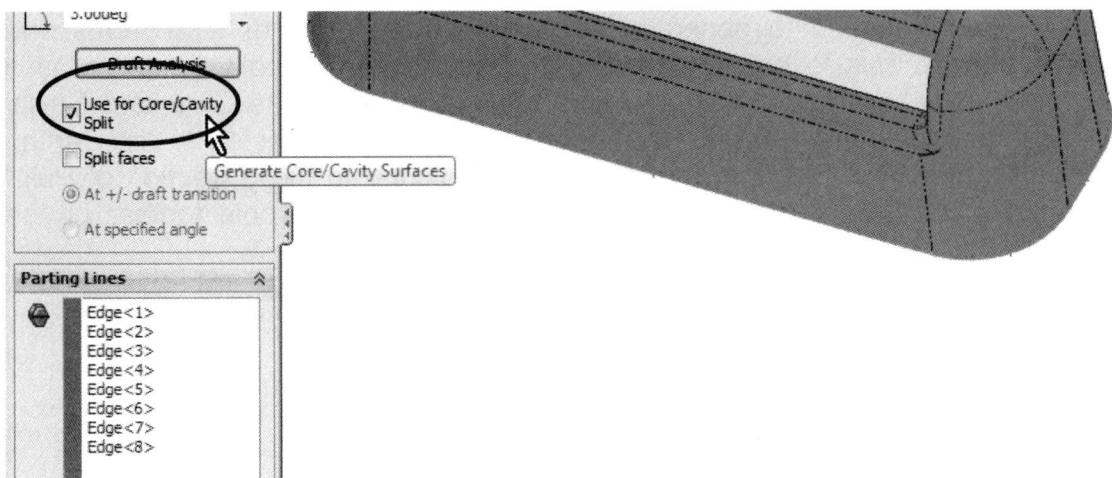

474. – After completing the parting line, a new feature 'Parting Line1' is added to the FeatureManager, and in the "Surface Bodies" folder two sub-folders are created, each with a surface for the Core and Cavity. These surfaces are automatically created with the "Parting Line" command. In this example, the "Cavity Surface Bodies" are the faces with a "Positive" draft (green) and the "Core Surface Bodies" are the faces with a "Negative" draft (red). The parting line remains visible on the screen (it can be hidden just like other features if wanted).

 The next step would be to close any holes in the model with "Shut Off Surfaces," but since our part has no holes, this step is not necessary.

475. – Now we need to generate the parting surface. In general terms, the parting surface has to be generated manually or automatically to serve as a boundary to separate the mold into core and cavity along the Core and Cavity surfaces previously generated. The parting surface is connected to the parting line and generally radiates away from it perpendicular to the "Direction of Pull." Select the "**Parting Surfaces**" command from the Mold Tools toolbar or the menu "**Insert, Molds, Parting Surfaces**." In this part the parting line lies in a flat surface, and this makes it easy to generate. Select the option "**Perpendicular to pull**" – the parting line is automatically selected – and enter a value of **1″** for the "Parting Surface" distance value. The option "Knit all surfaces" automatically merges all the faces generated into one. Click OK to finish.

After generating the parting surface, a new folder is added to the "Surface Bodies" folder called "Parting Surface Bodies" and the new surface is listed here.

Surfacing and Mold Tools

476. – The next step is to generate the tooling split. In this step we make the solid bodies for the core and cavity. To make these bodies, we need to make a sketch perpendicular to the "Direction of Pull" that fits inside the parting surface. The generated core and cavity will be defined by this sketch. We can make the sketch first and then make the tooling split, or start the "Tooling Split" command and make the sketch at that time. In this example, we'll make the sketch first. Select the parting surface and add a new sketch in it. Select the surface and use the "**Convert Entities**" command to project the surface edges and exit the sketch.

477. – Now, select the "**Tooling Split**" command from the Mold Tools toolbar or the menu "**Insert, Molds, Tooling Split**."

 The "Tooling Split" command is unavailable until a parting line feature is added to the model.

478. – When we use the "Tooling Split" command, we are first asked for a plane or flat face to add a sketch, or an existing sketch (if the sketch we just drew is pre-selected, this step is skipped). Select the sketch we just made in the graphics area or in the FeatureManager.

479. – After selecting the sketch, we can enter the "Block Size" for the core and cavity measured from the sketch plane. In the "Core," "Cavity" and "Parting Surface" selection boxes, the corresponding surface bodies are automatically selected. This is the reason why the surfaces are listed under the "Surface Bodies" sub-folders; alternatively we can manually select the surfaces, if needed. Enter a block size big enough to completely enclose the *Card Holder* part; in our case 2.25" up and 0.5" down will work. Click OK to finish.

 Knowing the size of the mold base that will be used, or the sizes available, usually helps when deciding how big to make the blocks. This way they are big enough to fit in the mold base and not bigger than needed.

480. – Now the core and cavity are finished. Hide the 'Parting Line' feature by selecting it and clicking in the "Hide" command. In the "Solid Bodies" folder we now have three bodies: one is the part, one is the core and the third is the cavity. At this point, the core and cavity bodies can be inserted into a new part file to continue designing the mold and adding the rest of the mold specific features, like cooling lines, injection ports, ejector pins, etc. using the same approach we used when working with a master model. To finish our design, save the core and cavity bodies to a part as '*Card Holder Core*' and '*Card Holder Cavity*'.

Our finished *Core* and *Cavity* parts look like this:

 In the original part, the solid bodies can be hidden to see the result without having to save the bodies to a new part file.

481. – For the second mold exercise, download the file *Hair Drier Cover-Mold* from www.mechanicad.com/download.html and open it.

 This part's external references have been broken to avoid potential conflicts with user generated files.

482. – This part is similar to the previous one in the sense that it can be made with a simple two-part mold, but this one has holes going through the part (vents) that the previous part did not. This will help us learn how to work with a part that has holes in it. The first thing we need to do is to verify if our part's faces have at least three degrees of draft. Select the "**Draft Analysis**" icon from the Mold Tools toolbar and select the Right plane as the "Direction of Pull."

From the analysis we can see that the ventilation holes and the extrusion built to assemble the cover ('Extrude-Boss1') don't have the required three degrees of draft, and therefore we need to fix them before we can make a mold. Click Cancel to continue (if we click OK, the Draft Analysis colors will remain visible).

368

483. – Select the 'Boss-Extrude1' feature and edit it.

484. – Activate the "Draft On/Off" option under the "Direction 1" group and enter a value of **3 degrees**. Click OK to finish.

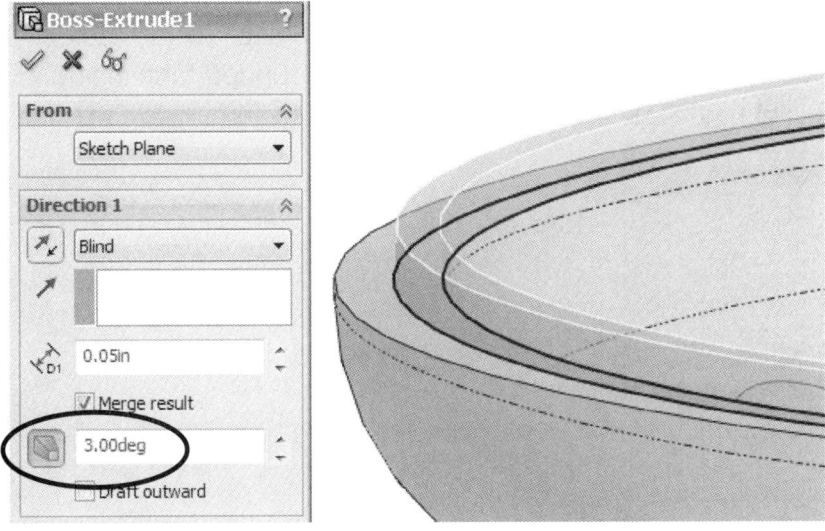

485. – Making a "Draft Analysis" again reveals a small cylindrical face on the inside that needs to be drafted. Cancel the "Draft Analysis" to continue.

486. – Upon closer examination we can see that there are a few smaller faces also along the surface that needs to be drafted.

To fix the draft and the smaller faces, we'll add a face fillet. Select the "**Fillet**" command with the "Face fillet" option. For the "Face Set 1," select the inside of '*Boss-Extrude1*', and for "Face Set 2," select the rounded face inside. Enter a 0.25" radius. The fillet blends both faces and eliminates all the faces between them.

Surfacing and Mold Tools

487. – Run the "Draft Analysis" tool again to reveal the remaining faces that need to be drafted using the same "Direction of Pull."

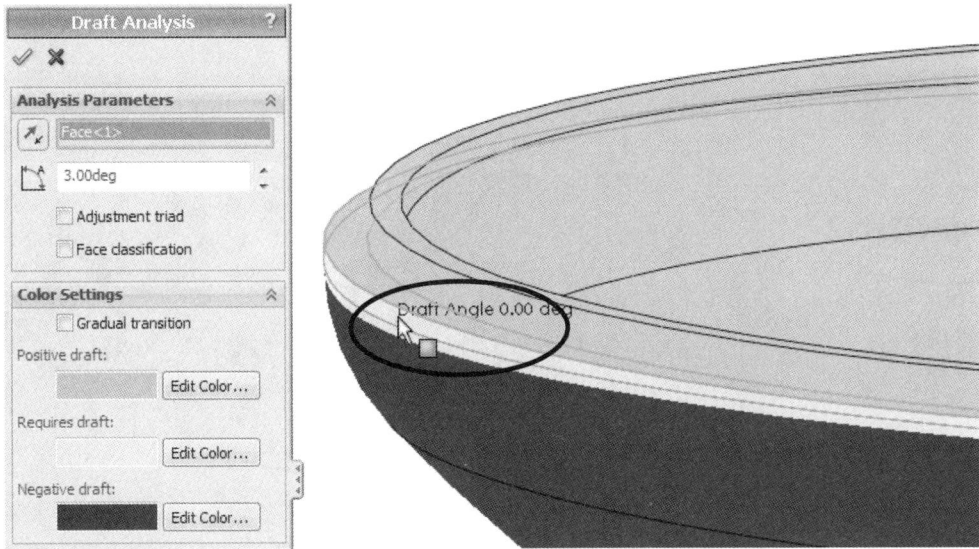

The only faces that need to be drafted are the ventilation holes and a narrow cylindrical face on the outside. This face cannot be drafted as the previous one using a face fillet. On the other hand, it's only 0.03" tall, and a face that small can be merged with the curved face when machining the mold. This is just another thing to consider. When designing plastic parts keep in mind how they are going to be molded, and if at all possible, involve the toolmaker in the design process to get his/her input before it's too late. He'll be glad you did, and you will be, too. ☺

For our example, we'll ignore this face and concentrate on the ventilation holes which are more critical. One thing we need to decide is if the holes will be made in the Core or the Cavity so we can add the draft with the correct "Direction of Pull." To make our mold easier to build, we'll add the holes to the Core (male part) to make the Cavity part completely round inside (you'll see it in a few steps).

488. – If we turn on the "**Draft**" option in the 'Cut-Extrude1' feature, the holes will become smaller than what we originally intended because the cut feature starts in the face where the part was originally split, and adding a 3 deg. draft will shrink the hole too much as it moves forward. Cancel this change as this is not the result we are looking for.

489. – To add a draft to these cuts, we need to create a new plane to be used as a "Neutral Plane." Make an auxiliary plane parallel to the Right plane as first reference, and a point at the top of the part for second reference as indicated. Click OK to finish.

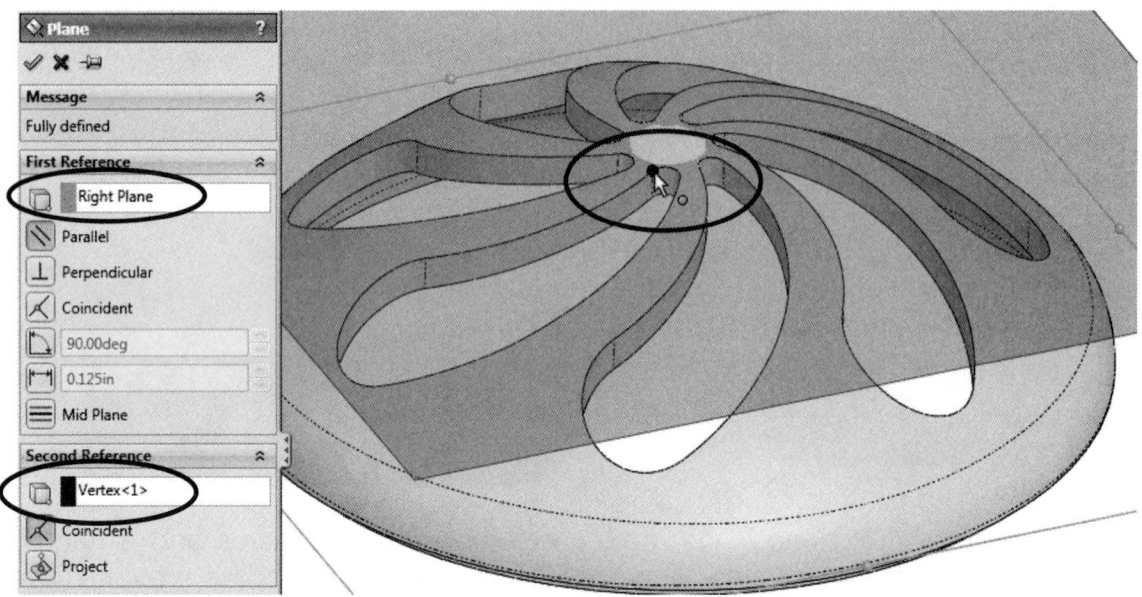

490. – Select the "**Draft**" command and select the plane we just made in the "Neutral Plane" selection box. Using the "Neutral Plane" option enter a 3 degrees draft. The arrow indicating the "Direction of Pull" must be pointing into the part, this way the draft will be made to build the holes in the core. Click "Reverse Direction" if needed.

Surfacing and Mold Tools

The "Faces to draft" are all the holes' inside faces. To select them right mouse click in one of the faces, and from the pop-up menu select the option "**Select Tangency**." Repeat in each hole to select all the faces. Click OK to finish and add the draft.

By adding the draft this way, the holes are wider inside and narrower outside, allowing us to mold the holes in the Core side as we intended.

 CHALLENGE: Instead of drafting all the holes, rollback, add the plane, draft the first hole and edit the pattern to include the hole *and* the draft.

491. – Run a "Draft Analysis" again to check all the faces have the required draft.

Now that all the faces (except the small one we're ignoring) have the required draft we can proceed to make the mold. Click Cancel to continue.

373

Sometimes it's difficult to identify which faces need draft from looking at this image and that's when we can use the "Face Classification" option in the Draft Analysis. When we activate this option the faces can be hidden or shown by color code, and at the same time we get a count for each case. After activating it we'll see a new color indicating the "Straddle faces." Straddle faces are defined as faces that have both positive and negative draft, typically cylindrical or curved faces (we'll learn more of that later).

To turn on/off a group of faces click in the Show/Hide icon next to each color. Turning off the positive and negative draft faces we can clearly see the faces that need draft, in our case the faces we chose to fix in the tooling process.

492. – Now we have to generate the parting line. Select the "**Parting Line**" command from the Mold Tools toolbar or the menu "**Insert, Molds, Parting Line**." Select the Right plane (or a flat face parallel to it) for the "Direction of Pull," enter 3 degrees as before, and click the "**Draft Analysis**" button.

In this case the parting line edges are not automatically selected. The reason is because the small face without draft (which we ignored…) is at the parting line and that causes a conflict that we have to resolve, as the software cannot tell for sure which side of the mold we want the faces to be in. Because of this we have to manually select the parting line.

Select the edges where the red faces meet the yellow. Notice the perimeter is made of multiple edges; be sure to manually select them all *or* right mouse click in one edge and use the "**Select Tangency**" option.

After selecting the parting line edges, the message at the top of the command (still with yellow background) says that the parting line is complete, but the mold cannot be separated into Core and Cavity, and we may need to create shut-off surfaces to close the holes in the part. Click OK to finish the parting line.

493. – Now we need to close the holes in the part to be able to split it into Core and Cavity. Select "**Shut-Off Surfaces**" from the Mold Tools toolbar or the menu "**Insert, Molds, Shut-Off Surfaces**."

After selecting the "**Shut-off Surfaces**" command, the open loops are automatically selected based on the "Direction of Pull" and the parting line settings. Be sure to leave the "**Knit**" option checked to have the new faces automatically merged with the rest of the Core and Cavity faces when we finish this command. By turning on the "Show Preview" option we can see the resulting surfaces. The message at the top of the command (now with green background) says that now the mold can be separated into Core and Cavity. If a hole had not been automatically selected, we'd have to manually select it. Click Ok to complete the command.

Surfacing and Mold Tools

494. – The next step is to generate the parting surfaces to separate the mold. Select the "**Parting Surfaces**" command from the Mold Tools toolbar or the menu "**Insert, Molds, Parting Surfaces.**" The option "Perpendicular to pull" option is automatically selected, as well as *Parting Line1*. Enter a value of **1"** for the "Parting Surface" distance and be sure the "Knit all surfaces" option is checked. Click OK to finish.

After completing the parting surface, we can see the "Core," "Cavity" and "Parting Surface" created and listed under the "Surface Bodies" folder in the corresponding mold sub-folders, and a single solid body. If we select the surfaces, they will become visible and remain visible until manually hidden. By making the surfaces visible, we can see them overlapping each other. In the holes we see the green and red surfaces overlap. Because the shut-off surfaces are knitted to both the Core and Cavity surfaces, the green and the part overlap in the Cavity side, and the red and the part overlap in the Core side.

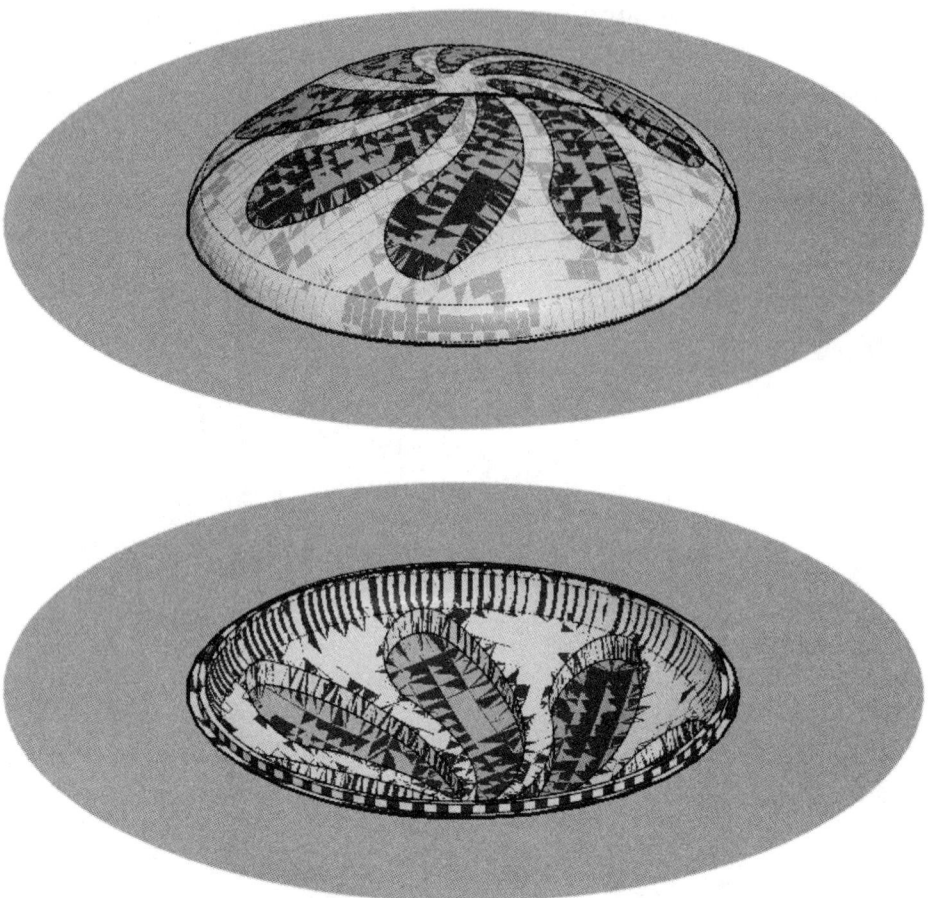

495. – Now we are ready to make the core and cavity. Select the "**Tooling Split**" command from the Mold Tools toolbar. In this example we'll make the tooling sketch at the same time we make the tooling split. Select the parting surface to add a sketch in it, use "**Convert Entities**" to project the surface's edge and exit the sketch as we did before to continue.

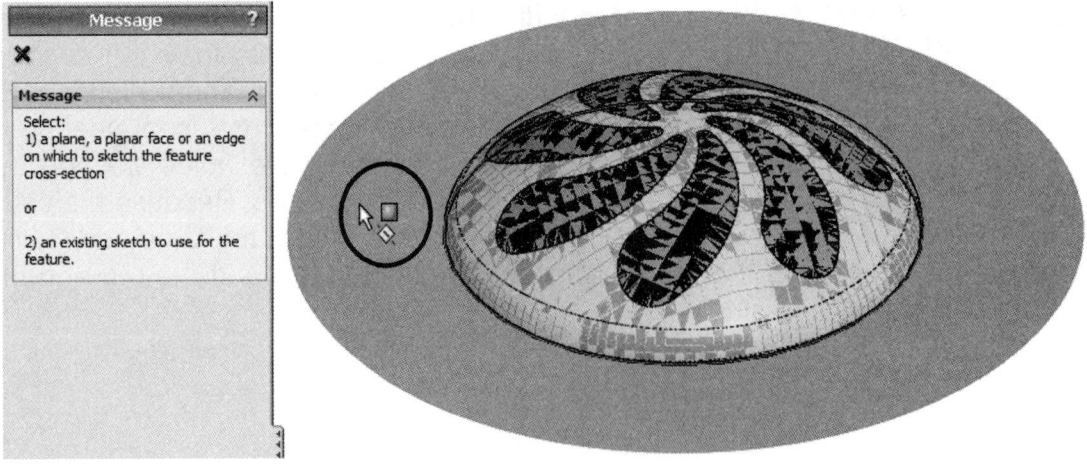

496. – After we exit the sketch, we return to the "**Tooling Split**" command; the surfaces are selected in the "Core," "Cavity" and "Parting Surface" selection boxes. Make the "**Block Size**" 1″ up and 0.5″ down. Click OK to complete the tooling split.

497. – To view the core, cavity and part bodies as an open mold, select the menu "**Insert, Features, Move/Copy….**" This command allows us to copy and/or move surfaces and solid bodies in the part (as if we were moving parts in an assembly). In our example we'll separate the core and cavity bodies away from the design part body only to show how this feature works and see how the bodies look. In reality there is no valid reason to do this other than visually inspecting the resulting bodies.

Select the top body (Cavity) and either enter a value to move it along the X direction, or drag the direction arrows in the graphics area, similar to exploding an assembly.

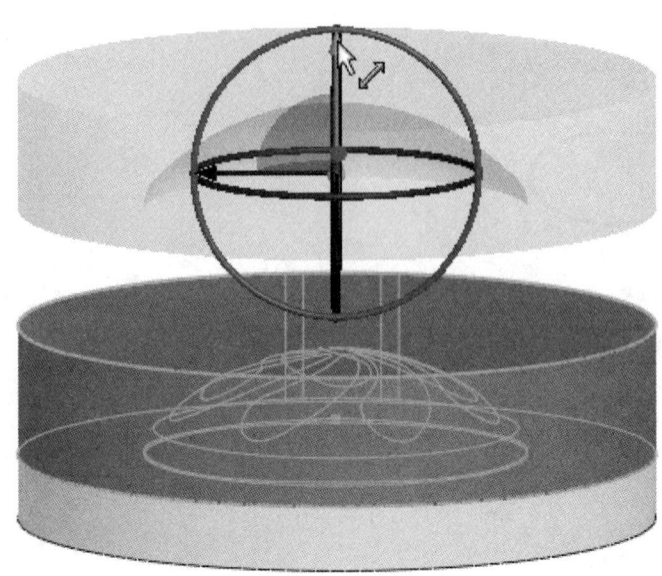

Repeat the **Move/Copy** command to move the lower body (Core). Make sure the "Copy" option is not checked.

 If needed, hide all the surfaces at the same time by selecting the "Surface Bodies" folder and picking "Hide."

Surfacing and Mold Tools

 When making multi body operations like combining bodies (where one or more bodies are absorbed), it's often useful to copy bodies in the same locations as the originals and retain the original bodies.

498. – The next step is to save the core and cavity bodies to separate files as we did with the previous part. Select the core and cavity bodies and save them to a file as 'Hair Drier Cover Core' and 'Hair Drier Cover Cavity'.

If we save a core/cavity/body to a new part after moving them with the "Move/Copy" command, the body in the new part will be located in the same position relative to the origin it had before saving it to a new part.

499. – Open the cavity part. If we pay attention, the holes are outlined in the cavity part. A part like is usually made with a Computer Numerical Control (CNC) machine, and for manufacturing purposes it's better to have a single surface than a surface split in multiple areas like this. One way we can fix this is by deleting the faces from the solid body, and patching it with a new one. Select "**Delete Face**" from the Surfaces toolbar or the menu "**Insert, Face, Delete**."

Select all the faces inside the Cavity that outline a hole. Use the "Delete and Patch" option and click OK to finish.

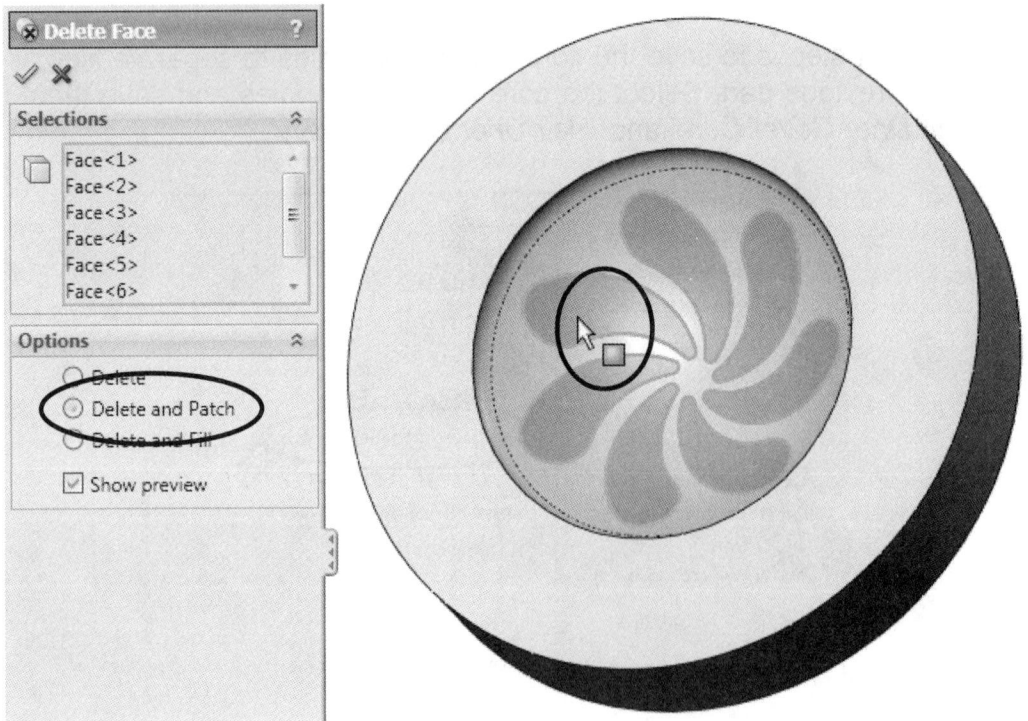

Surfacing and Mold Tools

And now we have a single surface in the Cavity that can be easily machined with a CNC. Save and close the Cavity.

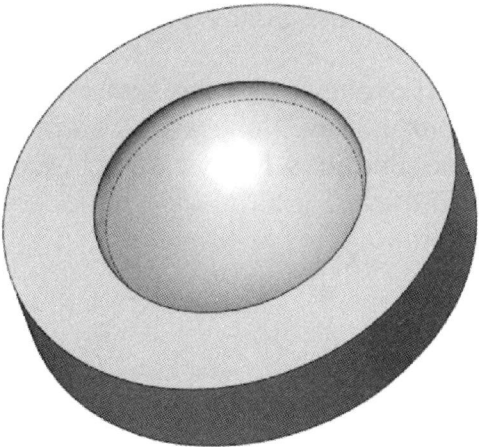

500. – Another common task is to add inserts to a mold. Opening the Core part, we see the protrusions that will make the holes in the cover extend past the top surface; these can be made adding inserts to the core, or building the entire core as a single piece. The problem with a single piece core is that it's harder to make, and if these protrusions wear out, it's more difficult and expensive to repair, whereas an insert can be replaced easier, cheaper and faster. This is a decision that can be answered with help from the tool maker and depends on the volume of parts to be molded, cost of making it one way or the other, etc. We'll see how to cut an insert (if needed/wanted) from the Core by using a split feature. Make a new sketch in the bottom of the part and use "**Convert Entities**" to project the outline of the inserts onto it (use "**Select Tangency**" to make selection easier).

We cannot select the top face with "Convert Entities" since it's smaller than the base because of the draft we added to release it from the mold.

501. – We can split the part directly using the sketch as we did when splitting the main body of the *Hair Drier*, but we'll show a different way to split a solid body using a surface. From the Surfaces toolbar select **"Extruded Surface"** or the menu **"Insert, Surface, Extrude."** Extrude the surface past the top of the Core as shown. Click OK to finish.

502. – Select the menu **"Insert, Features, Split"** and cut the part using the previous surface. Double click to give the insert's body a name and save it as *'Hair Drier Cover Core Insert'*. Use the "Consume cut bodies" option. Click OK to finish and hide the surface used to split the part.

Surfacing and Mold Tools

503. – To make the rest of the inserts, we'd follow the same procedure. In this part all the inserts are equal; we can make one insert and use a cut extrude feature to cut out the rest of the holes.

Save and close all parts.

504. – For the next exercise, we are going to use a part that will not automatically generate the correct parting line and we'll have to manually select it. Download *Hair Drier Mold Exercise* from www.mechanicad.com/download.html and open it.

385

This part is complete, including vents, power cord and switch cutouts; drafts have been added to the necessary faces and external relations have been broken to prevent possible conflicts with user generated files.

505. – In this part we'll make further use of the "Face Classification" option in the draft analysis. Select the "**Draft Analysis**" command using the Front plane as the "Direction of Pull" and enter 3 degrees draft.

Under "**Analysis Parameters**" turn on the "**Face classification**" checkbox to identify the model faces as "Positive," "Negative," "Requires draft" or "Straddle faces." "Straddle faces," as we stated before, refers to faces that have both positive and negative draft; this usually happens when a round face or a fillet crosses the parting line.

Surfacing and Mold Tools

506. – Click in the 'glasses' icons next to the green and red boxes to turn off the "Positive" and "Negative" draft faces and isolate the faces that require draft. Here we can see that only three faces do not have the required three degrees draft. At this time we'll proceed to make the core and cavity and ignore these faces. The reason we are not adding draft to these faces is because adding draft would generate the correct parting line automatically (which is good…), but since we need to learn additional functionality we will skip the draft and continue without it. Cancel the "Draft Analysis" to continue.

507. – To compensate for shrinkage in the mold when the plastic cools down, scale the part and make it 2% bigger. Select the "**Scale**" command; use the option "**Uniform Scaling**" about the "Centroid" and enter **1.02** as the scaling factor. Click OK to finish.

 Remember that material shrinkage depends on process, materials, geometry, etc. This is just an example.

508. – Select the "**Parting Lines**" command; use the Front plane for the "Direction of Pull," enter **3 degrees** for the draft angle and press the "**Draft Analysis**" button when done. A parting line is automatically selected, but since we left three faces with no draft, we need to review and make sure the parting line is where we want it (experience helps in making these decisions).

Surfacing and Mold Tools

Upon closer examination, in the front and back of the hair drier we see small faces on one side of the parting line and a larger face on the other side; in this case it's more convenient to make both of these faces on the same side of the mold. Unselect the edges between the green and yellow faces in the front and back of the part, and select the edge between the red and yellow faces. *(To show the Edge labels select them in the Parting Lines selection box for visibility.)*

Wrong parting line   **Correct parting line**

Repeat for the other side in the front of the hair drier…

Wrong parting line   **Correct parting line**

...in one side of the back of the hair drier (where the back cover fits)...

Wrong parting line   **Correct parting line**

... and the *other* side in the back of the hair drier.

Wrong parting line   **Correct parting line**

Surfacing and Mold Tools

The message in the "Parting Line" command is in yellow and says that the parting line is complete but we still need to create shut-off surfaces. Click OK to continue.

509. – Select the "**Shut-off Surfaces**" command from the Mold Tools toolbar or the menu "**Insert, Molds, Shut-off Surfaces**."

After selecting the command all the ventilation holes are automatically selected and closed, and our mold can now be separated into core and cavity. Click OK to continue.

510. – The last step before creating the core and cavity is to create a parting surface. Select "**Parting Surface**" from the Mold Tools toolbar or the menu "**Insert, Molds, Parting Surface**." Use the option "Tangent to surface" and enter a surface distance of **0.75"**. Make sure the "Knit all surfaces" option is checked. Click OK to finish.

392

Surfacing and Mold Tools

In this case, using the option "Perpendicular to pull" generates surfaces that are not desirable, and we would have to delete them, create new surfaces, knit them to complete the parting surface, and then move the knitted surface to the "Parting Surface Bodies" folder before we could make the tooling split.

511. – After completing the "Parting Surface" command, we can proceed to splitting the mold. Select the "**Tooling Split**" command from the Mold Tools toolbar; select the flat face of the parting surface or the Front plane to add a new sketch. When we work with surfaces, we can use "**Select Open Loop**" (right mouse click an edge) to pick all edges around the surface and then use "**Convert Entities**" to project all outside edges of the parting surface into the sketch. Exit the sketch when done to continue with the tooling split.

393

The tooling sketch must be bigger than the parting line and as big or smaller than the parting surface.

512. – Change to a Top or Bottom view to see the size of the tooling block. In the "**Tooling Split**" command make the "Block Size" big enough to fully enclose the part. Click OK to continue.

513. – Hide the 'Parting Line' feature, and all 'Surface Bodies'.

… and then hide the body at the top of the mold to see the cavity and the part.

Optionally we can change the color of the molded part's body (just the body's color) to make it easier to identify. Select the molded part, and from the pop-up menu select the appearance icon. From the drop down we can choose to change a face, feature, body or entire part's appearance. Select the "Body" option and change its color for visualization purposes.

Or select the body in the "Solid Bodies" folder and change its color this way.

Save and close the file.

CHALLENGE: Insert the Core and Cavity bodies into new part files.

- In the Cavity part, eliminate the vent hole markings to make a smooth surface (like we did with the back cover).

- In the Core part, cut an insert for one of the vent holes.

514. – In our last mold exercise we'll learn how to make a "**Side Core**." Think of a side core as a part split from the core or cavity to help us make a feature that would otherwise prevent the part from being released from the mold, like a hole perpendicular to the "Direction of Pull," an undercut, or a negative draft face in the positive draft side of the part. Download the part *Bucket Mold* from www.mechanicad.com/download.html (or use the bucket we made in the Surfacing lesson) and run a "Draft Analysis" with 3 degrees using the Top plane as "Direction of Pull." Use the "Face classification" option to show the "Straddle faces" in and around the holes for the handle. The blue faces will not allow the part to release from the mold using a two part mold, making this part a good example where we need to make a side core. After a part is molded, the side core is pulled first away from the mold, then the mold is opened and the part is released. Cancel the Draft Analysis to continue.

515. – From the previous analysis we see the lip at the top of the bucket needs a draft. Add a 3 degree draft to the outside face of the lip at the top of the bucket in the negative draft direction (down). Use the "Along Tangent" face propagation option to select the rest of the faces that need a draft. Click OK to complete.

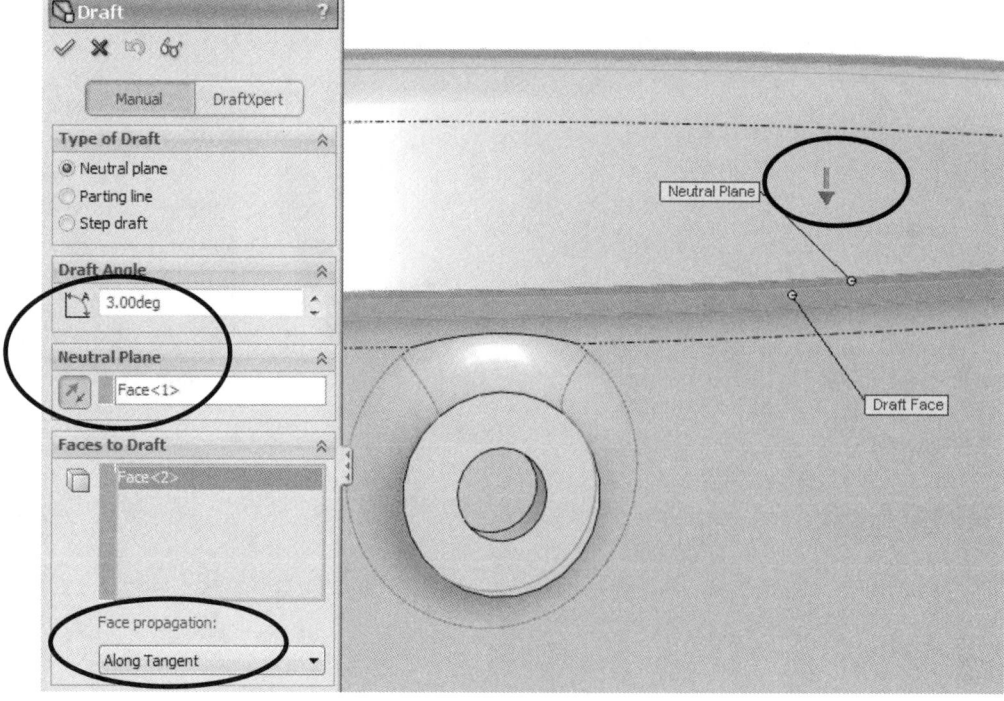

Surfacing and Mold Tools

516. – The next step is to add a draft to the side cores, since they also need to have it in order to release them from the part, but in this case the "Direction of Pull" is along the boss' axis. Edit the 'Boss-Extrude1' feature and activate the "**Draft**" option with 3 degrees and turn on the "**Draft outward**" option.

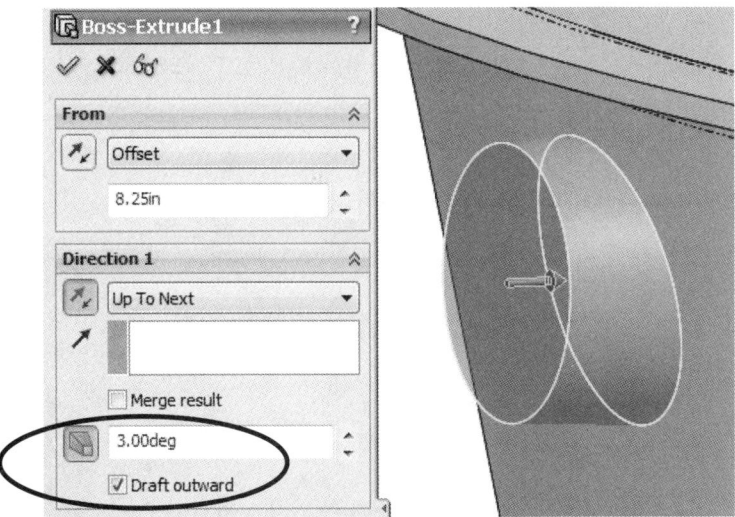

517. – Now edit the 'Cut-Extrude1' feature and also activate the "**Draft**" option but in this case with a 2 degrees draft. Leave the "Draft Outward" option off.

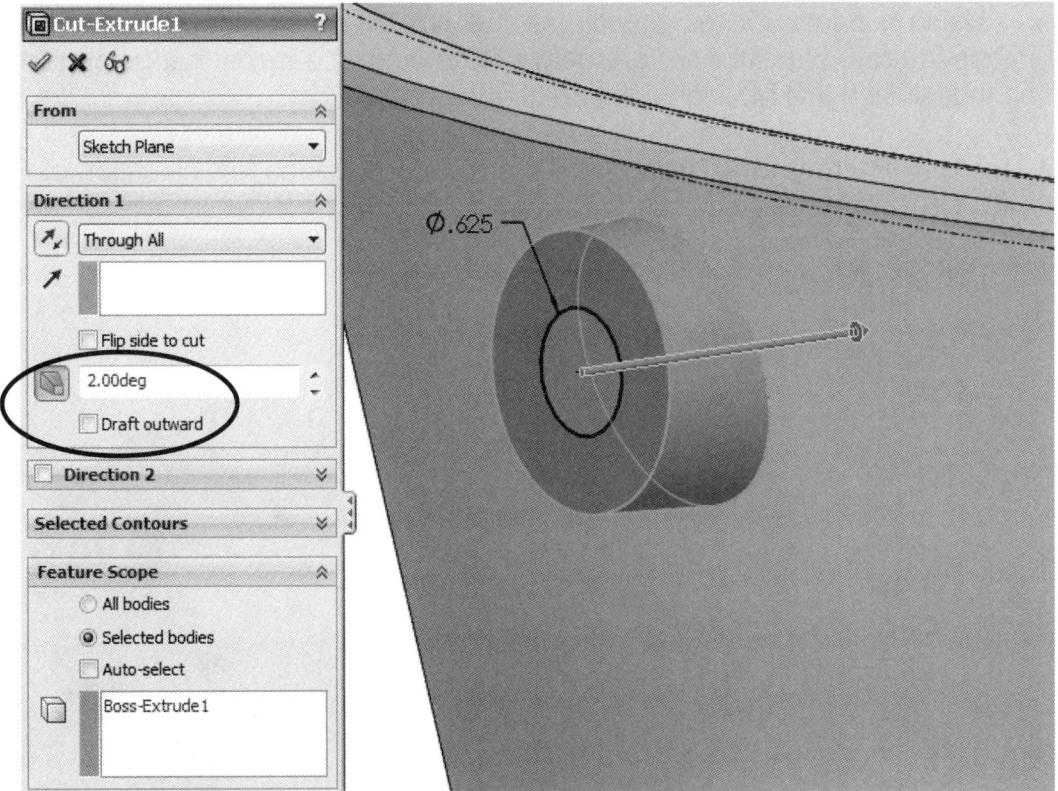

518. – Run a "Draft Analysis" using the flat face in the boss for "Direction of Pull" and 2 degrees. Now we can see the boss and hole have the draft angle required for the side core to release properly, and since the boss on the other side is a mirror of this it will also be correct. Cancel the "Draft Analysis" to continue.

 Using this face for the direction of pull will tell us that there are faces that need draft, but since we are only interested in the faces that belong to the boss using this face for direction of pull we are OK.

519. – Add a "**Parting Line**" using the Top plane or top face for "Direction of Pull" and click OK to continue.

520. – Add a "**Parting Surface**." Make the surface 2 inches "Perpendicular to pull" using the "Smooth" option. This option smoothes the transition between adjacent surfaces, giving us a better result in certain situations like this.

521. – Using "**Tooling Split**" add the tooling split sketch in the parting surface and using "**Convert Entities**" project the parting surface in the sketch.

401

Exit the sketch to continue the tooling split and make the block size 1″ up and 13″ down as shown. Click OK to finish.

522. – After creating the tooling split we have a core and a cavity. In our part the side cores will be split from the cavity. Switch to a Front view and hidden lines visible mode to see the area we are interested in. Add a new sketch in the Front plane as shown. The sketch is a closed profile starting at the parting line. The objective is to split a side core from the cavity using this sketch as a cutting tool. Exit the sketch when done.

Surfacing and Mold Tools

523. – Select the "**Core**" command from the Mold Tools toolbar or the menu "**Insert, Molds, Core**," and select the sketch we just made.

This command allows us to cut the side cores from either the core or the cavity bodies, essentially splitting it with more options. In the "Core" command, select the cavity's body, which is the one we want to make a core from, and in the "Parameters" options use the "Through All" end condition to cut the cavity. The preview will show the core split from the cavity. Click OK to split the first side core.

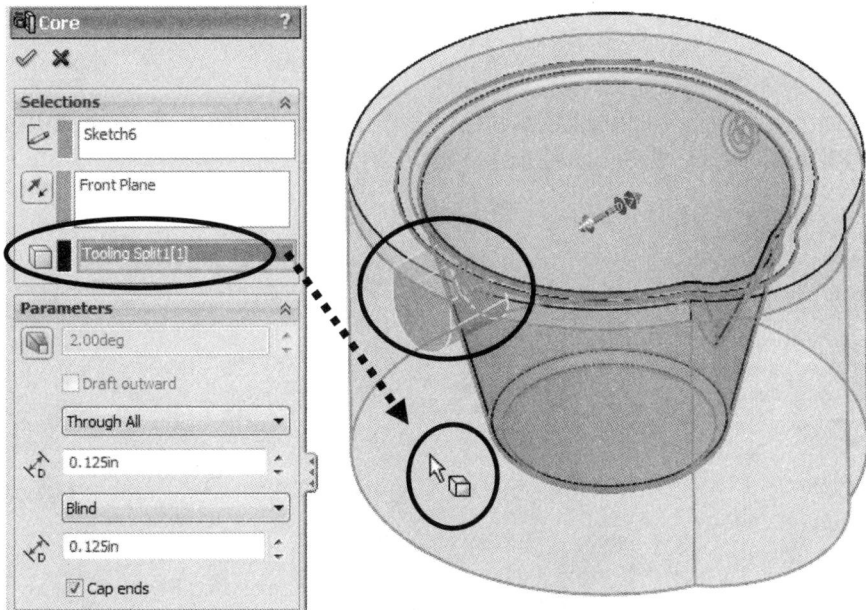

The core is split and added to a "Core bodies" folder in the "Solid Bodies" folder.

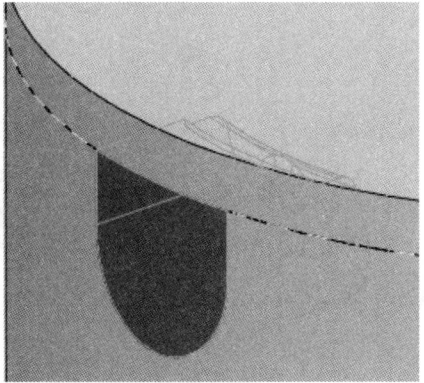

403

524. – Make the same sketch again in the Front plane and make a second Core, but now going in the other direction. Click OK to finish the second core.

The two side cores are highlighted after splitting them from the cavity body. (The bucket and the Core bodies have been hidden for visibility.)

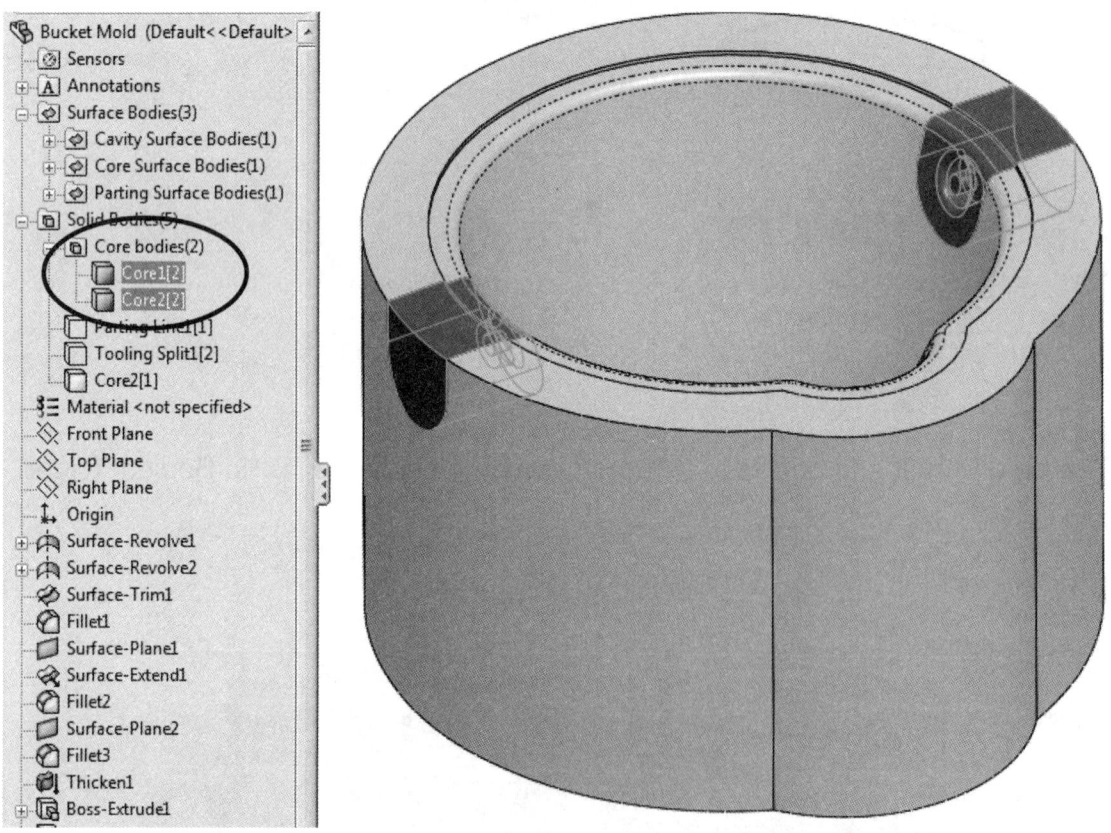

Surfacing and Mold Tools

525. – Hide all the surface bodies and use the "**Move/Copy**" command (menu "**Insert, Features, Move/Copy**") to separate and see the different bodies of the mold including the side core.

At this point the different bodies would be inserted into a new part to continue adding the remaining mold specific features. Save the part and close.

CHALLENGE: Save the core, cavity and side cores to external files and make an assembly with all the components.

Notes:

Final Comments

After going through the exercises in the book, the reader will have acquired a good understanding of several topics including sheet metal, welded structures, 3D Sketching, Top Down design, Editing tools, Multi Body parts, Surfacing, Mold tools and a handful of tips and tricks that can help a designer work faster and more efficiently.

Even though most of the topics included in this book are usually considered advanced, they are presented using simple examples that break down the concepts and make them easy to understand. Topics covered explore the most commonly used options to enable a reader to use them efficiently for the different design tasks at hand.

The Sheet Metal, Mold tools and Welded structures topics fall within the scope of the individual manufacturing trades, each of which has very specific tools, techniques and *fine details* that are (usually) learned after studying and by experience; take for example mold making: includes most of the tools available in SolidWorks, going from the very basic to advanced surfacing and more.

The amount of trade training that can be shown in a CAD oriented book is limited, since the objective of the book is to teach how to use SolidWorks and not a trade. If a reader has experience in one of these fields, he/she will quickly understand the purpose of specific tools, but we also tried our best to explain in a basic form trade terminology and processes so a reader unfamiliar with a trade can understand the purpose of a tool and the reason for certain operations.

We welcome all of your suggestions and ideas. As this book evolves new functionality and examples will be added, but rest assured we'll always try our best to make sure the models shown maximize functionality covered in as few pages as reasonably possible, helping you to get up to understand and practice fast. If you have any comments about this book, by all means please send it our way; we'll really appreciate it.

Please visit our website as we have other materials available that we are sure will be of interest to the reader.

Sincerely,

Alejandro Reyes,
Certified SolidWorks Professional, Instructor and Support Technician.

alejandro@mechanicad.com
Mechanicad Inc.

Notes:

Index

3D ContentCentral 113
3D Sketch 232, 253
3D Sketch Relations 233
Align with end faces 340
Along X 240, 255, 258
Along Z 240, 256, 258
Assembly Features 221
Assembly Transparency 183
Auto Relief 105
AutoBalloon 284
Base Flange 98
Bend Allowance 103
Bend Deduction 104
Bend Edges 200
Bend Notes 162
Bend Outside 124
Bends to unfold 126
Bodies to Keep 32
Bodies to Mirror 332
Bodies to Subtract 32
Break Corners 142
Broken 94
Broken Relations 57
Check Sketch for Feature 44, 47
Closed Corner 169
Collect All Bends 192
Collision Detection 217
Combine 333
Combine Bodies 23
Common Bodies 30
Component Pattern 214
Consume cut bodies 290, 321
Contour Selection 35
Contour Selection Tool 37, 38
Contours 36
Convert to Sheet Metal 166, 175, 199
Core 398, 399
Corner treatment 287
Corner Treatment 145
Cut list 259, 280, 289
Cut With Surface 247
Dangling 51, 54, 57
Default bend radius 103
Delete absorbed features 55
Delete Body 20
Delete Face 378
Derived Sketch 243
Design Library 130
Diagnose 60
Dimension Names 67, 133
Direction of Extrusion 304
Direction of Pull 350
Display Annotations 278
Display entity points in part/assembly sketches 44
Display/Delete Relations 58, 59
Draft 347, 351
Draft Analysis 347, 348, 364
Draft On/Off 304
Draft outward 304
Driving Feature 194
Dynamic Assembly Motion 211
Edge Flange 128, 168, 187
Edit Assembly 88
Edit Component 83, 88, 96, 112, 121, 156, 172, 183, 185, 193, 197, 208, 209, 210
Edit Flange Profile 128
Edit Linear Pattern 191
Edit Part 117
Edit Sketch Plane 52
End Cap 273
End Miter 262
End Trim 266
Equations 65, 68, 69, 71, 73, 74, 76, 107
Extend Surface 327
External Relations 57
Extrude From 331
Extruded Surface 303, 380
Face classification 382
Face Fillet 315
Feature Driven Pattern 193
Feature Scope 7, 19, 222, 332
Filled Surface 309, 310
Fix 61
Fix projected length 151
Flat pattern 160
Flat-Pattern 143
Flatten 157

Flexible Sub Assembly 219
Flip Tool 207
Fold 127, 192
Force Assembly Transparency 83
Form Tool 109
Forming Tool 107, 204
Forming tools 130
Global Variables 72
Gusset 271
Hem 196
Hide Body 17
Hide Cosmetic Welds 278
Hole Series 221
Hole Wizard 221
in context 82
In Context 59, 91
In Context Relations 57
InPlace 82, 96, 147, 211
Insert Components 96, 146
Insert into new part… 290
Internal Dimensions 134
Internal Part 86
Jog 150
Jog Offset 150
Jog Position 151
K-Factor 104
Knit Surface 313
Library Feature 131
Link to thickness 127
Link to Thickness 112
List Broken References 94
List External Refs 92
Local operations 7
Locate Profile 263
Locating Dimensions 134
Locked 92
Locked Relations 57
Lofted Surface 302
Maintain Assembly Transparency . 83
Master Model 319
Mate Reference 138
Material Inside 123
Material Outside 124
Merge arc segment bodies 287
Merge faces 144
Merge result …7, 8, 9, 10, 29, 31, 274, 312, 331
Miter Flange 122, 168, 176, 178
Move/Copy 400
Move/Copy body 375
Mutual Trim 307
Neutral Plane 352, 354
New Part .. 82, 96, 146, 171, 183, 197
New Weld Path 275
No External References 198
Normal Cut 112
Not Solved 57
Obround Relief 105
Offset from Surface 56
On Edge 62, 209
On Plane Relation 234
Opaque Assembly 83
Orientation Sketch 206
Out of Context 91
Over defined Sketch 57
Parent/Child 42, 50, 52, 53
Parting Line 358, 370, 395
Parting Surface 396
Parting Surfaces 360, 373
Pattern seed only 66
Planar Surface 308, 326
Projected Curve 248
Propagate feature to parts 222
Rectangular Relief 105
Revolved Surface 301
Rip Edges found 176, 200
Rollback 351
Rotation Angle 264
Save Bodies 290
Save Part (in External File 90
Save Part (in External File) 120
Scale 357
Select Open Loop 388
Select Tangency 369
Selected bodies 20
Selected Contours 35
Selection Filter 178
Set corner specific weld gaps 288
Sheet Metal 77
Sheet Metal features 98
Sheet Metal Parameters 102

Show feature dimensions 67
Shut-off Surfaces 386
Shut-Off Surfaces 372
Side Core 393
Simplify bends 145
Sketch Pattern 190
SketchXpert 59
Smart Weld Selection Tool 276
Solid Bodies 6
Split 319, 380
Start Condition 39
Stop at collision 217
Straddle faces 370, 382
Structural Member 259, 287
Structural Member Libraries 293
Surface Bodies 302
Swept Surface 337
Tear Relief 106
Thicken 316, 330
Tooling Split 361, 374, 388, 396
Top Down design 79, 80
Trim and attach 328
Trim side bends 123, 170
Trim Surface 305, 325
Trim/Extend 289
Trimming Boundary 267, 289
Try to form a solid 317
Twist Along Path 337
Underive Sketch 245
Unfold 126, 188
Use default radius 123
Vent 118
Weld Bead 274, 278
Weld Folder 278, 282
Weld Symbol 285
Weld Table 283
Weldment cut list 281
Weldment Profiles 294
Weldment Trim/Extend 266
What's Wrong 42, 43, 44, 46, 49, 52, 53, 54, 56, 57

Notes: